Hightown Grammar

the school as a social system

Hightown Grammar

the school as a social system

C. Lacey

Manchester University Press

Published by the University of Manchester at
THE UNIVERSITY PRESS
Oxford Road, Manchester M13 9PL

International standard book number 0 7190 0485 3

First published 1970
Reprinted 1971, 1972, 1974

Printed in Great Britain
by Butler & Tanner Ltd, Frome and London

Contents

Illustrations

To my father

Acknowledgments

My most sincere thanks are due to the staff and pupils of Hightown Grammar School. I received every co-operation from the head-master, senior master and staff of the school and at times the demands I made on their time and good will were very great.

I owe much to my colleagues in the Department of Social Anthropology and Sociology and members of the research team for their encouragement and criticisms. In particular, I thank Dr R. Frankenberg for his helpful supervision and Dr V. Pons and Dr B. Roberts, who read through an early draft of the PhD thesis on which this book is based and made many helpful suggestions.

My thanks are also due to Professor M. Gluckman, Professor P. Worsley, Dr R. Frankenberg and Dr V. Pons for their work in launching and directing the scheme, and to the Ministry of Education for making it financially possible.

The book also owes a great deal to Professor Worsley, whose careful criticism helped in preparing the manuscript for publication, to Mrs L. Smith and Mrs S. Marfleet, who voluntarily typed the first draft of the work, and to my wife, whose support and patient forbearance made the research possible.

Preface

This is a detailed study of a boys' grammar school in a north-western industrial town called Hightown.[1] Hightown Grammar School is the main avenue of secondary education leading to the universities and the professions within Hightown, and it has held this position for over half a century. The study deals with many aspects of the school: its changing function over the last fifty years; its position within the present educational structure; the way in which selection and anticipatory socialisation affect the pupils; the process of sub-culture formation within the student body, and the staff and staff–pupil relationships. The book is designed to give a multi-dimensional view.

Though I am presenting a case study of one school, its significance is not confined to the particularistic concerns of this one school. It extends to general problems in sociology and education. I agree with Frankenberg when he argues that an essential ingredient of the social sciences is '. . . a methodology in which the discussion of small segments of society in great detail is used to throw light on the general'. He continues, 'It is my firm view that only the particularistic can illuminate the universalistic.'[2]

Both these dimensions are examined. The school is viewed as a social system which is nevertheless embedded in a wider society. It is a socialising organisation which is an 'integral part of the process of social mobility' and 'an intrinsic part of community life'.[3] However, such analysis is only the proximal aim of the study. I lay bare the social mechanisms within the school in an attempt to explain the disappointing performance of working-class boys in grammar schools since the 1944 Education Act.[4] I do so in the belief that to understand this problem within the grammar school is to assist in solving the problem of the working-class pupil within the comprehensive system which is likely to replace the tripartite system. The insights gained in this study should not be thought inapplicable to the new comprehensive system.[5] The shape and character of the processes described in Hightown Grammar School are in part the result of pressures emanating from society. These same pressures will affect the comprehensive school. While the comprehensive system may provide an organisational framework more likely to achieve equal educational opportunity for all sections of the community, it will not happen automatically.

The research

This investigation was undertaken as part of a wider research project which was run by the Department of Anthropology and Sociology at Manchester University between 1962 and 1966 under the general guidance of Professors M. Gluckman and P. Worsley. The original proposal[6] had envisaged the detailed study of two grammar schools in the town, using a variety of field techniques but concentrating on participant observation and attempting to view the school as a social system. I joined the project in October 1962 and began work in the boys' grammar school. In March 1963, Mrs A. Lambert was appointed to work in a girls' grammar school.[7] Later the scheme was extended[8] and Mr D. Hargraves was appointed to make a similar type of study of a boys' secondary modern school.

The work of the team was co-ordinated by Dr R. Frankenberg and Dr V. Pons, and owes much to their direction and support. Seminars and informal discussions were held, and the researchers co-operated wherever possible in the design of questionnaires and in the sharing of fieldwork experiences. The additional knowledge and insight gained through these exchanges became part of the research process, but each field worker retained individual responsibility for his own research, both in the collection of data and in the presentation of results.

Other research in the field

The Manchester project was designed to fill an obvious gap in the sociology of education.[9] Most previous studies have focused on the educational system as a whole and its role in society[10] or on the correlatives of educational achievement, such as social class, intelligence or family size. In cases where the unit of study has been the school, the main concern has usually been to assess statistically the effect of social class[11] or sub-cultural and peer group values[12] on educational attainment. The principal concern has not been with the school itself as a social system.

The lack of published work in this sphere has been commented on by James Coleman: '. . . research in this area [of social systems] is not extensive, perhaps partly because of the difficulty of examining a social system, however small, in action.'[13] Coleman refers to only two other studies, those of Hollingshead[14] and Wayne Gordon,[15] as being closely related to his own. Since Coleman wrote, Cicourel and Kitsuse[16] have added their account of the effects of the administrative organisation, in particular of the counselling system, on the differentiation of pupils. The above studies have a close affinity to the present work, but were all conducted in a very different type of institution— the American public school.

In launching its first research project in the sociology of education the Manchester department was concerned to harness some of the skills and techniques developed in intensive studies of communities and small-scale societies, to the study of modern institutions. This was expressed as follows: 'The analysis of social relations within small groups has a distinctive contribution to make toward the understanding of how an institutional system operates. In stressing this, we have in mind the important contributions made by intensive small-scale studies in other areas of modern society—very notably, for example, in industry, where the parallel development of micro- and macroscopic studies over the past few decades has proved so valuable.'[17]

This contribution, we thought, would be especially fruitful within the context of the sociology of education, because so much excellent work has already been done and created a framework within which we could work.

Field work

Field work started at Hightown Grammar School in February 1963. My introduction to the school was gained through the good offices of the Chief Education Officer. It was made smooth by the decision to include teaching as an essential part of the field work.

The first two months were spent in getting to know the way around, meeting and talking to the staff and pupils, and explaining the purpose of my presence in the school. I also observed teachers giving lessons, at least one by each member of the staff. During this period my purpose was to locate a number of strategic areas that would enable me to gain a clear picture of the processes taking place within the school. The allocation of time then made was of critical importance, since my plans had to allow for long-term teaching commitments.

With the help of the senior master, I arranged a timetable that enabled me to gather information from the first year, the fourth year and the sixth year age groups and involved me in both teaching and observation. I spent twelve periods a week teaching, and twelve periods observing the teachers at work in the classroom. In addition to this, I had eleven periods a week free for marking, writing notes, working through the school records, collecting questionnaire material and talking to the staff. (The normal allocation of non–teaching periods was five or six.)

The periods of teaching and observation were distributed as follows:

Form	Participation	Observation
First year (1962 intake)	Taught six periods a week	Observed eight periods a week
Fourth year (1959 intake)	–	Observed four periods a week
Sixth form (1956 intake)	Taught six periods a week	–

This period of intensive field work lasted for eighteen months.

During the first term I also inaugurated two questionnaire studies. A panel study, which I based on the 1962 intake[18] (first year) and which included questions on sociometric choice, value orientations and career aspirations, and a questionnaire, which was given to each fifth year group after the GCE ordinary level examinations. This sought more detailed information on family background, school career and peer group affiliation. These two studies continued uninterruptedly during the period of this report (1962–66) and are still continuing.[19]

The data presented in this book are drawn mainly from the early period of intensive study (1962–64) and from the first three years of the panel study of the 1962 intake. This has been supplemented with material from the school records and the local education offices. Other minor enquiries were initiated for specific purposes, some of which I have used. During the field work period I attempted to immerse myself in the school and its activities. I helped to run a cricket team

xiv

and went on several school trips. I also lived within 300 yards of the school during (and since) the research.

Outline of the book

In considering the school as a social system, I have been concerned to avoid a major pitfall in system analysis—the presentation of an unchanging and totally integrated equilibrium model. For this reason I start my analysis on an historical level and consider the changing function of the school within the community. I recognise three stages in the development of the school, which culminate in the 'professionalising school'. In this period the school becomes the major avenue of social mobility in the community for a professional-managerial class of national dimensions. Academic competition within the student body intensifies and working-class students become the least successful of the class groupings in the school.

I follow this analysis with a description of the present-day structure of education in the community. The process of selection for the grammar school, from a hierarchy of junior schools, ensures that the intake to the grammar school consists of boys who have been used to playing the 'best pupil' role in their junior schools and who have thought of themselves as grammar school pupils.

The effects of selection and anticipatory socialisation are examined next. A model of the process of sub-culture formation within the student body of the grammar school is presented. This entails the differentiation of the student body in terms of the dominant school values and the subsequent formation of two distinct student sub-cultures; one pro-school and the other, called the anti-group sub-culture, reacting against the dominant school values (and the pro-school groupings). The development of these opposed sub-cultures is termed 'polarisation' and the process is studied over a four-year period, as the cohort under investigation moves through the school. Indicators derived from choice-of-friend questionnaires are used to assess the nature and extent of these opposed sub-cultures, which affect attitudes to academic work and patterns of behaviour.

The above model of the major processes within the school is refined and examined in more detail in the following chapters. Some of the assumptions on which the model rests are tested. The detail of inter-personal relationships within one stream is shown to reflect the twin, opposed pressures towards academic achievement and anti-academic activity.

Throughout, the focus of the study has been progressively changed. It has moved from an historical level to the present-day community, then to the school, then to the cohort and finally to the case study. At each stage or level of generality, an attempt has been made to carry over and consider in more detail the processes under investigation at the previous level. In particular, the analysis is integrated with a concern for the processes of 'differentiation' and 'polarisation' at each of these levels.

The change in focus within a single system is a useful heuristic device. The artificial closure of this system is corrected for in the final chapters.

Chapter 7 is organised around a paradigm involving factors emanating from the school, the home and the community. The paradigm allows the systematic introduction of material, on the influence of the above factors, into the discussion. The school is viewed as an arena for competing teams or units (comprising the child and his parents) with different psycho-socio-cultural resources. The case studies which are presented exemplify, in an exhaustive manner, the combinations of factors represented in the paradigm. A strictly enforced procedure for the selection of the case studies is used to prevent the distortion caused by 'apt illustration'. The analysis throws doubt upon the feasibility of 'equality of opportunity' in a stratified society.

Finally, I consider the staff and staff–student relationships. A descriptive analysis of the structure of staff relationships is followed by an analysis in which the previously discussed processes within the student body are related to the major social pressures affecting the staff. Staff–student relationships are pictured as the grinding interface between the two major sub-systems within the school. The leeway for experiment and change within the present system is seen to be extremely limited unless important structural changes are made in the role and career structure of the teacher.

NOTES

[1] Hightown is a pseudonym for the town in which the school was situated. Any reader with a little knowledge of the demography or the educational provisions of northern towns will speedily recognise it from the descriptive passages that follow. I feel it is extremely important that in any public discussion its anonymity should be preserved. All other proper names have been similarly disguised.

[2] R. J. Frankenberg, 'Taking the blame or passing the buck', paper presented to the British Association, Aberdeen, 4 September 1963.

[3] Norma Raynes, *The analysis of organisations as social systems*. Unpublished M.A. thesis, University of Manchester, 1963.

[4] See especially J. Westergaard and A. L. Little, 'Educational opportunity and social selection in England and Wales: trends and policy implications' in *Social objectives in educational planning*, O.E.C.D., Paris, 1967.

[5] Aaron Cicourel and John Kitsuse trace out very similar processes in their study of an American comprehensive school in *The educational decision makers*, Bobbs-Merrill, 1963.

[6] 'Proposal for the sociological study of grammar schools in Manchester', prepared by V. Pons and R. Frankenberg. The research was financed by a grant from the Ministry of Education. Both these studies eventually included work in a second school, which was used as a control. This arrangement also meant that the team collected data from all the local education authority grammar schools in Hightown.

[8] This extension became possible when I was appointed as an assistant lecturer in the Department of Social Anthropology and Sociology in October 1963. Mr Hargraves filled the vacant position on the scheme while I continued to work on the project part-time. During the first term of the appointment I was completely freed from teaching duties.

[9] See the following reviews of the literature: J. Floud, and A. H. Halsey, 'The sociology of education: a trend report and bibliography', *Current sociology*, vol. III, No. 3, 1958. W. W. Charters, 'The school as a social system', *Review of educational research*, vol. XXII, No. 1, February 1952. Both point to the lack of work in the area of the school as a 'system of interrelationships'.

[10] See the reader *Education, economy and society*, ed. J. Floud, A. H. Halsey and C. A. Anderson, Free Press, 1961, for examples.

[11] A. H. Halsey, J. Floud and F. M. Martin, *Social class and educational opportunity*, Heinemann, 1956.

[12] J. S. Coleman, with J. W. C. Johnstone and K. Jonassohn, *The adolescent society*, Free Press, 1961.

[13] Ibid., page vii.

[14] A. B. Hollingshead, *Elmtown's youth*, John Wiley, 1947.

[15] C. W. Gordon, *The social system of the high school*, Free Press, 1957.

[16] A. V. Cicourel and J. I. Kitsuse, *The educational decision makers*, Bobbs-Merrill, 1963.

[17] 'Proposal for the sociological study of grammar schools in Manchester', prepared by V. Pons and R. Frankenberg.

[18] I was able to continue observing this group for a period of three years.

[19] At the time of writing, the pupils who were in the first year panel study and on whom the most intensive data has been collected are in the sixth form. An additional investigation has been undertaken which was financed by the Social Science Research Council. This took the form of a questionnaire-interview study of parents, to collect more detailed information about home backgrounds. It included such items as parental job histories, kin and friendship networks, and attitudes towards the school. The intention has been to compare the parents' view of the educational process with that obtained from the vantage point of the school.

1 The community and the school: an historical dimension

Hightown is part of a large northern conurbation. It has the highest population density in a county in which all county boroughs have very high population densities. This despite the fact that Hightown has experienced the greatest percentage decrease in population in the county: from 1931 to 1951 the decrease was 20 per cent.[1] In fact, since the 1920's, when the population was nearly a quarter of a million, Hightown has been losing population at the rate of approximately 2,000 a year, and by 1964 the population total was estimated at only 150,000.

The community

Industry in Hightown is varied and the town itself is situated in a conurbation of even greater industrial diversity. This has protected the town against severe unemployment at a time when many of its more specialised and prosperous neighbours suffered badly. Transport and communications are the most important industries, and the docks are the largest employer. Engineering, clothing and textiles, building and construction, and chemicals are also important. Up to the present, employment opportunities have shown more resilience to change than would be expected from the population figures. Despite the loss of just under a quarter (23·9 per cent) of its population between 1921 and 1951, the number of people working in Hightown increased from 82,000 to 86,000. This apparent contradiction needs an explanation and it illustrates some of the structural changes that have taken place and are still taking place in Hightown.[2]

During the late 1800's and early part of the twentieth century, many of the owners and senior managers of Hightown's industrial firms left the area and moved south to the remoter and more desirable

1

'county' areas. The grounds of the large houses which they vacated along 'millionaires' mile' were used for middle-class housing estates and schools, and for a museum and a park. The middle-class areas of Brightside and Clearview were developed rapidly. At the same time there were important changes in the structure of industry. Many family firms disappeared and local ownership gave way to larger bureaucratic establishments, many of which had their head offices outside Hightown, in the central metropolitan area of the conurbation. This familiar pattern of development was accompanied by growth and differentiation in white-collar employment. By the late 1930's practically all the land in the desirable outer parts of the town was built up, and Hightown was no longer able to absorb an increasing number of clerical, managerial and professional workers. Census figures reveal that this class contributed the bulk of the migrants to the ring of suburbs beyond the town. A comparison of the social class composition with that of a neighbouring suburban area illustrates the degree to which the scarcity of land for building and consequent migration deprived Hightown of middle-class population (see social classes I and II in table 1). The northern neighbour has in fact been a recipient of much of the population leaving Hightown.

TABLE 1

SOCIAL CLASS DISTRIBUTION (PER CENT), 1951

	I	*II*	*III*	*IV*	*V*
Hightown	1·4	9·8	52·2	15·7	20·9
Northern neighbour	4·9	26·2	50·4	9·1	9·4
England and Wales	3·3	15·0	52·7	16·2	12·8

Source: Census of Great Britain, 1951; one per cent sample tables

The two categories disproportionately represented in those migrating from Hightown are (1) people living in Hightown but working outside the town, and (2) those who were socially mobile as a result of the expansion of managerial, professional and white-collar jobs. Since the 1950's, however, Hightown has also been losing working-class inhabitants. The local authority has rehoused approximately 10,000 in an overspill council estate some seven miles out. In addition, since the late 1940's the Board of Trade has refused as a matter of policy to grant development certificates to new industry within Hightown. This had not produced any marked effect before the 1951 census.

It would seem therefore that when information for the 1960's be-

2

comes available[3] it will reveal that the social class composition of Hightown has changed less in recent years, because the town has been losing a more representative sample of its population than in earlier years. The number of people employed in its industries will have decreased. (Six major employers of local labour have either closed down or moved out since the 1951 census.)

Finally, it should be noted that a rebuilding programme is now under way and that much of the central area, formerly denuded of population because of demolition during the slum clearance scheme, is now being repopulated. This will not halt the outflow of population, but should slow it down. These migrations have left an enormous problem of urban renewal. Large areas of decaying terraced houses

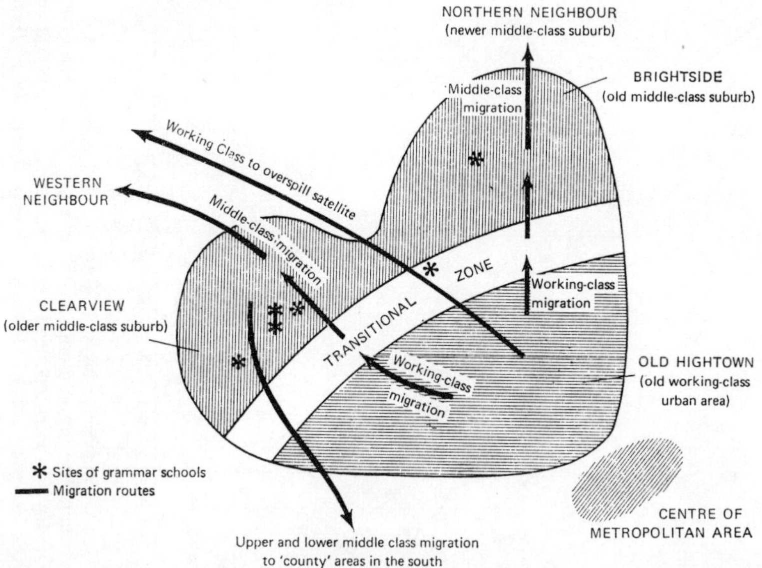

Fig. 1. Hightown: the main ecological areas, the migration routes and the sites of grammar schools.

and dilapidated industrial building remain to be cleared, while the size of the rate-paying population that must shoulder this task decreases yearly.

Although the main focus of this study is Hightown Grammar School, we have to bear in mind the nature of the changes over recent decades in the community of which the school is part. Not only do these changes indirectly affect the functioning of the school, they also

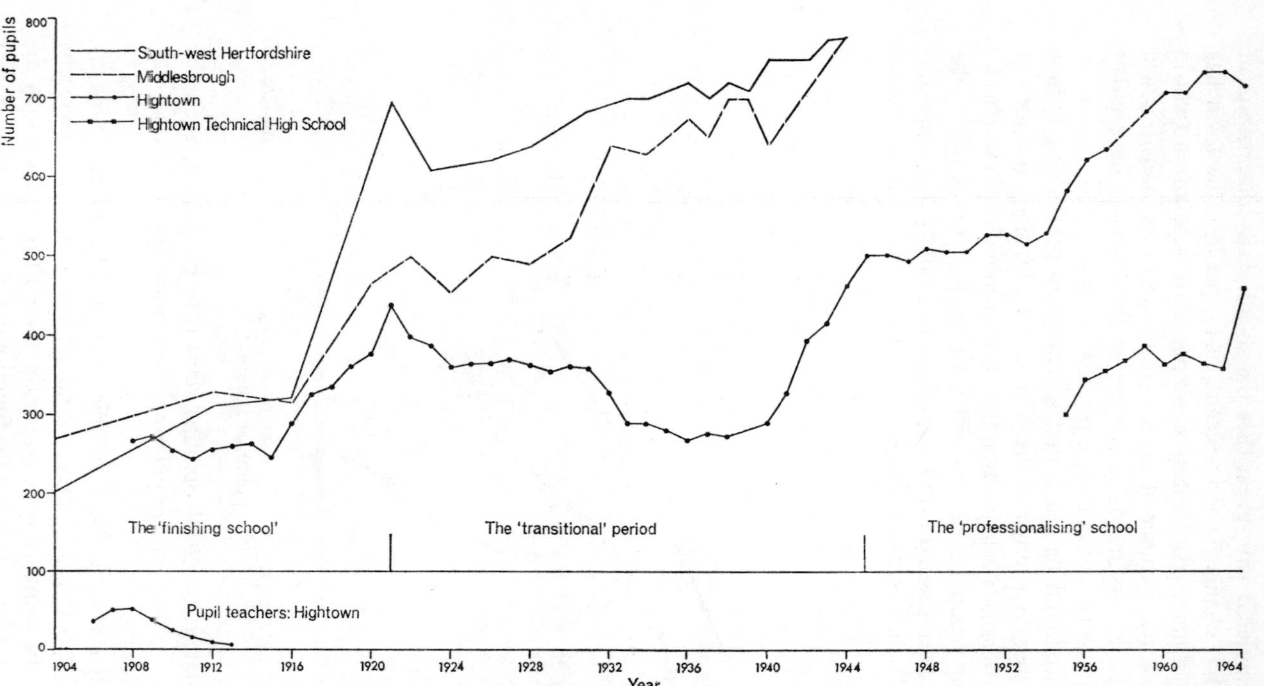

Fig. 2. Provision of grammar school places for boys: Hightown, 1908–65; south-west Hertfordshire, 1904–55; Middlesbrough, 1905–44. The differences are significant. The graph compares the growths of the principal (and for long the only) grammar schools in towns of approximately equal size. In 1951 Hightown had a population of about 178,000, south-west Hertfordshire had about 155,000 and Middlesbrough about 146,000. However, these differences are only illustrative. Whereas Hightown's population has recently decreased by about 2,000 a year, south-west Hertfordshire has experienced a rapid increase. Hence the differences shown in the early part of the graph grossly underestimate the differences in grammar school provision in the two areas.

affect people's attitudes towards the school. For example, the chief education officer was worried that the average IQ in Hightown was falling, and a practising teacher was convinced that the majority of boys in the school were not suited to grammar school education. 'It's cruel to them and not fair on us,' he said.

While it would not be accurate to describe Hightown, or even old Hightown, as a working-class ghetto, it certainly retains many of the characteristics of a residual or 'core' working-class culture. This will be an important consideration in the analysis.

Hightown Grammar School

Hightown Municipal Secondary School was formed in 1904 by the amalgamation of a number of existing post-elementary schools already established by the town. The schools amalgamated were the Central Scholarship Higher Grade School (boys' section), the Pupil Teacher Centre (male section) and the day school at the Technical Institute. In its early years, selection was by examination, at the age of twelve, of boys from the local elementary schools. Twenty-four per cent of places were free scholarship places and the remainder paid a fee of £3 per annum. Pupils had to undertake to complete a three-year course.[4]

The Technical Institute had been established in 1896 but, because of the already existing craft apprenticeship system, the day classes had never been very successful. The institute was therefore easily able to provide accommodation for the new school's 230 pupils, and the principal of the Technical Institute combined his position of principal with that of headmaster of the new secondary school. The Municipal Secondary School did not get its own headmaster until 1913 and, because its new school building in Birch Place was used as a military hospital during the first world war, did not get its own building until 1920.

The move to the new building in 1920 enabled the number of pupils to be increased to 440, and in 1921 the school agreement was amended to retain pupils to the end of the session in which they became sixteen years old. By this time the number of scholarships had increased and only a limited number of pupils paid the fees, which had risen to £7 10s. per annum.

In 1918 the school captain obtained the first Higher School Certificate and in 1925 a sixth-former gained the first open university scholarship. However, academic standards were still generally low compared with the rest of the country. In 1927 only 2 per cent of the boys on the register stayed on for the full Higher School Certificate, compared with 10 per cent for comparable schools in the rest of the country.

The depression of the 1930's had a serious effect on the development of the school. Scholarships were curtailed, dropping from an average of 99 per year over the previous ten years to 59 in 1931, and to 39 and 47 in 1932 and 1933. The school roll dropped from over 400 in the 1920's to 278 in 1934, and it was to remain around this low level until the second world war. The war years show a spectacular rise in the school's numbers—from 280·in 1942 to 460 in 1945. There was a corresponding rise in the size of the sixth form, which reached 40 in 1945.

In keeping with trends in the rest of the country, this expansion continued after the war. However, despite the rapid growth in numbers, the proportion of boys staying on at school after the age of 15 remained one of the lowest in the country. Similarly, the proportion of Grammar School boys staying on into the sixth form remained low despite the efforts of a new and energetic headmaster. In March 1963, when I started work in the school, there were 730 boys, of whom 116 were in the sixth form, and 614 in the four streams up to ordinary level. For a local education authority grammar school of four streams, a sixth form between 150 and 200 would have been more normal.[5]

The present site of the school, Clearview, was a remnant of one of the small estates in the area. It consisted of 25 acres of park land which had been purchased by the education committee in 1937. Owing to difficulties during the war and the post-war period, the present school building was not completed until 1956. This new building has many advantages over the old. It stands in its own grounds, which accommodated several rugby and football pitches as well as an area of park land. The school has its own gyms, laboratories, dining halls, assembly hall and workshops. It has spacious classrooms and is surrounded by an attractive area of park land and detached and semi-detached houses. The previous building in Birch Place was inferior in practically every respect; its dilapidated frontage of tall metal railings, dark basement and high, narrow windows gave it the appearance of a converted workhouse rather than that of a modern school. The Chief Education Officer of Hightown wrote in

6

1956 that the school in Birch Place had always 'lacked many of the features which ought to have contributed to its reputation', adding that 'the achievements of the school, and its reputation, have come about despite the condition in which the school has worked, in a building too small, on a site too confined, and amid the noise and dirt of a highly industrialised city'.

Despite this criticism and its poor condition, the building in Birch Place was not immediately demolished. From 1956 to 1963 it housed the new Hightown Technical High School which had been established in the old Technical Institute building. The accommodation of the Technical High School in the building in Birch Place inevitably gave it second-class status in the public's eyes. The very fact that it had on two occasions moved into buildings deemed unsuitable for the Grammar School gave the community reason to embrace the popular idea that technical schools are educationally inferior alternatives to grammar schools.

In 1962 it was announced that the Technical High School was to be rehoused in a new, specially designed, building on the same site as the Grammar School. To make room for it a number of old houses (which the Grammar School had hoped to acquire for its Scouts and sixth form) were demolished, and the Grammar School lost a foot-ball pitch. The considerable feeling aroused among parents of Grammar School pupils by this move of the education committee—and the underlying suspicion that the real motive behind the move was to enable the two schools to be turned into a single comprehensive school—gave rise to a protest movement.[6] It is sufficient to note here that a great deal of opposition to the move was generated and that this was largely due to the clear difference in status that existed between the Technical High School and Hightown Grammar School. The difference still exists, but a number of indicators point to a levelling of their respective statuses, although it is doubtful whether this process will be able to proceed far before both schools are affected by an impending reorganisation.

In conclusion, we can summarise as follows. Hightown lies in an inner segment of a conurbation which has suffered a net loss of population since the 1920's. The nature of the loss has been difficult to establish with precision, but the evidence available points to a disproportionate loss from the middle classes. The net population loss and the failure of the middle class to establish itself in the town in large numbers are important factors affecting the development of

7

the school, factors which will be examined in more detail in the following chapter. Despite the problems facing it, the analysis reveals that Hightown Grammar School has established itself as the most prestigious local-authority secondary school for boys in the city.

NOTES

[1] All figures are rounded to the nearest one per cent or nearest 1,000.

[2] I am indebted for a number of points in the following analysis to: John Lee, 'The journey to work', an unpublished report, Manchester University.

[3] At the time of writing (1968) the information necessary to check this conclusion has not yet been published.

[4] The fees and the length of the school course were the main features of an 'agreement' signed by the parents before their sons could attend the school. Parents who broke the agreement, usually by taking their sons away before they had completed the course, were liable to be fined.

[5] *Early leaving report*, Ministry of Education, C.A.C.E., H.M.S.O., 1954, page 26.

[6] The combined efforts of the Grammar School parent–teacher association, the 'Old Hightownians' and the headmaster were unable to get the decision reconsidered. However, the protest movement also attracted support from the community and engaged in fund raising activities. Sufficient funds were raised to engage a solicitor but even this move failed to influence the council.

2 The development of the school

As we have seen, Hightown Grammar School was established in 1904 as Hightown Municipal Secondary School for Boys and achieved full grammar school status in 1932. Up to 1944 the school grew slowly and suffered a number of setbacks, and it was only after the second world war that it started on a period of uninterrupted growth and of steady improvement in academic standards. By the 1950's it was established as a vigorous and reputable grammar school.

Its development can be depicted in terms of a series of struggles: to obtain entrants of sufficiently high standard and in sufficient numbers; to retain pupils in competition with outside opportunities of employment; to maintain standards of scholarship and to attract staff of good grammar school calibre. This is in marked contrast to the growth of most grammar schools during this period. In the following sections Hightown is compared with Middlesbrough and Watford Grammar Schools,[1] which were specifically chosen as contrasting types by Floud, Halsey and Martin.

the two . . . should be of contrasting social character in order that post-war educational reform might be seen at work under both favourable and unfavourable conditions.[2]

As shown in Fig. 2, Hightown constitutes a more extreme contrast to Watford than does Middlesbrough.

The subsequent analysis of the development of Hightown Grammar School will be approached in the following manner:

Stage 1
(*a*) 1904–15
(*b*) 1916–21 } 1904–21: the 'finishing school' period.

Stage 2
(*a*) 1922–31
(*b*) 1932–40 } 1922–45: transitional period.
(*c*) 1941–45

Stage 3

(*a*) 1946–54
(*b*) 1955–65 } 1946–65: the 'professionalising school' period.

These stages and sub-stages in the development of the school have been chosen for descriptive and analytical reasons.

TABLE 2

SOCIAL CLASS COMPOSITION OF HIGHTOWN GRAMMAR SCHOOL
(PER CENT)

	(*a*)	(*b*)	(*c*)
	1905 H.M.I.'s report	1915 H.M.I.'s report	1917–20 leavers
	Social composition of school		*Leaving sample (reflects social composition of school)*
	Left during the period (1905–8)	*Left during the period (1915–18)*	
Professional, managerial and owning	15·2	20·0	12·7
Retail trade, clerks, etc.	49·2	44·0	55·3
Artisans	35·6	36·0	32·0
Totals	100·0	100·0	100·0
N =	230 (24 unknown)	246	284 (11 unknown)

The sub-stages represent periods of stability, or of increase or decline in the school population. All were, however, linked to policy decisions (for example, in 1921 the new four-year agreement meant that the yearly intake was cut back to three forms and the school population decreased and stabilised at a new level), so that the sub-stages can be combined to form significant developmental stages in the life of the school. It will also be argued that between 1904 and 1965 there were changes in the social function of the school and the above stages represent significant periods in this development.[3]

The 'finishing school', 1904–21

The reports of H.M. Inspector of Schools and the leavers' records provide sufficient information to reconstruct some aspects of the social composition of the school during this period (see table 2).

The table shows that the social class composition of the school has been fairly constant over this period. Certainly, no underlying trend

10

TABLE 3

SOCIAL CLASS COMPOSITION OF HIGHTOWN GRAMMAR SCHOOL
(1905–17) COMPARED WITH SOUTH-WEST HERTFORDSHIRE AND
MIDDLESBROUGH GRAMMAR SCHOOLS (PER CENT)

	S.W. Herts 1904–18	Middlesbrough 1905–18	Hightown 1905–17
Professional, managerial and owning	31·3	29·8	15·9
Retail trade, clerks, foremen	54·2	46·4	49·7
Skilled and unskilled workers	14·5	22·8	34·5
Totals	100·0	100·0	100·0
N =	873	993	760

TABLE 4

SOCIAL CLASS OF MALES (OCCUPIED AND RETIRED)
AGED 15 AND OVER, 1951 (PER CENT)

	I	II	III	IV	V
Hightown	1·4	9·8	52·2	15·7	20·9
Middlesbrough	1·8	10·8	44·4	18·6	24·4
S.W. Herts	6·1	17·1	53·9	12·6	10·3

Source: Census of Great Britain, 1951; one per cent tables

is discernible in the data, and the fluctuation in size of the 'professional, managerial and owning' category could be due to demographic chance or small variations in the criteria of classification.[4] When the three sets of figures for the period are averaged and compared to similar data (see table 3) presented by Floud, Halsey and Martin for south-west Hertfordshire and Middlesbrough, there are some important differences.

The high proportion of boys of working-class origin (34·5 per cent) in Hightown was not paralleled by Middlesbrough Grammar School until the 1920's and by south-west Hertfordshire until the late 1940's. This high working-class intake was no doubt related to the large number of scholarships available. Already in 1912 nearly 60 per cent of the boys had scholarships, compared with about 30 per cent in Middlesbrough and south-west Hertfordshire. It was probably also influenced by other factors, such as the existence in nearby towns of established direct grant schools, which creamed off middle-class

11

pupils, and the social composition and cultural characteristics of the local community, which were predominantly working class.

An indication of the post-war social class compositions of the three communities is given in table 4. As a result of competition from direct grant schools and the characteristics of the local community, the school had great difficulty in attracting and keeping suitable students for the full course. This was in spite of the high provision of free places, which continued to grow and is in contrast to both the Hertfordshire and Middlesbrough schools, which were under pressure to increase their size. In the case of the south-west Hertfordshire school, the demand was such that it would have been possible to do this even though free places were reduced. It is apparent then that Hightown represents a polar extreme to south-west Hertfordshire, with Middlesbrough in a middle position. Hightown Secondary School was a relatively poor school in an educationally depressed area.

The problem of attracting pupils of a sufficiently high calibre and at the right age (11+), was acute for a number of years, and contributed directly to the problem of early leaving. Pupils who joined the school at the age of 13 frequently left at 15. To have remained at school might have meant sacrificing the chance of the best local jobs.

TABLE 5

AVERAGE AGES AT ENTRY AND LEAVING
HIGHTOWN GRAMMAR SCHOOL*

The number of years for which these averages are recorded
is small

	Entry	*Leaving*
1912	12 years 9 months	15 years 9 months
1916	12 years 2 months	–
1918	11 years 10 months	–
1925	–	15 years 8 months
1928	11 years 5 months	15 years 5 months
1937	–	16 years 4 months

* From school records. These years were selected to show (*a*) the decrease in the age of entry and (*b*) the later increase in the age of leaving.

In 1909, when about a quarter of the boys were leaving at the end of their second year, the headmaster complained to the governors that commercial and business houses, and even the corporation, considered 16 too old for a boy to start work. He felt that the corporation could give a lead, not by giving preference to secondary school boys,

12

but by devising a test that will 'give due weight to training above the elementary school standard'. By 1911, the headmaster found it necessary to take practical steps to increase the incentive to stay on at school. He contacted the managers of six of the major banks in the area and arranged that boys from the school who were awarded apprenticeships at these banks could stay on for an extra year, in order to take matriculation. They would then have the length of their apprenticeship reduced by one year. With at least one bank he was able to arrange to nominate boys for the bank's waiting list, before the matriculation examination, so that boys thus nominated could go straight into the bank, without having to wait an indefinite period for a vacancy. Although these arrangements probably affected a small number of boys, the average age of withdrawal remained about the same (15¾ years). The large increase in the size of the school came (in 1916) because of the lower age at which pupils entered the school and because the yearly intake was increased.

In 1912 the headmaster's report to the governors records that the average age of the intake had fallen from 13 years 3 months to 12 years 9 months. Between 1912 and 1918 the average age of entry again fell from 12 years 9 months to 11 years 10 months.[5] Since the age of leaving remained constant, this caused an increase in the school population of about seventy, and in 1917 the intake was increased by thirty boys.

This rapid increase in the size of the school during and after the first world war was part of a nation-wide expansion and was also noted in Middlesbrough and south-west Hertfordshire. It is important to realise that, although the Middlesbrough expansion took place in the context of a constant proportion of scholarships (20 per cent) and the Hertfordshire expansion (which was proportionately and numerically greatest—320 to 700) took place concurrently with a slight decrease in the proportion of scholarships, the expansion in Hightown occurred only as the proportion of scholarships rose to nearly 80 per cent.

It is clear that the attempt to establish and develop secondary education in Hightown must be regarded as a struggle in the face of a rather apathetic response from the local community. The aim of the headmaster was to increase the length of the school course so that the *normal* school career would link with a regional system of external examinations leading to higher education. Once achieved, this would increase the status of the school, would legitimise the 'higher' forms

13

of knowledge it was attempting to impart, and would eventually change the major local function of the school. The way would be open to the higher professions and universities.

The headmaster's local attempts to legitimise the content and length of his courses by making agreements with a few prominent employers was only partially successful, as the number and range of local employers was too great and their methods of recruitment remained on the whole haphazard and open to other, more powerful local influences—for example, parental connections and rapid variations in manpower requirements. If a good job became available a few months before the end of the school course or the examinations, it was often worth leaving and even paying a fine equivalent to several weeks' wages in order to secure the job. For example, in 1919 a county fee-payer was withdrawn by his father, a dispenser, to take a job as an assistant pharmaceutical chemist at Butcher & Simmons. His father paid a fine of £3 for taking the boy away from school at

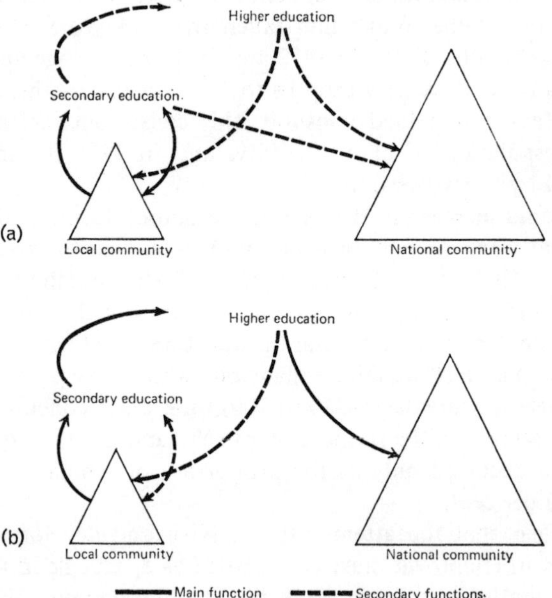

Fig. 3. Hightown Grammar School: (*a*) the 'finishing school' function, 1904–21— the links with higher education and the national community are tenuous; (*b*) the 'professionalising' function, 1945 onwards—the secondary school is now seen primarily as a route to higher education and to professional or managerial jobs in the national community.

the age of 15 years 2 months, in this case seven months before finishing his three-year course. This was also true of boys who were staying on with the intention of matriculating, and sometimes even for those staying on as pupil teachers.

The major function of the school during this period can be described as the 'finishing school function' (see Fig. 3). The school was used as a jumping-off place, one of higher status than the ordinary or higher elementary school, from which it was possible to obtain the best clerical, commercial, technical and trade apprenticeships in local industry. For this purpose a two-year course was often as good as a three-year course. Given the conditions in local industry, academic qualifications were to a large extent ignored in favour of a 'secondary school boy' with a good family. In practice this frequently meant a fee-payer whose parents could intercede with the employer or, better still, claim some tenuous link[6] (see table 9). It is true that a small number stayed on to take examinations. In 1909—a very successful year—sixteen out of twenty-three passed matriculation, seven in the first division, and one boy won an exhibition to a university. It is also the case that a small fraction of the intake went eventually to training colleges, commercial colleges and colleges of art.[7] However, these hardly represent a significant minority. Reports of their examination results do not dominate the headmaster's reports, which are pre-occupied with average ages of the intake, average ages of with-drawals and numbers completing a three-year course.

The 'finishing school function' was more marked among the fee-payers than among the scholars. The fee-payers were on the whole less able to exploit the academic potentialities of the school and were frequently less motivated to do so. Their parents were more often well placed locally and able to exploit their wealth, kinship or business connections to provide a local career for their sons.[8] This combination of factors brought about a marked inferiority in the staying qualities of fee-payers (see table 6).

Although by 1917–20 the difference between fee-payers and scholars was not so marked, it is clear that the former were still less likely to complete the course and stay on at school. Table 7 shows that this marked academic inferiority is not carried across into the sphere of occupational opportunity except in the proportion of each group obtaining clerical jobs. On the other hand, the predominance of scholars obtaining higher clerical jobs is almost exactly offset by the higher proportion of fee-payers going into their fathers'

TABLE 6

'LENGTH OF SCHOOL LIFE' OF FEE-PAYERS COMPARED WITH SCHOLARS

(a) From headmaster's report to the governors, 1912

	Did not complete three years	Completed three years	Stayed on for fourth year or more	Totals
Fee-payers	20 (38·5%)	26 (50%)	6 (11·5%)	52
Scholars	1 (4%)	6 (24%)	18 (72%)	25
				77

(b) The more complete record from the report cards of school leavers (1917–20) confirms this analysis

	Did not complete three years	Completed three years	Stayed on for fourth year	Totals
Fee-payers	35 (33·7%)	45 (43·2%)	24 (23·1%)	104
Scholars	31 (18·6%)	70 (41·9%)	56 (33·5%)	167
				271

TABLE 7

JOBS OBTAINED BY FEE-PAYERS AND SCHOLARS ON LEAVING SCHOOL, 1917–20

Jobs obtained on leaving	Fee-payers (%)	Scholars (%)
Technical	11	10·0
Higher technical	23	8·9
Clerical	17	35·5
Higher clerical and banks	2	10·7
Skilled apprenticeships	11	8·3
Others	9	6·5
Further education	12	10·7
Unemployed and deceased	2	3·6
Sent to elementary school	3	3·0
Father's business	10	3·0
Totals	100	100·2
N =	100	169

businesses. Similarly, although scholars predominate in obtaining ordinary clerical jobs, the predominance of fee-payers getting higher technical jobs almost exactly cancels this advantage. The jobs designated as 'higher technical' were non-manual technical occupations where there was an indication that extensive on-the-job or night-school training would be received, for example junior analytical chemists, articled engineers and apprentice draughtsmen. They were in no way inferior to clerical jobs and must in some cases have

16

ranked with higher clerical jobs. It is worth recording that of twenty higher clerical jobs obtained, eleven went to boys who stayed on at school and the other nine to boys who completed the course. None went to early leavers. It is therefore apparent that by this time—1917 —the local banks, etc., were becoming much more examination-conscious and local influence counted for less. This movement had not yet spread to industry.

A similar disparity to that found between fee-payers and scholars is found between two groups within the middle class. When the professional, higher technical, clerical and miscellaneous categories are grouped and assumed to constitute the qualified elements of the middle class—opposed to the businessmen, managers, foremen and shopkeepers, who constitute the proprietary[9] middle class—it can be shown that the 'proprietary' group is more highly represented among the early leavers. This relationship holds for both fee-payers and scholars within these two groups. It is important to note that the clear disparity between the 'qualified' and 'proprietary' groups with respect to length of school career is *not* mirrored in the jobs they were able to achieve on leaving school.[10]

The evidence suggests that the local influence and connections of the 'proprietary' group were able to make up for their poorer performance at school when it came to obtaining jobs. It therefore supports the 'finishing school' hypothesis because it demonstrates that the group best placed to exploit the 'finishing school' mechanism did so by joining the school for short periods and leaving to acquire local jobs in no way inferior to those acquired by the academically more conscientious group.

Before closing the discussion of this stage in the development of the school, it is important to look at the performance of the various class groups (see table 8). This can be done only with respect to length of school life, since records of examinations are not systematically recorded on the record cards. Table 8 shows conclusively that, as one would expect, early leaving becomes more prevalent and staying on at school less common from the upper middle class through the lower middle class to the working class. The performances of fee-payers and scholarship boys are combined in table 8, but the relationship also holds if scholars are considered separately. Table 9 shows that the class differentiation in 'completing' or 'not completing' the course was even more marked among the 'scholars' than among the school population as a whole.

TABLE 8

'LENGTH OF SCHOOL LIFE' OF THE BOYS
IN EACH CLASS CATEGORY, 1917–20*

Father's occupation	Early leavers (three years) %	Completed (= three years) %	Stayed on (three years) %	Totals %
1 *Upper middle class:* professional and higher technical business owners and managers	15·6	43·7	40·7	100 (32)
2 *Lower middle class:* clerical, foremen, shop and miscellaneous non-managerial	24·7	44·7	30·6	100 (150)
3 *Working class:* skilled manual, unskilled manual	27·0	49·5	23·6	100 (89)
				N = 271

Excluded from this table: (1) Occupations not stated	11
(2) Transfers to other grammar schools	13
	N = 295

* This table is presented in a more detailed form in Appendix 2.

TABLE 9

'LENGTH OF SCHOOL LIFE' FOR THE SCHOLARS
IN EACH MAJOR CLASS CATEGORY (LEAVERS 1917–20)

Scholars	Early leavers %	Completed %	Stayed on %	Totals %
1 Upper middle	–	37·5	62·5	100
2 Lower middle	16·9	47·2	36·0	100
3 Working	23·5	50·0	26·5	100
				N = 182

The evidence presented in this section confirms the major components in the 'finishing school model' described earlier. The school was not, at this stage, a dispenser of academic certificates which were all-important in the subsequent careers of its pupils. In many spheres, the general status obtained from having gone to secondary school, the influence of one's parents, or simply the chance of being the person available when a job came on offer, were more important than the academic certificate. Pupils left early and paid a fine rather than miss the chance of a job. The headmaster complained that the local employers did not pay sufficient heed to the academic qualifications he dispensed, and consequently the school could point to few

18

examples of rewards available to those who persevered at their studies. In many respects, high academic achievement was a luxury, except to those who traditionally utilised and valued such skills.[11] Naturally, the sections of the population which could most afford 'luxuries' were the ones who indulged most in this one, and the class distribution of pupils staying on conforms closely with the class gradient.

The main purpose of this book is to explain and clarify the social mechanisms that account for the correlation between social class and educational achievement. At this juncture we have been concerned largely with its documentation. Later in this chapter we shall examine fluctuations in the correlation in terms of the changing function of the school and the changing role of education in the larger community. Subsequent chapters will trace the implications of this explanation into all aspects of the social organisation of the school.

The transitional period, 1922-45

In 1921 a new four-year agreement became operative and practically the whole of the third year stayed on for a fourth year. The school's numbers rose to a new peak of 440. They did not reach it again until 1944, for in the next year the intake was cut from four to three streams (120 pupils to 90) to make room for a further agreement which, it was expected, would cause most pupils to spend five years in the school (i.e. for most pupils, until they were 16).

These two new agreements finally created the organisational link with higher education which was the aim of the headmaster during the period 1904 to 1921. But although the organisational framework of the school was now linked up with the main stream of higher education, the job of persuading pupils to take advantage of it still remained. It proved a difficult task in the face of economic recession and reductions in expenditure on education. The size of the school stagnated at around 360 pupils, and even this level was dependent on practically 100 per cent of scholarship places. By 1925, fee-payers had almost disappeared.

The Board of Education circular of 1932, limiting the number of scholarships to 50 per cent of the previous year's intake, hit the school exceptionally hard. In 1931 it had temporarily reduced its intake from 90 to 62 because a large number of boys had been kept down to repeat their first year. Only 31 scholarships were therefore available in 1932—two-thirds less than usual.

A second economy measure, the idea of special places for which a parent's contribution was required on a sliding scale, also worked to reduce the demand for grammar school places, although the degree to which it affected the intake is not known.[12] During this period, fee-payers were given the maximum encouragement to join the school; despite this, and a reduction in the overall size from 360 to 270, the fee-payers never amounted to much more than 16 per cent of the total (see Fig. 4).

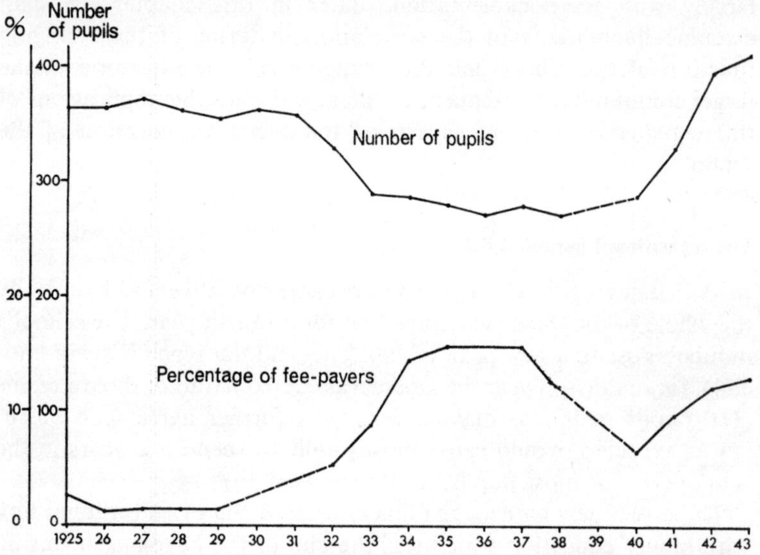

Fig. 4. The percentage of fee-payers and number of pupils at Hightown Grammar School, 1925–43.

The effects of the 1932 circular demonstrate the shaky foundations and the insecure nature of grammar school education in Hightown. In south-west Hertfordshire the pressure from fee-payers was such that the governors (unsuccessfully) requested the Board of Education to allow them to reduce the number of *free* places, and until 1940 the proportion never rose about 30 per cent. Even in Middlesbrough, the number of free and special places did not rise to 80 per cent until 1940. In Hightown, the education committee could not reduce the number of scholarships and special places below 84 per cent without endangering the existence of the school.

20

During this period the whole content and emphasis of the headmaster's reports to the governors underwent a noticeable change. From 1923 onwards, there were detailed reports on examinations, school certificates and, later, Higher School Certificates, and the number of boys staying on beyond matriculation (at 16 years of age).

Despite the difficulties the school was facing, an increased number of boys were able to exploit the 'prestige' route to universities. The importance the school attached to academic success at this time can be gauged from the fact that when a sixth-former won the first State scholarship, in the 1930's, the whole school was given a day's holiday. The school won three State scholarships during this period (after 1945, it won four or five a year).

By the end of the period, there was increasing evidence that the community was beginning to see the school as a gateway to higher education and the higher professions rather than, as previously, a 'finishing school' through which preferential entrance to local job opportunities could be obtained:

1 The demand for grammar school education increased among fee-payers and scholars.
2 The size of the sixth form increased from ten or twelve boys in the late 1920's to 45 in 1944.
3 The number of successes in higher education increased and they became an important reference group.

The records for 1934–39 have been selected to illustrate the trends that matured during this period. The size of the school had diminished, so that to obtain a reasonable sample of leavers (303) a five-year period had to be selected. The records for the early war years could not be used, because evacuation had disrupted the school and the records were not complete.

Once again, the proportion of working-class boys in the school

TABLE 10

SOCIAL CLASS COMPOSITION OF HIGHTOWN GRAMMAR SCHOOL
(PER CENT)

Year of leaving:	1917–20	1934–39	1934–36	1905
Upper middle class	12·7	17·0	20·6	15·2
Lower middle class	55·3	48·3	43·5	49·2
Working class	32·0	34·7	35·9	35·6
Totals	100	100	100	100
N =	284	294	131	230

remained relatively constant (see table 10). This is also true if the period 1934–36 is taken on its own. These years are significant because the pupils were all recruited before the 1932 reductions in expenditure. The table also demonstrates the failure of working-class pupils to gain places in the grammar school in a proportion greater than that established in 1905.

The importance in the change of representation between the upper middle class and the lower middle class is difficult to assess. It may represent a change in the proportion of upper middle class parents using the school, as opposed to direct grant schools outside Hightown. It may also reflect a change in the structure of industry and commerce in the town, for it is noticeable that whereas in 1917–20 the professional and higher technical category outnumbered the business and managerial category by almost two to one, the reverse is true in 1934–39. However, there can be no doubt about the significance of the working-class/middle-class figures. In a town where migration was mainly from the middle class, the working class failed to increase its proportional representation in the school.

During this transition period, Hightown stands between south-west Hertfordshire and Middlesbrough in the proportion of working-class pupils in the school population (see table 11). One characteristic

TABLE 11

THE SOCIAL CLASS COMPOSITION OF HIGHTOWN GRAMMAR
SCHOOL (1934–39) COMPARED WITH THAT OF MIDDLESBROUGH
AND SOUTH-WEST HERTFORDSHIRE FOR SIMILAR PERIODS (PER CENT)

	Middlesbrough (1935–38 intake)	S.W. Herts (1934–38 intake)	Hightown (1934–39 leavers)
Upper middle class	16·1	19·1	17·0
Lower middle class	33·8	61·5	48·3
Working class	45·6	16·1	34·7
Totals	95·5	96·7	100
Not known	(4·5)	(3·3)	
N =	575	366	294

that stands out from the records is that in this period the relative *performances* of the three class groupings changed notably. Although full information covering the whole of the period is not available from the Middlesbrough and south-west Hertfordshire schools, the information on parts of the period, 1934–38 and 1935–38, confirms the Hightown figures. In Hightown, the *change* in the relative performances of the three class categories can be expressed only by

22

recording length of school life, because examination results were not set down on record cards between 1917 and 1920. However, *length of school life*[13] is a reliable indicator of success in secondary schools for this period.

Table 12 reveals that whereas in 1917–20 working-class boys were more likely to be early leavers and less likely to be members of the

TABLE 12

LENGTH OF SCHOOL LIFE FOR 1917–20 COMPARED WITH
THAT FOR 1934–39 (PER CENT)*

	1917–20		1934–39	
	Early leavers	*Stayed on*	*Early leavers*	*Stayed on*
Upper middle class	15·6	40·7	20·4	34·7
Lower middle class	24·7	30·6	25·0	19·7
Working class	27·0	23·6	24·7	21·6

* The percentage of each class group that completed the course can be obtained by adding the 'early leavers' and 'stayed on' categories, and subtracting from 100 per cent. The 'completed' category is omitted, to facilitate comparison between 1917–20 and 1934–39.

sixth form than lower middle class boys, by 1934–39 the working-class boys were *less* likely to be early leavers and *more* likely to stay on than lower middle class boys. This is a reversal of the normally expected trend. Lower middle class children are normally expected

TABLE 13

PERCENTAGE OF CHILDREN IN EACH CLASS CATEGORY
OBTAINING SCHOOL CERTIFICATE, MATRICULATION OR HIGHER
SCHOOL CERTIFICATE IN HIGHTOWN GRAMMAR SCHOOL, 1934–39

	No exam (a) %	*School* Certificate (b) %	Matriculation (c) %	HSC (d) %	Number of boys
Upper middle class	33·3	66·7	31·3	16·7	45
Lower middle class	43·3	56·7	14·9	11·2	134
Working class	40·2	59·8	20·6	12·4	97
					276

Excluded: (1) Transfers to other grammar schools, 14.
         (2) Not classifiable by social class, 9.

(a) *No examination*, either through failing the examination or leaving before it was possible to take the examination.
(b) *School certificate examination*, successful candidates. The 'No exam' and 'School certificate' columns add horizontally to 100 per cent.
(c) *Matriculation* exemption. A higher level of achievement in the school certificate examination which was recognised as a university entrance requirement.
(d) *Higher School Certificate*. A higher level examination usually taken two years after school certificate.

to perform better than working-class children. This finding becomes more important when the examination results for the period are considered. They show that the slight superiority of working-class children in completing the normal school course is consistent with their examination results (see table 13).

The table shows that in every category (school certificate, matriculation and Higher School Certificate) working-class boys have a higher proportion of passes. If this reversal of the usual performance of working-class boys were the only case of its kind, it would still require an explanation in terms of the changing strengths of the social factors involved and an estimation of how they were related

TABLE 14

PERCENTAGE OF CHILDREN IN EACH CLASS CATEGORY
OBTAINING SCHOOL CERTIFICATE OR HIGHER SCHOOL
CERTIFICATE IN SOUTH-WEST HERTFORDSHIRE AND MIDDLESBROUGH

	School certificate %	HSC %	Number of leavers
(a) *S.W. Herts, 1934–38*			
Upper middle class	82	13	79
Lower middle class	69	14	133
Working class	82	11	54
			266
(b) *Middlesbrough, 1935–37*			
Upper middle class	76	4	49
Lower middle class	61	5	108
Working class	69	6	139
			294

to the changing function of the grammar school in Hightown. However, as the figures presented by Floud, Halsey and Martin[14] make clear, this reversal of fortunes also occurred in south-west Hertfordshire and Middlesbrough. Table 14 shows that in south-west Hertfordshire the small working-class contingent performed as well as *upper* middle class boys at school certificate level but slightly worse than them at Higher School Certificate level. In Middlesbrough they performed at well above the lower middle class level at school certificate and above both the lower and upper middle class boys at Higher School Certificate. They were also the numerically largest contingent in this school.

Before finally accepting these figures as a genuine reflection of the changing fortunes of the class categories within the schools under scrutiny, it is necessary to examine a number of intervening variables which, although significant in themselves, may put the explanation on a rather different footing:

1 The low performance of the middle class could be due to the fact that a high proportion of the middle-class boys are fee-payers. As we have seen, fee-payers do not perform as well as scholars.
2 The high performance of the working class could be due to the fact that a proportion of marginally qualified working-class children declined their places in the grammar school owing to the economic situation, which affected the working-class families disproportionately. The resulting working-class contingent was thus more highly selected.
3 The class structure of the community might have changed.

In Appendix 3 these points are considered in turn and seen to be, of themselves, insufficient explanation of this reversal of the normal class fortunes. The evidence from the three schools under consideration shows that the working-class category performed better in examinations than the lower middle class (if the total school population is taken into account). The poorer performance of fee-payers and the over-representation of fee-payers among the upper middle and lower middle class only partially explains this. In addition, the evidence fails to support the view that the phenomenon can be completely accounted for by working-class boys being selectively discouraged from taking up positions in the school. Some explanation of the working-class boys' exceptional performance is required. The hypothesis must be consistent with the more substantial findings of the research and in line with general changes in class structure and in the relations between classes that are known to have taken place.

By 1934–39 the school had an established record of academic success in further education to which the staff could refer when encouraging their pupils. It could be demonstrated that academic achievement, above the levels required for local employment, offered them the chance of a worthwhile career. This had not been possible before. Further education was now a viable alternative to local career mobility. In addition, local career opportunities appear to have been at a low ebb, owing to the economic recession (28 boys were recorded as unemployed after leaving school and for 80 others no jobs were recorded). In these new circumstances, it may be argued, the three class categories found themselves in a rather different relationship. In this new context of increased motivation towards academic achievement, the upper middle class remained much as before, orientated towards academic success and possessed of the material and cultural resources to achieve it. The lower middle and working class, while receiving a new impetus towards academic achievement, lacked to a far greater extent the material and cultural equipment to fulfil themselves. Any slight advantages the lower middle class possessed here were likely to have been outweighed by the remaining attraction of the local career opportunities, in which it traditionally had a dominant position.[15] In other words, the traditional superiority of the lower middle class in the 'finishing school' stage became a liability as the major function of the school changed to 'professionalising'.

This equality in the educational fortunes of the two class categories, as represented in the school, could not be expected to last long; after the second world war the lower middle class resumed its old dominance.

The professionalising school, 1945-65

As we have seen, this period in the school's growth saw a number of major developments: a substantial increase in overall size;[16] an even larger proportional growth in the size of the sixth form;[17] the move to new, larger school premises that were the most modern and best equipped in Hightown. These developments reflected the continual growth of processes in the wider society described in the previous stages:

1 The recognition by parents that the educational system provided the most promising avenues for career advancement. This led to increased competition for grammar school places in the only school[18] generally available with an established and direct route to further education—in particular, to the universities.
2 The gradual assumption on the part of the majority of the Grammar School teachers[19] that the school's *main* function was to send its pupils into further education, and in particular to the universities.
3 Awareness by the Hightown education authorities of factors 1 and 2 above, and hence the realisation that they could achieve

26

a prominent reputation in the educational field by investing in a larger, successful grammar school.

The war years had seen a rapid growth in the size of the school. This growth was part of a nation-wide expansion in secondary education, and had taken place despite the difficulty of organising a school which was divided partly in evacuated premises and partly in Hightown.

When the 1944 Education Act abolished fees and established an all-embracing system of secondary education purporting to provide education according to age, ability and aptitude, the stage was set for still further expansion, a raising of standards and, it was widely thought, a much greater participation of the working classes. Although the early part of this post-war period (1946 to the early

TABLE 15

DISTRIBUTION OF SOCIAL CLASS CATEGORIES IN HIGHTOWN GRAMMAR SCHOOL FROM RECORD CARDS, 1962–65

		Number		Percentage
Upper middle class	Professional and higher technical	37	} 112	31·3
	Business and managerial	75		
Lower middle class	Clerical	25	} 107	29·9
	Miscellaneous non-manual	31		
	Foremen and shopkeepers	51		
Working class	Skilled manual	91	} 139	38·8
	Semi- and unskilled manual	48		
Not classifiable		27		
Totals		385		100·0

1950's) may have seen an increase in working-class participation, the period for which the records of school leavers have been examined, 1962–65, show that by 1957 Hightown Grammar School was recruiting almost the same proportion of working-class boys as in 1905![20]

Table 15 shows that the major increase was in the recruitment of upper middle class boys, and this was achieved at the expense of lower middle class participation. Between 1905 and 1965, lower middle class participation dropped from 49·2 per cent to 29·8 per cent, while upper middle class participation increased from 15·2 per cent in 1905 to 31·2 per cent in 1962–65. The most radical and persistent change, however, was the increase in the participation of the 'proprietary middle class' group, at the expense of the 'qualified middle class' group. This is shown in table 16.

TABLE 16

INCREASING RATIO OF 'PROPRIETARY' TO 'QUALIFIED' AT
HIGHTOWN GRAMMAR SCHOOL, 1917–65 (PER CENT)

	1917–20	1934–39	1962–65
Proprietary	28·2	31·1	35·2
Qualified	39·8	33·7	26·0
Ratio of 'proprietary' to 'qualified'	0·71	0·92	1·36

These changes are directly related to the pattern of migration from Hightown described earlier in this chapter. White collar workers (especially those with jobs outside Hightown) and professional workers have been prominent among those migrating from Hightown. Since both these categories are included in the category of the qualified middle class, it is this group whose representation is most diminished. The increased participation of the proprietary middle class is also related to the increased pressure on small local businessmen to see that their sons achieve qualifications. This was particularly noticeable of Jewish parents, a number of whom explained to me that since their businesses could not support their sons, the boys' futures lay in academic achievement.

The inability of working-class boys to increase their participation cannot be explained in the same way. Working-class migration has not kept pace with middle-class migration.[21] It is partially explained by the post-war development and growth of the Technical High School, which has a predominantly working-class intake (67 per cent).[22] It must be pointed out, however, that the Technical High

TABLE 17

SOCIAL CLASS DISTRIBUTION OF FREE AND SPECIAL PLACES (PER CENT)

	Grammar School			Grammar School + Technical High School
	1917–20	1934–39	1962–65	1962–65
Upper middle class	5·7	17·2	31·2	21·3
Lower middle class	54·9	44·0	29·8	29·6
Working class	39·5	38·8	38·8	49·1

School[23] replaced two central schools, which gave some boys post-elementary education up to the 1944 Act. Thus, although the overall proportion of working-class boys in Hightown receiving 'grammar type' education has increased (see table 17), it has done so only through the expansion of the bottom level of grammar school education. Working-class boys do not have a greater share of the places in the most prestigious and most successful school.

If the class distribution of the share of free and special places for Hightown Grammar School is examined, the position of working-class scholars can also be seen to have remained constant. Once again, it is only by considering the Technical High School that an increased participation of working-class boys can be demonstrated. In this respect, Hightown is similar to Middlesbrough and south-west Hertfordshire, both of which also failed to show any increase in the proportion of working-class boys gaining free places. In fact, the numbers had actually decreased by 1953. In south-west Hertfordshire, where the largest proportion of places were thrown open to competition (66 per cent) by the 1944 Act, the proportion of free places gained by working-class boys fell from 50 per cent in 1943 to 42 per cent in 1950–53. In Middlesbrough, where the Act freed only 20 per cent of places, the proportion gained by working-class boys fell from 53 per cent in 1935–38 to 45 per cent in 1953, after temporarily climbing above that level in 1948–51.[24]

TABLE 18

COMPARISON OF THE RELATIVE SUCCESS OF THE VARIOUS CLASS
CATEGORIES IN COMPLETING THE SCHOOL COURSE

Completion of five-year course (doubtfuls classified as 'stayed on')

	Did not complete %	*Completed* %	*Stayed on* %	*Number*
(*a*) 1962–65				
Upper middle	4·0	23·0	73·0	100
Lower middle	7·9	33·4	58·8	102
Working	13·3	39·3	47·4	135
Average				
(nearest 1%)	9·0	33·0	59·0	337
(*b*) 1934–39				
Upper middle	17·1	41·5	41·5	41
Lower middle	20·4	55·3	24·3	103
Working	20·4	57·0	22·6	93
Average				
(nearest 1%)	20·0	53·0	27·0	237

The failure of working-class boys materially to increase their participation in these grammar schools, despite the 1944 Act, is perhaps unexpected. There is evidence to show that it is part of a more general phenomenon,[25] and the relative success in examinations of the various class categories during this post-war period also reveals an increased class differentiation, compared to the period 1934–39. If completion of the normal five-year course is taken as a criterion, the results shown in table 18(a) are obtained. The figures show a marked increase in class differentiation as compared with the 1934–1939 figures, even if fee-payers are omitted from consideration.

A comparison of table 18(a) and 18(b) also demonstrates the degree to which the school had moved from a 'finishing' to a 'professionalising' role. Only 9 per cent of the boys left school without completing the course, compared with 20 per cent in 1934–38, and 59 per cent stayed on, compared with only 27 per cent in 1934–39. Success, in terms of examinations passed, also shows the trends of increased levels of performance and increased differentiation (see table 19).

TABLE 19

ACADEMIC SUCCESS OF THE MAJOR CLASS CATEGORIES, 1962–65
LEAVERS, HIGHTOWN GRAMMAR SCHOOL

	Some A level passes	No A level passes			
	1–3 A levels %	*5 + O levels* %	*1–4 O levels* %	*No O levels* %	*Number*
Upper middle	56·0	17·0	16·0	11·0	100
Lower middle	37·6	9·9	37·6	14·8	101
Working	27·3	9·9	39·4	23·4	132
Average (nearest 1%)	39·0	12·0	32·0	17·0	333

The level of performance for this period is more difficult to compare with the 1934–39 figures. Probably the only safe comparison is the number of boys leaving without sitting an examination of any kind. In 1934–39, this was about 34 per cent; in 1962–65, it had halved to 17 per cent. The proportion gaining a Higher School Certificate in 1934–39 compared with those gaining one A level in 1962–65 shows an increase from 14 to 39 per cent. A better comparison, at this level, would be with those gaining two or more A levels in 1962–65 (i.e. with minimum university entrance). Since this was 36 per cent, the increase in standards is still obvious, if not accurately represented. The increased class differentiation in Hightown between 1934–39 and 1962–65 is also apparent in Middlesbrough and south-west Hertfordshire (see Appendix 4, table 72).

During the 'professionalising' period, then, the major function of the school was to provide the educational link to higher education, and its academic standards achieved reached new heights. The increased competition in the educational field brought on by the rich rewards society offers educational attainment meant that, within the grammar school, those with the most ability to exploit this avenue triumphed over those with fewer resources. A marked class differentiation has thus re-established itself.

NOTES

[1] Described by Floud, Halsey and Martin in *Social class and educational opportunity*.

[2] Floud, Halsey and Martin, *op. cit.*, page xiii.

[3] I had hoped to make a more exhaustive study of the school records to document these changes. Unfortunately, some of the records were destroyed by fire in March 1963, just as the research was getting under way. The fire mainly affected the very early and very recent records. The second world war period was also unreliably documented, owing to evacuation. Information from the school records for this chapter was derived from the following sources: 1905—H.M.I.'s report; 1915—H.M.I.'s report; 1917–20—school-leaving record cards; 1934–49 —school-leaving record cards; 1962–65—school-leaving record cards; headmaster's reports.

[4] The 1917–20 leavers were classified on the basis of the scheme used by Floud, Halsey and Martin in *Social class and educational opportunity*. The number of categories used in the H.M.I.'s reports were reduced in an attempt to make them comparable with the above.

[5] In 1912, 28 per cent of the pupils in the school came from outside Hightown, and even in 1920 12 per cent of the school still came from outside, although the proportion decreased very rapidly after this.

[6] Tumin points out a similar phenomenon in Puerto Rico (M. M. Tumin, *Social class and social change in Puerto Rico*, Princetown, 1961, page 67): 'Three groups, then, owners of businesses, managers (white collar) and owners or managers of firms, make access to their ranks available with less regard for formal education than other groups. These three seem to constitute the proprietary middle classes of Puerto Rico, as against the semi-professional and clerical staffs in the middle class. This suggests that for some of the more esteemed and better paying propositions, avenues of entry, other than formal education, are also available.'

[7] 1917–20, 29/295 went on to universities, training colleges, colleges of commerce and technical institutes, i.e. 9·8 per cent. Only 6·4 per cent went to university or training college.

[8] As has already been mentioned, it is probable that the few Hightown parents with both wealth and academic ambitions sent their sons to school outside Hightown.

[9] This division of the middle class corresponds closely to that used by Tumin, *op. cit.*, page 27. It differs in that foremen are included in the proprietary grouping in the above.

[10] The tables relating to this analysis are included in Appendix 1.

[11] Professional and clerical workers had the highest rates of staying on at school, 43·5 per cent and 39·3 per cent respectively.

[12] Whatever its strength as an inhibitor of growth, its efficiency as an economy measure was negligible. Hightown saved £66 6s. 8d. a year on the scheme in Hightown Grammar School.

[13] *Age* of leaving school is not nearly so reliable an indicator (see page 201) because during this period the age range in each form was quite extensive. Age is therefore not a reliable indicator of having completed the course. 'Length of school life' is, in fact, a compound index and relates accurately to the school course. For example, a boy who spent five years in the school but failed to reach the fifth form and failed to take school certificate, because he repeated a year, would be recorded as an early leaver. On the other hand, a boy who spent four years in the school and took school certificate at the end of his fourth year would be judged to have completed the course.

[14] Floud, Halsey and Martin, *Social class and educational opportunity*, page 133, table 32.

[15] Unfortunately, this hypothesis cannot be substantiated, using the technique of examining the jobs obtained, because the information is too scanty. As stated earlier, the jobs of 108 pupils are either not recorded or stated as unemployed; a further sixteen are recorded simply by the names of firms and cannot therefore be classified.

[16] See Fig. 2. During this period the numbers on the role increased from 500 to 720.

[17] During this period the sixth form grew from 47 to 121, with a record number of eighteen in the third-year sixth.

[18] The Technical High School developed a sixth form during this post-war period and established itself as a route to the universities as well as to higher forms of technical education. However, this remained a very small development compared with the Grammar School.

[19] In his speech to the parents of new pupils, the headmaster always emphasised that the school course was seven, not five years. 'Those that leave after taking O level have not completed the school course.'

[20] Working-class participation has been extremely constant throughout the life of the school: 1905, 35·6 per cent; 1917–20, 32·0 per cent; 1934–39, 34·7 per cent; 1962–65, 38·8 per cent.

[21] Working-class boys at Hightown Grammar School who moved to the overspill satellite did not, in most cases, leave the school. They continued to travel in by bus or motor scooter.

[22] See Appendix 4, table 71.

[23] It must also be noted that, although the Technical Grammar School had two or sometimes three streams up to O level, the sixth form was extremely small and rarely amounted to many more than thirty boys.

[24] Middlesbrough and south-west Hertfordshire differ in that, although in south-west Hertfordshire the participation of working-class boys in the total school population (including fee-payer and scholar) rose from 25 per cent in 1943 to 42 per cent in 1950–53, in Middlesbrough the proportion of working-class boys

rose from 49·3 per cent in 1939–44 to 54 per cent in 1948–51, but fell again to 44·6 per cent in 1953.

[25] A. Little and J. Westergaard, 'The trend of class differentials in educational opportunity in England and Wales', *British Journal of Sociology*, 15 (4), 1964. For a more general discussion of the evidence see A. H. Halsey, 'The sociology of education', in *Sociology*, ed. N. J. Smelser, Wiley, 1967, page 427.

3 The present-day educational provision: its overall structure in Hightown

In the previous chapter we have been concerned with the historically changing function of the Grammar School within Hightown. Now we must turn to examine the contemporary situation. My purpose is to illustrate the way in which a complex of factors sifts and then selects children, first for their junior schools and then, more importantly, for their secondary schools. Special attention will be paid to how the Grammar School selects its intake but it is important to realise that the eleven-plus examination is only the last hurdle in a process that starts, in some respects, with the birth of the child.

The structure of education in Hightown is in many ways typical of a large number of local education authorities throughout the country. There is a distinct, and informally acknowledged, hierarchy of schools at both the junior and secondary levels. Pupils from junior schools in middle-class and in the better working-class areas obtain a disproportionately high share of the Grammar School and Technical School places. Within any given district, parents rank the local schools. This has practical implications, since catchment areas often overlap, and parents then have a choice of school.

Table 20 illustrates the degree of variation in the eleven-plus success between junior schools in Hightown. This success rate is an important factor in determining a school's local standing. The table also demonstrates clearly that junior schools maintain levels of success in the eleven-plus examination that are recognisably distinct from each other in the eyes of the parents and intending parents of the neighbourhood. It is, thus, meaningful to refer to a '30 per cent' or a '50 per cent' school (i.e. a school that usually gets about 30 or 50 per cent of its students through the eleven-plus). The six schools in the table were selected to illustrate the range of these levels. They were not selected on the basis of the consistency of their examination results.

34

TABLE 20

SIX SELECTED HIGHTOWN JUNIOR SCHOOLS, SHOWING NUMBERS AND
PERCENTAGES OF ELEVEN-PLUS SUCCESSES

	1956 %		1959 %		1962 %		1965 %	*Fluctuate about* (%)
R.C. Preparatory boys'	$\left(\frac{12}{14}\right)$	86	$\left(\frac{10}{11}\right)$	91	$\left(\frac{11}{11}\right)$	100	$\left(\frac{8}{8}\right)$ 100	90
Brightside Junior mixed	$\left(\frac{9}{13}\right)$	62	$\left(\frac{18}{27}\right)$	66·7	$\left(\frac{23}{36}\right)$	63·8	$\left(\frac{29}{33}\right)$ 87·8	70
Birch Hall Junior mixed	$\left(\frac{50}{83}\right)$	60·3	$\left(\frac{57}{110}\right)$	51·8	$\left(\frac{30}{78}\right)$	38·5	$\left(\frac{39}{63}\right)$ 61·8	50
Park Hall Junior mixed	$\left(\frac{21}{78}\right)$	26·6	$\left(\frac{25}{86}\right)$	29·1	$\left(\frac{17}{49}\right)$	34·7	$\left(\frac{13}{46}\right)$ 28·3	30
Old Town Junior mixed	$\left(\frac{10}{67}\right)$	14·9	$\left(\frac{6}{101}\right)$	5·9	$\left(\frac{12}{92}\right)$	13·0	$\left(\frac{8}{63}\right)$ 12·7	10
St B's	$\left(\frac{0}{48}\right)$	0	$\left(\frac{1}{39}\right)$	2·6	$\left(\frac{1}{34}\right)$	2·9	$\left(\frac{1}{33}\right.$ 3·0	2

In this respect they can be taken as fairly typical of junior schools in areas where no rapid changes are taking place through redevelopment. On the other hand, there are schools where recent changes in the local population have produced change in the examination results. Spring Lane's results reveal a fairly constant improvement since 1956:

	1956	1959	1962	1965
Spring Lane[1]	(1) (29) 3·4%	(15) (45) 33·4%	(14) (45) 30·4%	(26) (47) 55·4%

Parents do not, of course, have any precise knowledge of the percentage of passes in various schools from year to year, but in any one district educationally conscious parents know, for example, that Birch Hall is a 'better school' than Park Villa, or that Spring Lane is improving its standard but is not yet on a par with Birch Hall.

Middle-class parents who are education-conscious try to register their children at the best junior school in the area at the age of three, in order to secure a place. In doing so, they inadvertently ensure that the school remains the best junior school in the area, for, with the encouragement and academic orientation that these children receive from home,[2] they are more likely to pass the eleven-plus.

Eleven-plus results provide a reasonably reliable guide to the

35

fortunes of each junior school. These fortunes change slowly and are more influenced by the selective movement of population than the abilities of individual headmasters or teachers (which is not to say that their influence is negligible). Old Hightonians teaching in the Grammar School remember a time when the junior schools situated in the inner area of the city (which were in fact *their* old schools), e.g. Park Villa, obtained most of the scholarships and enjoyed a high prestige in the district. The prestige of these schools has declined as those in the outer area have established themselves and grown to prominence.[3] The change is closely correlated with the movement of population and ecological change described in chapter 2.

The influence of the structure of primary education on the recruitment of teachers is too well known to need much comment. The newer, better equipped, high-prestige junior schools in the suburbs recruit easily and have fewer changes of staff,[4] while those at the bottom of the league find difficulty in recruiting suitable teachers.[5] They attract a disproportionately large number of first appointments or of unqualified staff, who frequently leave when they have gained enough experience to compete for a post in the suburbs. Those that stay do so for a variety of reasons. Some are idealistically motivated and competent; others are compelled to remain by their lack of qualifications, questionable ability or peculiar personality. This selective flow[6] of teaching talent reinforces population movement and parental selection to produce a rigid, highly differentiated and stratified hierarchy of schools.[7]

The ways in which parents obtain and use information about the quality of schools differs from area to area. For instance, the working-class area of Old Hightown contrasts markedly with Clearview, a middle-class suburb. In Clearview, information about the quality of schools is gleaned by parents, very frequently the mother, long before the child is due to start infant school. Every year, at the time eleven-plus and scholarship results are coming out, local interest is at a height. There are frequent conversations in shops, among friends and in local organisations about the fortunes of the neighbouring children and schools. The following comment is typical of many conversations overheard during the study: 'I hear poor Joan's girl hasn't passed. How dreadful for her! She was at St A's, wasn't she? They seem to have had a bad year, because poor Mrs Williams's boy has failed from there too.'

Within the Clearview area, local organisations such as the churches, tennis club and children's pre-school play groups provide clearing houses for the accumulation and dissemination of information and gossip relating to the schools. Many teachers live in the area and some of them teach locally, belong to the local organisations and send their children to local schools. They provide a valuable source of information about the schools.

Indices of parental concern with education[8] are the large and active parents' associations attached to the Clearview junior schools—for example, the parents' association of one school financed the building of a swimming pool from fund-raising projects. The parents also support three nursery play groups (or nursery schools), one of which is run privately, another by a group of parents (parents' co-operative) who employ a nursery teacher and send their children to the nursery school, while the third is run by the local Anglican church. All three are well attended and have long waiting lists.

In Old Hightown I found no instances of a nursery school run by the local community, nor of any parent–teacher associations. Interviews revealed that parents were concerned about their children's education but lacked the well structured knowledge of the Clearview people. Their friendship and kin networks did not include teachers of the local schools, and their sources of information were therefore less reliable and did not provide a clear picture. In these circumstances, considerations other than educational criteria are often important in determining the choice of a junior school. I have recorded instances where propinquity or the site of a major road have been more influential than the uncertain perception of academic priority.

The examination taken by all Hightown pupils before they pass from junior to secondary schools, usually at the age of 11, is used to select pupils for a number of secondary schools. The possibilities for boys living in Hightown are as follows:

1 Hightown Grammar School.
2 Hightown Technical High School.
3 Roman Catholic direct grant grammar school.
4 Other direct grant grammar schools in and outside Hightown (high prestige schools).
5 Secondary modern schools.

The boys who are selected for the four first alternatives in this list are said to have 'passed the eleven-plus', while those who go to the secondary modern schools are said to have 'failed'.[9]

37

Hightown Grammar and Hightown Technical select from non-Catholic boys from the whole of Hightown, but the latter also gives about 10 per cent of its places to pupils from the county education authority outside the town. The Roman Catholic direct grant school selects *via* its own examination, as well as the eleven-plus, taking pupils from Catholic schools over a sizeable part of the conurbation and from well beyond the town boundaries. The number of places allocated to Hightown boys is usually about thirty a year.

Similarly, the direct grant schools in and outside Hightown select from wide areas, and those with the highest prestige 'cream' the entrants from far beyond the limits of the conurbation. Only a small proportion of Hightown boys enter these schools—ten in 1956, eighteen in 1959, sixteen in 1962—but this proportion is selected from the best scholars of the year. This loss is strongly resented by the Grammar School masters, who are the people most affected by it. When I pointed out to one master that it usually amounted to fewer than twenty boys out of an intake of 120, he replied, 'You've got to realise that the loss of these twenty boys means the loss of twenty sixth-formers, and twenty university places to the school.' It is, of course, true that these pupils are often specially encouraged and even coached by parents and junior schools. They represent part of the social and educational elite, which is, as we have seen, very sparsely represented in Hightown.

The proportion of any year group selected for grammar school education varies slightly, but was about 15 per cent in 1956. In recent years the proportion has increased as the population has declined and the number of boys taking the eleven-plus examination has fallen. The other 85 per cent go to secondary modern schools, Protestant or Roman Catholic, which have local catchment areas. Although some of the secondary modern schools do run GCE courses for a small proportion of their more able pupils, and many more put boys in for commercial examinations at a lower academic level, none can compete with the grammar schools in educational standards or social prestige. Nor is there any overlap, for not even the highest ranking secondary modern can compete with the lowest ranking grammar school—the Technical High School. (This is not, of course, to say that individual pupils from the secondary modern schools do not sometimes end up better qualified than some of the pupils from the grammar schools. Some do.)

Table 21 shows how the pupils taking the eleven-plus in 1956, 1959

TABLE 21

THE ALLOCATION OF PUPILS WHO PASSED THE ELEVEN-PLUS EXAMINATION TO DIFFERENT TYPES OF GRAMMAR SCHOOL

The top 300 pupils from the eleven-plus examination, arranged in rank order, prior to final testing of borderline cases

1956	0–50 (top 50)	51–100 (2nd 50)	101–150 (3rd 50)	151–200 (4th 50)	201–250 (5th 50)	251–300 (6th 50)	Total
Hightown Grammar	34	27	29	17	11	–	118
Technical High School	1	4	11	16	17	–	49
Direct grant grammar schools	6	3	1	–	–	–	10
Other grammar schools*	1	1	1	–	1	–	4
Roman Catholic direct grant grammar school	8	15	5	–	–	–	28
Not allocated (failed):							
Roman Catholic	–	–	3	9	7	}50	91
Others	–	–	–	8	14		
Totals	50	50	50	50	50	50	300
1959							
Hightown Grammar	28	26	22	21	7	12	116
Technical High School	1	7	11	11	30	16	76
Direct grant grammar schools	7	4	4	2	1	–	18
Other grammar schools*	4	5	5	5	2	–	21
Roman Catholic direct grant grammar school	10	8	8	11	3	1	41
Not allocated (failed):							
Roman Catholic	–	–	–	–	2	10	12
Others	–	–	–	–	5	11	16
Totals	50	50	50	50	50	50	300
1962							
Hightown Grammar	23	26	21	18	16	6	110
Technical High School	3	2	9	11	12	12	49
Direct grant grammar schools	6	6	3	1	–	–	16
Other grammar schools*	–	5	4	4	2	1	16
Roman Catholic direct grant grammar school	18	10	10	3	–	–	41
Not allocated (failed):							
Roman Catholic	–	1	3	11	11	8	34
Others	–	–	–	2	9	23	34
Totals	50	50	50	50	50	50	300

* 'Other grammar schools' refers to ordinary grammar schools outside Hightown, i.e. pupils removed from Hightown after taking the eleven-plus.

and 1962 were allocated to the different types of school. It is readily apparent that of the two local education authority schools, Hightown Grammar attracts the bulk of the most able boys. Combining the above figures for 1956, 1959 and 1962, we get:

	Top 50	Second 50	Third 50	Fourth 50	Fifth 50
Hightown Grammar	28·3	26·3	24	18·7	10·7
Technical High	1·7	4·7	10·3	12·7	19·7

In order to interpret table 21 in more detail, it is necessary to outline the eleven-plus procedure in Hightown. The details vary from year to year,[10] but the principle has remained the same since shortly after the second world war. All pupils in the correct age bracket (most children are 10+ when they take the test) take the examination, except the educationally sub-normal and those who have already opted out of the State system. (Officials believe that the latter category is very small—most of the parents want their children to take the eleven-plus in case they fail to gain a place in the direct grant or public school of their choice.) The total age group is given two IQ tests (IQ 1 and IQ 2) and final scores are obtained by adding these to the headmaster's assessment.[11] In the past, the headmaster's assessment was equivalent to a single IQ score, but now it is given the weight of two IQ scores. The rank order is then arranged on this combined score.

TABLE 22

PARENTAL FIRST CHOICES: OPTIONS FOR HIGHTOWN GRAMMAR SCHOOL OR THE TECHNICAL HIGH SCHOOL, 1956, 1959 AND 1962*

| | Boys who were ranked in the 11+ in the: | | |
	First 100 places	*Second 100 places*	*Third 100 places*
1956			
Percentage opting for:			
Grammar School	61	56	40
Technical High School	5	24	44
1959			
Percentage opting for:			
Grammar School	54	43	46
Technical High School	8	22	32
1962†			
Percentage opting for:			
Grammar School	49	43	47
Technical High School	5	20	26
Average for 1956, 1959 and 1962			
Percentage opting for:			
Grammar School	55	50	44
Technical High School	6	22	35

* This table differs from table 21 in that table 21 shows the actual allocation, i.e. after removals, direct grant places, etc., have been taken up, and after a number of changes have been made to parental options. For example, in 1956 all allocations were made according to parental options until the 165th place ('top border-line'). Below this line, but above the 'bottom border-line', seven who opted for Hightown Grammar School and seven who opted for the Technical High School were not given places; seven who opted for Hightown Grammar School were given places in the Technical High School, and two who opted for the Technical High School were given places in the Grammar School.

† The 1962 options are characterised by an unusually large number of Roman Catholics in the top 100 places (28 in 1962, compared with 18 in 1959).

Table 22 is compiled from this final rank order. Pupils who have been successful in obtaining a place in a direct grant school, or who are leaving the district, are then crossed off the list. Starting from the top of the list, the remainder are allocated, where possible, to the school of their choice—the Technical High School, the Grammar School or the Roman Catholic direct grant school. When all the places allocated to the local education authority by the Roman Catholic school are filled, a line is drawn and all those who went to Roman Catholic junior schools are allocated to Roman Catholic secondary modern schools[12] (e.g. below the 124th boy in 1956).

When a certain proportion of places at the Grammar School and the Technical High School have been filled, a second line is drawn ('top of the border zone') and all the boys below this line, but above a third line ('bottom of the border zone'), are put through a further selection procedure before allocation either to the Grammar School and Technical High School or to secondary modern schools. This procedure has varied from year to year. It may consist of a further examination (an English test and arithmetic test—EQ and AQ) or an interview, or both.

In the four years' eleven-plus results that I examined—1956, 1959, 1962 and 1965—the Grammar School places have always been filled before the Technical High School's. This has meant that some boys in the border-line zone, who put down the Grammar School as their first preference, had to be allocated to the Technical School. This, in itself, is a clear indication of the difference in prestige of the two schools in the parents' eyes.

Examination of table 22 reveals a marked tendency, repeated each year, for those who do best in the eleven-plus examination to opt for the Grammar School, while those who do less well opt for the Technical High School. While it is possible to attribute the overall preference for the Grammar School to its higher prestige, it seems unlikely that this graded preference can be attributed to the single diffuse factor of community prestige. The average number of boys choosing the grammar school, in the three years examined, drops from 55 per cent in the 'top 100' to 44 per cent in the 'third 100', while the number choosing the Technical High School increases from 6 to 35 per cent. The higher prestige of the Grammar School in the community accounts for the larger number of preferences for it in each division of 100; it does not explain why the options for the Technical High School increase, while on average those for the

Grammar School decrease, as one moves from the top to the bottom of the scale.

It should be noted that if the boys allocated to direct grant schools are taken into account, the slope is even more pronounced, because they all opted for the Grammar School and are distributed disproportionately in the top of the eleven-plus results. They have been excluded, however, in order to make a simple comparison between those principally interested in the two local education authority schools. The problem is conveniently expressed diagrammatically (see Fig. 5).

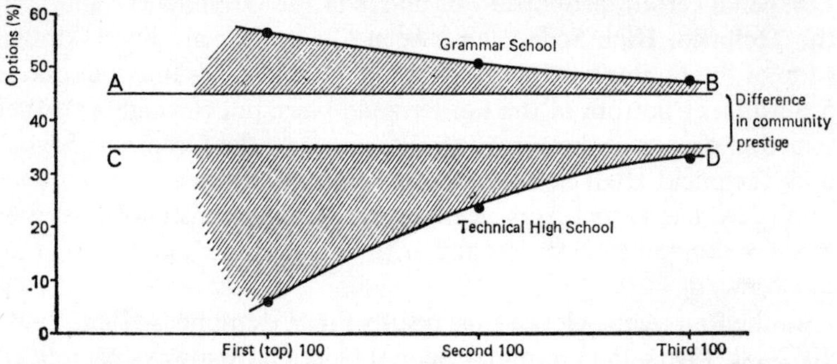

Fig. 5. Options for Hightown Grammar School and Hightown Technical High School.

The Grammar School and Technical High School options are approximately asymptotic to lines *AB* and *CD* respectively. The difference in community prestige between the two schools is represented by the gap between lines *AB* and *CD*. The difference in the number of options for the two schools is represented by the shaded areas above *AB* and below *CD*. Some explanation is required. It can be demonstrated that two factors are required for this: (1) the unequal distribution of the various social classes in the eleven-plus results, coupled with the middle-class propensity to choose grammar schools rather than technical schools,[13] and (2) the process of pre-selection and anticipatory socialisation in junior schools.

These two factors are complementary and neither in itself provides a full explanation. But whereas both elements of the first are well documented in sociological literature,[14] the second has either been ignored or seen as largely dependent on the first. The aim of this section is to demonstrate the existence of a large measure of pre-selection and anticipatory socialisation.

The association between middle-class parental background and a preference for grammar as opposed to technical secondary education has usually been established on large samples, representative of the total social class structure and involving children who are eventually destined for secondary modern as well as grammar schools. The sample we are considering differs in that its members are destined for selective secondary education and have a biased social class distribution (compared with the Hightown population). Within this group, social class background is not sufficiently vigorous to explain the pattern of options demonstrated by table 23.

TABLE 23

SOCIAL CLASS BACKGROUND (MANUAL/NON-MANUAL) OF BOYS WHO OPTED FOR HIGHTOWN GRAMMAR SCHOOL AND HIGHTOWN TECHNICAL HIGH SCHOOL IN THE TOP 100 PLACES OF THE ELEVEN-PLUS RESULTS*

	Opted for Grammar School	Opted for Technical High School	Total
Non-manual	22 (91·6%)	2 (8·4%)	24 (100%)
Manual	27 (90%)	3 (10%)	30 (100%)
Totals	49	5	54

* I was able to complete this table because I had information from the Technical School records and from the Grammar School records of parents' occupations.

The table shows that children whose fathers have non-manual and manual occupations opt disproportionately for the Grammar School if they are in the top 100 places of the eleven-plus. The question we have to answer is: why do sons of manual workers in the top 100 places of the eleven-plus opt differently from the rest of their social class peers? The answer lies in the pre-selection and anticipatory socialisation that goes on in the junior school, and in the stability of the performance and reputation of the schools that provide the majority of the successful eleven-plus candidates.

Over the years, the teachers responsible for the scholarship classes know, within limits, how many passes they can expect. Since they also develop an intimate knowledge of the pupils in the class, they—and to a lesser extent, the pupils—know who (if any) in the class can be expected to pass the eleven-plus. Pupils who know themselves to be in this category are more likely to choose the Grammar School, and in fact are often expected to do so.[15] Pupils who are on the edge of this group are more likely to choose the Technical School, partly because they feel they might be better off there, with its less academic curriculum, and partly because they have come to accept this as an appropriate objective.[16]

The teacher helps to create this structure and the expectations that go with it. It is not necessarily done deliberately, but simply develops out of the teacher's normal task of instructing and disciplining his class.[17] However, one of the main strands around which this structure develops is academic performance. A measure of how accurately teachers can predict academic performance (eleven-plus success) is, therefore, to some degree a measure of the extent to which the structure exists and of how accurately expectations are fulfilled.[18]

An indication of the accuracy with which teachers are able to predict success is obtained from the yearly estimates submitted by all headmasters to the local education authority. In 1956 they consisted solely of estimated numbers of passes, but in 1959, 1962 and 1965 headmasters were asked to recommend two categories: 'definitely

TABLE 24

BOYS DESIGNATED AS (*a*) DEFINITELY SUITABLE, (*b*) POSSIBLY SUITABLE, (*c*) UNSUITABLE FOR GRAMMAR SCHOOL: THEIR SUCCESS IN THE ELEVEN-PLUS EXAMINATION IN HIGHTOWN IN 1956, 1959, 1962 AND 1965

	No. of candidates	(a) Definitely Suitable	Passed	(b) Possibly suitable	Passed	(c) Unsuitable	Passed
1956	1,262	331	204	–	–	931	15
1959	1,446	270	214	210	50	966	7
1962	1,108	219	187	169	44	720	2
1965	1,053	229	184	155	58	669	4

TABLE 25

PERCENTAGES OF BOYS PASSING THE ELEVEN-PLUS*

	(a) Definitely suitable	(b) Possibly suitable	(c) Unsuitable
1959	79·3	23·8	0·7
1962	85·5	26·2	0·3
1965	80·4	37·4	0·6

* 1956 has been left out because of the different method used in collecting estimates. A neighbouring authority has recently changed from the eleven-plus examination to teachers' assessment. In the first year it ran both the assessment and the examination. It claimed well over 80 per cent agreement between the two methods. In the light of the above tables, this seems very probable.

44

suitable' and 'possibly suitable' for grammar school education. Tables 24 and 25 record this information.

The low percentages in the 'possibly suitable' column of table 25 show that headmasters tend to err on the side of over-optimism. Certainly, few children with a chance of success in the examination are left out of the 'possibly suitable' category. This is confirmed by the very low percentages in the 'unsuitable' column. Although these tables show a high degree of correlation between the prediction and the results, the overall figures give only an approximate idea of the accuracy to which some schools consistently predict their results. In general, the 'better' schools with most of the eleven-plus passes predict more accurately than the unsuccessful ones. In 1959, for example, the ten most successful schools (those that obtained seven or more passes) got 97 out of 99 boys recommended as 'definitely suitable' through the exam. In these schools, being classified as 'definitely suitable' is tantamount to having a place in a grammar school. For the less successful ones, prediction is more difficult. It is often hard to say whether the odd child, destined to be placed in the border zone, will be selected or not. For example, the predicted results of St B's school are as follows:

	1956	1959	1962	1965
Definitely suitable	14	3	4	2
Passes obtained	0	1	1	1

Even if the 1956 result is excluded, the prediction is poor, only 33 per cent of 'definitely suitable' candidates passing.

These tables demonstrate that it is the 'definitely suitable' student who passes the eleven-plus. Table 26 shows that he goes disproportionately to the Grammar School (as against the Technical High School). Whereas the 'possibly suitable' candidates are divided fairly evenly between the technical and grammar schools, the 'definitely suitable' candidates go disproportionately to the Grammar School, in ratios varying between three and six to one.

Thus analysis shows the considerable accuracy with which children in junior schools are pre-selected (predicted) for grammar school education, and suggests that anticipatory socialisation is a probable consequence of this process. 'Definitely suitable' pupils choose the grammar school, while 'possibly suitable' ones are less likely to do so. The 'possibly suitable' have learnt through their junior school experience that the grammar school is a less appropriate objective

TABLE 26

HOW 'DEFINITELY SUITABLE' AND 'POSSIBLY SUITABLE' CANDIDATES
ARE ALLOCATED TO HIGHTOWN GRAMMAR SCHOOL AND TECHNICAL
HIGH SCHOOL

	Definitely Suitable %	Possibly Suitable %
1959		
Grammar School	166 (77·6)	26 (52)
Technical High School	48 (22·4)	24 (48)
Totals	214 (100)	50 (100)
1962		
Grammar School	160 (85·6)	23 (52·3)
Technical High School	27 (14·4)	21 (47·7)
Totals	187 (100)	44 (100)
1965		
Grammar School	141 (72·7)	24 (41·4)
Technical High School	53 (27·3)	34 (58·6)
Totals	194 (100)	60 (100)

for them. Their standard of work, their general attitude and behaviour are more appropriate for the less exalted level of secondary education represented by the Technical High School.

The junior schools supplying the grammar schools in Hightown fall into a status hierarchy. The factors causing this differentiation are many, and some, like the social class intake, the quality of the teachers and the quality of the external examination results, are mutually reinforcing and self-perpetuating.

The stability of the hierarchy of junior schools is demonstrated in table 20 over a nine-year period. I have shown that this stability gives rise to a set of expectations within the school, which raises the question of the extent of anticipatory socialisation in junior schools.[19] This, in itself, becomes a factor of importance in success or failure in the eleven-plus and in the choice of secondary school.[20] It is of importance to the Grammar School because it means that the intake consists in many cases of boys who have long thought of themselves as probable grammar school pupils,[21] which in turn affects the way they conduct themselves on their arrival at the Grammar School.

NOTES

[1] Spring Lane was built after the war and draws its pupils initially from a nearby council estate. More children now come from a nearby middle-class area.

[2] Throughout this book I leave aside the question of 'nature *v.* nurture'. I take the view that although the inherited factor in intelligence is important, it is not a sufficient explanation of the differences in educational attainment between working-class and middle-class children. In fact, table 7 (page 79) of the *Early leaving report* shows that class differences produced a bigger discrepancy between the eleven-plus results and subsequent GCE results than did the measured differences in intelligence at eleven-plus.

[3] See Floud, Halsey and Martin, *Social class and educational opportunity*, page 99.

[4] At one time, some schools concealed over-staffing by employing part-time teachers, taking pupils at an earlier age, etc. This practice has now been prevented by the strict surveillance of local education authority officials. Pressure brought to bear on local Brightside schools by parents who wished the school to take their children earlier than 5 has now been deflected into developing other types of pre-schooling.

[5] See Howard S. Becker, 'The career of the public school teacher', *American Journal of Sociology*, March 1952, page 470.

[6] One effect of two-tier teacher training has been to protect these schools from complete drain of teaching talent. See Bryan Roberts, *The effects of college experience and social background on professional orientations of prospective teachers*, unpublished PhD. thesis, Chicago, December 1964.

[7] See also Brian Jackson and Dennis Marsden, *Education and the working class*, London, Routledge & Kegan Paul, 1962, page 84, for a description of this aspect of primary schools in Marburton.

[8] I later argue that these activities must be explained in terms of socio-cultural resources and not just parental concern.

[9] See O. L. Banks, *Parity and prestige in English secondary education*, London 1955.

[10] In recent years there has been a tendency to attach greater weight to the headmaster's assessment and less to the objective part of the test. At one time, the whole group was given four objective tests, IQ 1, IQ 2, EQ and AQ, and the headmaster's assessment amounted to only one-fifth of the total score. The border-line cases were then allocated by interview. At a later stage, IQ 1 and 2 constituted the main test and the headmaster's assessment counted as a third of the total. Most recently, it counts as half the total. Previous research (see Floud, Halsey and Anderson, *Education, economy and society*, page 214) shows that this trend is likely to have weighed more in favour of middle-class boys.

[11] The headmaster's assessment is quantified as follows. The headmasters of all Hightown junior schools are asked to rank their entry (boys and girls separate) on the basis of school work. The top boy in this rank then gets the top mark of any boy from his own school which was scored in the IQ tests. The second boy in the headmaster's list gets the second mark from the IQ list, irrespective of whether he scored it himself or not. The third boy gets the third IQ mark as his headmaster's assessment, and so on. This method ensures that the weight of headmasters' assessments is in line with the actual performance of their schools.

[12] Until recently grammar school places for Roman Catholics were in short supply in Hightown. Since 1962, more grammar school places have been made available at St A's and Cardinal L's. Some Roman Catholic parents probably do not know that their children have achieved a sufficiently high standard in the

E

eleven-plus to attend the local education authority grammar schools. About five or six Catholics find their way into Hightown Grammar School each year, but this is usually because their parents have contracted out of the Roman Catholic system at the junior school stage.

[13] Middle-class parents tend to choose grammar rather than technical education and middle-class pupils predominate in the 'top 100' places of the eleven-plus. This would provide an explanation of the unequal distribution of options demonstrated in the graph.

[14] J. W. B. Douglas, *The home and the school*, London, 1964, page 40. H. T. Himmelweit, 'Social status and secondary education since the 1944 Act: some data for London' in David Glass, *Social mobility in Britain*, page 141.

[15] The expectations are acquired over a long period of time. An illustration of this process concerns two cubs who were examined for their 'house orderly' badges some three months before they were due to take the eleven-plus examination, and nearly a year before they entered secondary schools. They were both middle-class boys who lived in the same district, and went to the same school. During the afternoon I observed the boys at a number of tasks, for example, cleaning windows, sewing on buttons and cooking a simple meal. One boy imme-diately impressed by his self-assurance, competence and politeness. The other struggled with his tasks, frequently giggled, made silly remarks and, in all, only narrowly passed this essentially practical test. In conversation afterwards, the competent boy revealed that he *expected* to go to B school, a high-prestige direct grant school. His sister had gone there, so had several boys from his school and he felt fairly confident he could make the grade. The other boy said he was going to go to the Technical High School. He said he liked and was good at practical things and, therefore, preferred the technical side. In fact, he had shown that he was relatively poor on the 'practical' side, but had learnt, mainly from his junior school, that this was the standard to which he could aspire.

[16] A more surprising example of this phenomenon—the development of an informal norm that a certain level of intellectual achievement is appropriate to a functionally different but ostensibly equal alternative—was reported from a small women's teacher training college. The student who came top of her year was found to be registered for courses in infant teaching. She was called before the principal, who tried to convince her that it was not only to her advantage to change to the secondary level, but also her duty.

[17] See chapter 4 for an account of this process within the Grammar School.

[18] This measure is obviously an indirect one. In theory, it would be possible for teachers to refrain from passing on any information about the relative perfor-mances of their pupils; in practice it seldom happens. Different teachers probably use the information in varying degrees (e.g. in fostering competition). A direct assessment could of course be designed.

[19] The extent of anticipatory socialisation and the mechanisms that produce it in junior schools deserve further investigation.

[20] J. W. B. Douglas, *The home and the school*, page 64. Thirty-eight per cent of future grammar school children were said by their primary school teachers to be very hard-working, but only 8 per cent of the future secondary modern school children were similarly assessed.

[21] The category 'definitely suitable' used in this chapter will be seen to cor-respond, to a large measure, with what I have called 'the best pupil role' in chapter 4.

4 Differentiation and sub-cultural polarisation

In chapter 3, I stressed the importance of the selective and socialising function of junior schools. Here[1] we shall examine what happens to the pupils who leave these schools to enter grammar school. Since it is the only local education authority boys' grammar school[2] and selects its pupils from the whole of the town, Hightown Grammar is well placed for such an investigation.

This chapter provides a link between the broad historical analysis of the changing function of the Grammar School (chapter 2) and the more detailed analyses of its micro-sociological mechanisms which are the subject of later chapters. The link takes the form of a model of differentiation and sub-culture formation within the school. The model will be developed and modified subsequently before being used to throw fresh light on the early development of the school.

The approach will be in three stages:

1 A description of some of the sociological characteristics of boys entering the school.
2 (*a*) A descriptive analysis of some aspects of the informal structure that developed in one class in the school, with particular reference to two case studies.
   (*b*) An attempt to establish a model which describes the passage of pupils through the school.
3 An attempt to verify the model through the use of quantitative indices—in particular, the concepts of differentiation and polarisation which are developed in 2 (*b*).

The overall aim is to provide a picture of the stratification and subsequent sub-culture development, associated with academic streaming.

1 The intake

We have seen that Hightown Grammar School is a highly selective institution. It is important, therefore, for us to investigate the ways in which the selection affects the composition of the newly recruited first-year classes. Their composition affects the subsequent sub-cultural development of the group. The particular factors that will concern us are:

(*a*) The way selection restricts the intake to a particular type of student.

(*b*) The way selection isolates the successful candidate from his fellow pupils and friends at his junior school.

(a) *The effect of selection on the intake*

The evidence I have been able to gather[3] supports my contention that the new intake to a grammar school will consist largely of 11 year olds who have been accustomed to playing what I have called 'best pupil' role in their junior schools and who, in their new environment, are often separated from their former school friends. The extent to which this is true of any grammar school will, of course, depend on a large number of factors, such as the percentage of grammar school places available and the number and size of junior and grammar schools in the catchment area.

We have seen that the local education authority of Hightown sends 15–20 per cent of its 11 year olds to grammar schools each year. Evidence from a variety of sources—junior school reports, autobiographies, and the statements of junior school teachers—clearly shows that these contingents include the vast majority of top scholars, team leaders, school monitors, head boys and teachers' favourites. For example, in the 22 junior school reports of the 1962 intake that recorded a class position, only one boy was placed in the bottom half of the class (20/34). Similarly, of the 41 junior school reports of the 1959 intake recording class positions, the lowest position recorded was 19/39, and this was accompanied by the remark 'Tries hard, keen and interested'. In short, they are the 'best pupils'.

(b) *How selection isolates the successful candidates*

The boys entering Hightown Grammar are selected from a large number of junior schools. Table 27 shows that the selection test tends

50

to scoop a few pupils from each school. Over half the boys come from schools that send six or fewer pupils.

TABLE 27

HIGHTOWN GRAMMAR SCHOOL INTAKE, 1962, CLASSIFIED ACCORDING TO SIZE OF JUNIOR SCHOOL CONTINGENTS

Mean size: 3·5 boys per contingent

	Size of contingents				
	1–3	4–6	7–9	10–12	Total
Number of junior schools	24	5	4	2	35
Number of pupils	42	25	30	21	118

The relative isolation of pupils from their former schoolmates is only partially illustrated in table 27. When the boys arrive at Hightown Grammar they are divided at random into four classes, which further increases the likelihood of their being separated from former schoolmates. These classes are also house groups, and the pupils in them remain together for prayers, school meals and registration as well as lessons.

The degree of isolation of the first-year boy is illustrated by the responses to a 'friendship choice' questionnaire, asking whether boys had friends in their first-year class who had attended the same junior school as themselves. Fifty-eight boys out of 118 questioned had no friend from the same junior school in their class. Thus almost half the first-year intake spend the great majority of their time at school in a class where they are isolated from previous friends.

This isolation[4] means that there is no basis for a common identification other than membership of the school. Combined with their 'best pupil' background, it has the initial consequences for the boys of (1) high commitment to the school and its norms, (2) rivalry among themselves. Both are manifested in a number of ways. First-year boys adhere rigidly to school uniform, caps and blazers are proudly displayed, and they attend school functions and clubs in disproportionate numbers. Their behaviour in the classroom is characterised by eagerness, co-operation with the teacher and competition among themselves. 'Please sir, Willy Brown is copying my sums' is a remark that could only come from a first-year boy.

I once tried to measure the response rate to a narrative and question-and-answer lesson given by a history teacher. So many

51

responded to each question that I could not record them. As the tension mounted, boys who did not know the answers looked around apprehensively at those who did. The latter, in a state of high excitement, smiled triumphantly at the ignorant ones, and stretched their arms and bodies to the utmost as they eagerly called 'Sir!' 'Sir!' 'Sir!' every time the master glanced in their direction. When he said 'All right, Green, you tell us,' there were quiet sighs and groans as those who had not been called upon subsided into their seats. The whole performance was repeated as soon as the next question was asked.

During such spells, the desire to participate was so great that some boys would put up their hands and strain for notice, even though they had no idea of the answer. If asked to give it, they would either make a gesture implying that they had suddenly forgotten, or subside with an embarrassed and confused look, to the jeers and groans of the rest of the class, who would then redouble their efforts to attract attention.

The type of enthusiasm characteristic of a first-year class was occasionally found in second- or third-year forms, but there were a number of observable differences. The second and third years were more likely to 'play dead' and allow five or six people to 'do all the work'. If the master succeeded in getting a larger proportion to participate, there was always a residue of boys who hardly took part at all or who did so only by giving obviously wrong or facetious answers. There was a possibility that the form would use any excitement of this kind to sabotage the lesson or play the fool: a boy might stretch so hard as to fall out of his desk, another accidentally punch the one in front as he put his hand up, and the form's 'funny man' would display his wit in response to an ambiguous question—sometimes isolating the teacher by referring to a private class joke.

First-year forms are thus widely regarded by teachers as the easiest and most rewarding to teach. They are typically allocated to young, inexperienced masters or those who have difficulty with discipline. Misdemeanours are largely the result of high spirits, over-eagerness or forgetfulness rather than conscious malice. Hopes are high and expectations as to school performance and subsequent careers unrealistically rosy.

2 The model

(a) *The informal structure: two case studies*

As soon as the highly selected first-year population meets at the Grammar School and is allocated to the four first-year classes, a complex process of interaction begins. It takes place through a variety of encounters. Boys talk and listen to each other; talk and listen to teachers; listen to conversations; notice details of accent, gesture, clothing; watch others at work and at play in various situations and in innumerable different permutations.

During the first few days much of this interaction appears to take place in a fairly random way, influenced mainly by the physical and organisational arrangements. Soon, patterns of selection begin to emerge. Various initial interactions yield information and experience, which are retained by the individual and provide some basis for the interpretation and partial control of other interactions. This partial control is extremely important because it soon gives rise to a recognisable, although unstable and changing, structure.

When I started observing the first-year classes in March 1963, the members of each class had been together for only about six months, but each class already had a definite structure of which the pupils clearly had detailed knowledge. When a master called a boy to read or answer a question, others could be seen giving each other significant looks which clearly indicated that they knew what to expect. On one occasion, for example, a master asked three boys to stay behind after the lesson to help him with a task calling for a sense of responsibility and co-operation. He called out 'Williams, Maun and Sherring'. The class burst into spontaneous laughter, and there were unbelieving cries of 'What! Sherring?' The master corrected himself. 'No, not Sherring, Shadwell.' From the context of the incident, it was clear that Sherring's reputation was already inconsistent with the qualities expected of a monitor.

On another occasion, Priestley was asked to read, and the whole class groaned and laughed. A fat boy, he had been kept down from the previous year because of ill-health (catarrh and asthma) and poor work. He grinned apprehensively, wiped his face with a huge white handkerchief and started to read very nervously. For a few moments the class was absolutely quiet, then one boy tittered; Priestley made a silly mistake, partly because he was looking up to smile at the boy who was giggling, and the whole class burst into laughter. Priestley blew his nose loudly and smiled nervously at the class. The teacher quietened them and Priestley continued to read. Three lines later a marked mispronunciation started everyone laughing again. This performance continued, with Priestley getting more and more nervous, mopping his brow and blowing his nose. Finally, the master snapped, with obvious annoyance, 'All right, Priestley, that's enough!'

This short incident, one of several during the day, served to remind . Priestley of his structural position within the class and to confirm the opinions and expectations of both class and teacher towards him. His behaviour was consistent with his performance in the examination at the end of the autumn term when he was ranked twenty-ninth out of thirty-three.

During this period of observation, I also noticed the significance of the behaviour of another boy, Cready. Cready first attracted my attention because, although his form position was similar to Priestley's (twenty-sixth), he habitually associated with a strikingly different group. He behaved very differently in class and had a markedly different reputation.

Cready was a member of the school choir. It so happened that the English master, whose classes I was observing, was also the music teacher, and he had arranged the class so that the members of the school choir sat in the row next to the piano and his desk (row 4). To be a member of the choir, one had to have a good voice and be willing to stay in school to practise during lunch time and at four o'clock, once or twice a week, for certain periods of the year. In the next two rows were members of the first-form choir. To be in this a boy had only to be willing to sing. In the last row (row 1) were boys who could not or would not sing at all.

During the first three lessons I observed, Cready answered four of the questions put to the class. On two of these occasions, he had discussed the answer with the boy next to him before putting up his hand. If Cready got an answer wrong he was never laughed at. Priestley answered two questions in the same period. He got one of them wrong and was laughed at by the class. As I observed later, if Priestley attempted to discuss an answer with the boy next to him, he was reprimanded.

Table 28 illustrates how the seating arrangements in the class affected the pattern of interaction with the teacher.[5] A sociogram for the class showed an apparent inconsistency. During lessons, Priestley was frequently in the middle of a group of mischievous boys. If there

TABLE 28

RECORD OF TEACHER–PUPIL INTERACTION:
AVERAGE FOR THREE LESSONS

| | Row number | | | |
Type of interaction	1	2	3	4
Answers to questions (per boy)	0·5	0·7	1·3	3·6
Rebukes per boy	1·6	1·2	0·5	0·4
Questions from boys (totals)	3	1	2	10

was a disturbance, he was in it. I expected him to be fairly popular with some of the boys who led him into trouble, but none of them picked him as a friend. He chose five boys as his friends but only one reciprocated.

The other boys used Priestley to create diversions and pass messages, and because he was so isolated he was only too pleased to oblige. He could never resist the temptation to act as if he were 'one of the boys'. But when he was caught out they deserted him and laughed at rather than with him. He was truly the butt of the class.

These incidents, seen in the context of the structure of the class, show how he had fallen foul of the system. He was not in control of his own situation, and anything he tried to do to improve his position only made it worse. His attempts to answer questions provoked laughter and ridicule. His attempts to minimise the distress it caused —a nervous smile round the room, a shrug of the shoulders, pretending that he had either caused the disturbance on purpose or did not care—served only to worsen his position with the teacher.

He compensated for social and academic failure by learning the stocks and shares columns of the *Financial Times* every week. This enabled him to develop a reputation in a field outside the sphere in which the school was competent to judge. He would emphasise its *real* importance to his future career and thus minimise the effect of his scholastic failure. Even this did not improve his standing at the school, least of all with the staff. It merely explained his laziness, bad behaviour and lack of concern with school work. 'Oh, Priestley. He's just biding his time with us—from what I hear his future is assured anyway. He's just lazy,' said the English master.

If I had had to forecast the future performance of these two boys on the evidence, I would of course have expected Cready to do better in the following examinations and Priestley, if anything, worse. Their positions in class in the first and second-year examinations were as follows. The second-year forms, 2E, 2A, 2B and 2C, were streamed; 2E was the top form and 2C the bottom.

| | First-year exams | | | | Second-year exams | | |
	Form	Autumn	Spring	Summer	Form	Autumn	Spring	Summer
Priestley	1A	29	30	26	2C	12	27	16
Cready	1A	26	10	10	2E	11	12	10

It is interesting to note their family background. Priestley was Jewish,[6] second in a family of three, and lived in an area of expensive detached houses. His father was a clearance stock buyer. Cready, on the other hand, lived on a council estate, was fourth out of six in the family, and his father was a quality inspector in an abrasives factory.

Cready and Priestley did not, therefore, conform with the established correlation between academic achievement and social class. Cready, a working-class boy from a large family, was making good, while Priestley, an upper middle class boy from a smaller family, was failing academically. This negative case highlights an important point: there is a degree of autonomy in the system of social relations in the classroom which can transcend external factors and even differences of intelligence. External factors, such as social class, and intelligence have to be fed through the internal system of relations within the classroom. If the possessor of advantages in the external system fails to feed them in correctly (some factor in the internal system might intervene) they can be misunderstood or even ignored. On the other hand, positive rewards can come from skill in manipulating internal relations;[7] they can make up for lack of external advantages, and even intelligence, as measured by an IQ test.

The positions of Cready and Priestley are only explicable in the light of this type of analysis of the system of social relations inside the classroom. The system is open to manipulation by those who are sensitive to its details. Hence Cready, who had all the major external factors stacked against him, was able to use the system of social relations to sustain and buoy himself up. He was friendly with some of the most prestigeful and successful members of the class. He built up a reputation for reliability, neatness and helpfulness with his form master in his work and in attendance at the choir.

Despite all the advantages he brought to the situation, Priestley had fallen foul of the system. Although separated from his friends in the second year, he shared their contemptuous view of first-formers. His overbearing and rather condescending attitude to many of his new first-year classmates lost him their sympathy and friendship. His attempts to gain influence by playing the fool or 'acting up' in class, which would have been appropriate in a second-year group, estranged him further. He was not only failing but also speedily losing any motivation to succeed in the sphere in which the school was competent to judge him.

It should be reiterated that this is not an attempt to disprove the established correlations between social class and academic achievement, but to highlight the fact that there are detailed social mechanisms and processes responsible for bringing it about, mechanisms which are not completely determined by external factors. Studying them will enable us to add a new dimension to our understanding of the general process of education in schools.

(b) *Differentiation and polarisation*

I now suggest a model which describes the passage of pupils through the grammar school. Two terms should first be explained: differentiation and polarisation. By *differentiation* I mean the separation and ranking of students according to a multiple set of criteria which makes up the normative, academically orientated, value system of the grammar school. Differentiation is defined here as being largely carried out by teachers in the course of their normal duties.

Polarisation, on the other hand, takes place within the student body, partly as a result of differentiation, but influenced by external factors and with an autonomy of its own. It is a process of sub-culture formation in which the school-dominated, normative culture is opposed by an alternative culture which I refer to as the 'anti-group' culture. The content of the anti-group culture will, of course, be very much influenced by the school and its social setting. For example, it may range from a folk music CND group in a minor public school to a delinquent sub-culture at a secondary modern school in an old urban area. In Hightown Grammar School it fell between these extremes and was influenced by the large working-class and Jewish communities of Hightown.

Differentiation. There are a number of scales on which a master habitually rates a boy. For the purpose of the analysis, two will be considered:

(a) *Academic scale.*
(b) *Behaviour Scale.* This would include considerations as varied as general classroom behaviour and attitudes; politeness; attention; helpfulness; time spent in school societies and sports.

The two are not independent. Behaviour affects academic standards not only because good behaviour involves listening and attending, but because a master becomes favourably disposed towards a boy who is well behaved and trying hard. The teacher therefore tends to help him and even to mark him up. I have found in my own marking of books that when I know the form (i.e. the good and bad pupils), I mark much more quickly. For example, I might partly read an essay and recognise the writing: 'Oh, Brown. Let's see, he tries.hard. Good, neat work, missed one or two ideas—seven out of ten.' Or 'This is a bit scruffy—no margin, not underlined; seems to have got the hang of it though. Who is it? Oh, Jones, that nuisance—five out of ten!'[8]

Polarisation. There is another reason why good behaviour is correlated with academic achievement. A boy who does well and wishes to do well academically is predisposed to accept the grammar school's system of values, that is, he behaves well. The system gives him high prestige, and it is therefore in his interest to support it; the correlation between membership of the choir and performance in class illustrates this point (see table 28). He is supporting his position of prestige. On the other hand, a boy who does badly academically is predisposed to criticise, reject or even sabotage the system where he can, since it places him in an inferior position.[9]

A boy showing the extreme development of this phenomenon may subscribe to values which are actually the inverted values of the school. He obtains prestige for cheeking a teacher, playing truant, not doing homework, for smoking, drinking and even stealing. As it develops, the anti-group produces its own impetus. The boy who takes refuge in such a group because his work is poor finds that the group commits him to a behaviour pattern which means that his work will stay poor—and in fact often gets progressively worse.

The following extracts from an essay entitled 'Abuse', written by a first-form boy for his housemaster, illustrate a development of anti-group values which is extreme for a first-year pupil:

I am writing this essay about abuse in the toilets. . . . What they [the prefects] call abuse and what I call abuse are two different things altogether.

All the people where I live say I am growing up to be a 'Ted' so I try to please them by acting as much like one as I possibly can. I go around kicking a ball against the wall that is nearest to their house and making as much noise as I can and I intend to carry on doing this until they can leave me alone. . . . It seems to me the Grammar School knows nothing about abuse for *I would much rather be a hooligan and get some fun out of life than be a snob always being the dear little nice boy doing what he is told* [my italics].

In section 1 above, we saw that at the beginning of the first year the pupils constitute a relatively homogeneous, undifferentiated group. They are uniformly enthusiastic and eager to please, both through their work and in their behaviour. The pupils who are noticed first are the good ones and the bad ones. Even by the spring term, some masters are still unsure of the names of quiet pupils in the undifferentiated middle of the classes they teach.

It is somewhat rare for an anti-group to develop in the first year. Although one or two individuals may develop marked anti-group values, they are likely to remain isolates. In the 1962 first year, I was able to recognise only one, Badman, the author of the essay. He wished to be transferred to a secondary modern school.

The usual course of events associated with a marked degree of (relative) failure in the first year is for the child to display symptoms of emotional upheaval and nervous disorder, and for a conflict of standards to take place. Symptoms that occurred in the first year intake of 1962 included:[10]

Bursting into tears when reprimanded by a teacher.
Refusal to go to school or to particular lessons, accompanied by hysterical crying and screaming.
Sleeplessness.
Bedwetting.
Playing truant from certain lessons or from school.
Constantly feeling sick before certain lessons.
One boy rushed to the stage in assembly clutching his throat and screaming that he could not breathe.
Consistent failure to do homework.
High absence record.
Aggravation of mild epilepsy.

The fifteen cases recorded probably represent all the instances of major disturbance, but a large number of minor ones probably never become known to the school.

The individual cases cannot be discussed here, but their general significance is important to the model under discussion. We have seen that the eleven-plus selects the 'best pupils' from the top forms of the junior schools. These forms have been highly differentiated in preparation for the examination. Often, the pupils have been 'best

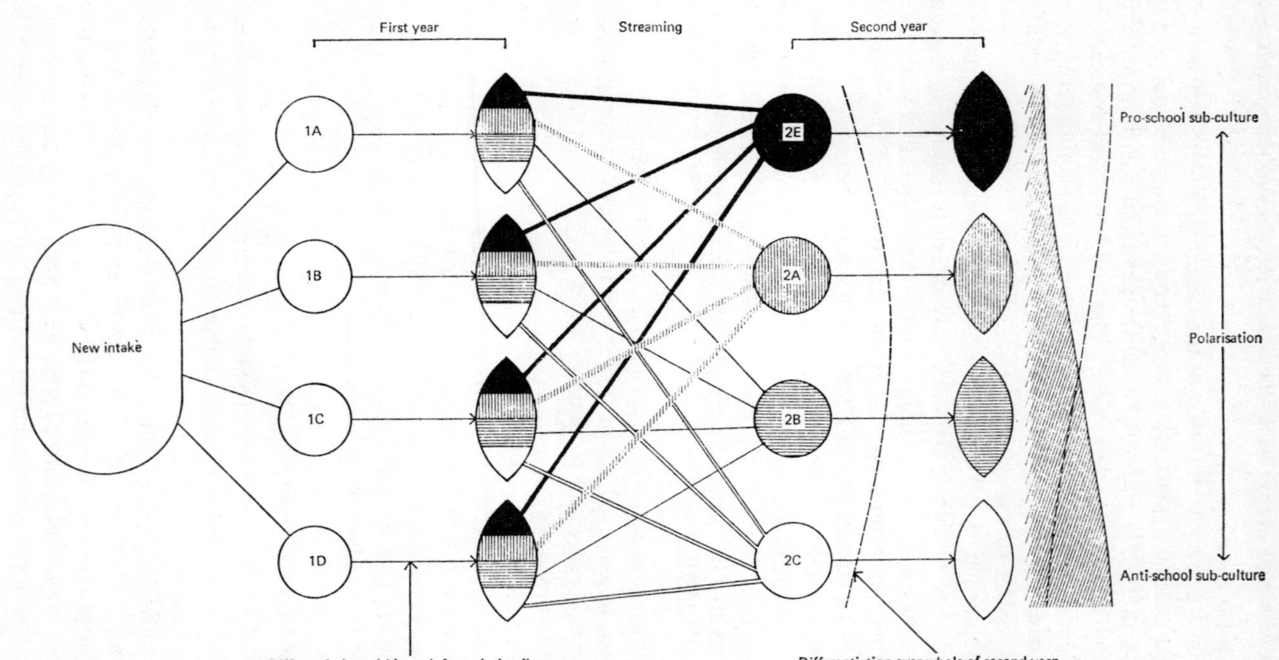

Fig. 6. Differentiation and polarisation associated with the streaming that takes place at the end of the first year.

pupils' for some time and have internalised many of the expectations inherent in that position. Their transfer to the grammar school means not only a new environment, with all that such a change entails—new classmates, new teachers and new sets of rules—but also for many of them a violation of their expectations as 'best pupils'. It is when this violation of expectations coincides with 'unsatisfactory' home backgrounds that the worst cases of emotional disturbance occur.

In the second year the process of differentiation continues. If streaming takes place between the first and second years, as it did in the year group I studied,[11] it helps speed the process and a new crop of cases of emotional disturbance occurs. In the 1963 second year most of them were associated with boys who were failing to make the grade in the top stream and boys who were in the lower half of the bottom stream. Early on, the symptoms are mainly individual; later, after a prolonged period of interaction and the impact of streaming, they are expressed mainly in group attitudes. After six months in the second year this bottom stream was already regarded as a difficult form to teach because, to quote two teachers, 'They're unacademic, they can't cope with the work'; 'Give them half a chance and they'll give you the run-around'.

The true anti-group starts to emerge in the second year, and it develops markedly in the third and fourth years. It is then that strenuous efforts are made to get rid of anti-group pupils. Considerable pressure is put on the headmaster by the teachers who take the boys. He in turn transmits it to the board of governors. In most cases, application to leave will also be made by the boys and their parents. In Hightown, the board of governors was often loath to give permission for a boy to leave or transfer, for two reasons: (1) the governors were also the governors for the secondary modern schools in the area and could not readily agree to passing on disciplinary problems from the grammar school to the secondary modern; (2) they were generally suspicious of grammar school teachers and felt reluctant to risk an injustice to a pupil who was often a working-class boy.

Nevertheless, some requests cannot easily be refused, for example, cases of ill health, family hardship or consistent truanting. There are also a number of cases of unofficial leaving: the boy has actually left school and taken a job, but is still being marked as absent in the register. It is difficult to estimate the extent of the total loss accurately, but, from each of two intakes which have been thoroughly investigated, somewhere between ten and fifteen pupils left or were transferred to secondary modern schools before taking O level or reaching the age of 16.

A similar process can be observed in the sixth form and results in a crop of leavers in the first-year sixth. The extent to which differentiation develops and is internalised in the sixth is illustrated by a remark made to the economics master. He had just rebuked a boy in the Upper Sixth Modern and told him that unless he worked harder he would not pass economics A level. 'Well, the way I look at it is this. If some of the boys in the General form [the bottom stream in the sixth] can get it—and they usually do—then I should be all right.'

3 Quantitative indices

The indices developed below are prepared from two questionnaires completed by all members of the 1962 intake. One questionnaire was given at the end of the first year and one at the end of the second. The indices are designed to illustrate the processes of differentiation and polarisation. On both occasions the boys were asked who had been their close friends over the last year. They were asked to restrict themselves to boys in the school and to six choices, unless they felt they definitely could not do so.

The first and second years

There was virtually no difference in the average number of choices *received* per boy in the four *unstreamed* first-year classes (table 29).

When the boys were streamed on academic criteria at the end of

TABLE 29

AVERAGE NUMBER OF FRIENDSHIP CHOICES RECEIVED
PER BOY IN EACH FIRST-YEAR CLASS*

Form	Choices per boy
1A	4·1
1B	4·1
1C	4·2
1D	4·5

* The choices are 'received' from boys in their own form and from the other first-year forms.

the first year, these *same* friendship choices were related to the new forms 2E, 2A, 2B, 2C (table 30, column (a)).

TABLE 30

AVERAGE NUMBER OF FRIENDSHIP CHOICES RECEIVED PER BOY
AT THE END OF FIRST YEAR AND SECOND YEAR, FOR EACH OF
THE SECOND-YEAR CLASSES

Average number of choices per boy in each class

Form	(a) *First year**	(b) *Second year*
2E	4·8	4·8
2A	4·5	4·6
2B	3·9	4·0
2C	3·3	4·3

* The choices in column (a) were made at the end of the first year and are the same as those averaged in table 29, but they have been averaged for the classes the pupils were about to enter.

The choices in column (b) were made at the end of the second year and are averaged for the classes in which the pupils have spent the year.

Not only do the figures reveal striking differences, but these differences are related to academic achievement. At the end of the first year, the higher up the academic scale a boy was placed, the more likely he was to attract a large number of friendship choices.

At the end of the second year, the boys were asked the same question. The response was equally striking. Column (b) of table 30 shows that the year spent among a new class of boys has hardly changed the overall positions of 2E, 2A and 2B, although the actual friendship choices for any one boy will have undergone considerable change. However, 2C has undergone a substantial change. The increase from 3·3 to 4·3 for 2C represents an increase of something like thirty choices, in a class of thirty boys. That the new popularity of boys in 2C is brought about by the growth of a new set of norms and values or the beginnings of the anti-group sub-culture is demonstrated by table 31. The boys of 2C have become popular for the very reasons they were unpopular in the first year.

The boys of 2E and 2A who, according to our hypothesis, *should* be positively influenced by the academic grading, since they are successful in relation to it, show that it does have a marked positive influence on their choice of friends (e.g. 2E make 26 choices into 2A, fourteen choices into 2B and only seven into 2C). There is no element in the organisation of the school that could bring this about. Similarly, 2A make 28 choices into 2E, sixteen into 2B and only six into 2C.

F

TABLE 31

DISTRIBUTION OF FRIENDSHIP CHOICES ACCORDING TO CLASS:
SECOND YEAR, 1963 (1962 INTAKE AT END OF SECOND YEAR)

Read *across* for choices made, *down* for choices received by each class

Form (number in each class in brackets)	*2E*	*2A*	*2B*	*2C*	*Others*	*Total of choices made*	*Percentage of choices in own class*
2E (31)	91	26	14	7	12	150	60·7
2A (31)	28	94	16	6	14	158	59·5
2B (28)	20	17	63	23	20	143	44·0
2C (30)	9	4	18	92	13	136	67·7
Total (of choices received)	148	141	111	128	58	588	

In 2B a change takes place. Their choices into 2E and 2A have the
expected form but there is an unexpectedly large number of choices
into 2C—23, more than into 2E or 2A. Similarly, the boys of 2C
show a marked tendency to choose their friends outside 2C from 2B,
rather than from 2E and 2A. There must be a basis, other than the
school-imposed academic values, on which these friends are chosen.
This alternative set of norms and values I have already referred to as
the anti-group sub-culture.

Table 32 shows that, in the second year, academic achievement is
related to social class. To some degree this is a problem of working-
class and middle-class culture. That it is not the whole answer is

TABLE 32

DISTRIBUTION OF THE SONS OF NON-MANUAL AND
MANUAL WORKERS BETWEEN THE FOUR SECOND-YEAR STREAMS

Form	*Non-manual–manual ratio*	*Ratio*
2E	18 : 14	1·3
2A	18 : 13	1·4
2B	13 : 14	0·9
2C	8 : 23	0·3

demonstrated by reminding ourselves of table 30, which shows
clearly that anti-group development took place between the end of
the first year and the end of the second. If it were solely a social class
phenomenon, it would have been apparent at the end of the first
year.

This analysis is confirmed by another set of data which are, in many ways, complementary to the first. The second-year questionnaire asked 'What boys do you find it difficult to get on with?' Once again, the subjects were allowed to give up to six names unless they felt they could not possibly confine themselves to six. This time, however, many boys refrained from putting any names down and only a few put six. Enough names were mentioned to establish a pattern of unpopularity. Once again, the largest number of choices were made into the informants' own class (see table 33). The number

TABLE 33

DISTRIBUTION OF CHOICES OF UNPOPULAR BOYS:
SECOND YEAR, 1963

Form	2E	2A	2B	2C	Others	Prefects	Total of choices made	Average number of choices received
2E	38	4	4	26	3	0	75	1·71
2A	5	33	1	9	22	1	51	1·45
2B	7	4	24	20	1	0	56	1·14
2C	3	4	3	42	3	6	61	3·23
Totals (of choices received)	53	45	32	97	29	7	243	

of choices into other forms was always less than seven, with one notable exception: 2C received 26 from 2E, nine from 2A and twenty from 2B, so receiving the highest number of unpopularity choices—97 compared with 53 for 2E, the next highest.

The preponderance of choices into 2C is explained by the anti-group development in 2C. These boys are now regarded as bullies and 'tough eggs' who, in Badman's terminology, would rather be hooligans and have a good time than be nice little boys. They are aggressive, loud-mouthed and feared by many who are successful in terms of the dominant school norms.

An expectation that is altered by academic streaming is the school leaving age. Boys who are successful will expect to continue after O level at 15 or 16 into the sixth form. At the end of the first year the boys were asked 'At what age would you like to leave school?'

The results demonstrate the overall optimism of the first year. Only 25 per cent wanted to leave at the end of the fifth year, 75 per cent desiring a sixth-form career. In practice, only something like

50 per cent ever achieve this. When the figures are broken down into the second-year classes, they reveal, even so, considerable foresight (see table 34).

Even the relatively low value of 2E compared with 2A is fairly realistic in that, since 2E take the GCE at the end of four years, compared with the normal five for 2A, 2B and 2C, many will expect to complete their sixth-form career at $17\frac{1}{2}$ compared with the normal $18\frac{1}{2}$. The fact that, at this stage in their school career, they had not been told officially that they would be going into 2E next year affects

TABLE 34

AVERAGE AGE AT WHICH BOYS IN EACH CLASS
WOULD LIKE TO LEAVE SCHOOL

Form	Before streaming at end of first year	After streaming at end of second year
2E	17·4	17·4
2A	17·7	17·3
2B	17·3	17·4
2C	17·0	16·7

the situation only marginally. By this time the process of structuring and differentiation had gone on long enough for most boys to know whether they would go into 2E or not. In the same questionnaire, 28 of the 32 boys who eventually went into 2E indicated that 2E was the second-year class of their choice.

By the end of the second year, the averages of the desired leaving ages revealed a number of puzzling features. 2E remained the same, while the average age for 2A fell below 2B. 2B's average, in fact, increased to the same level as 2E's; 2C's average value decreased, but not as much as one might expect. The situation has been complicated by an additional factor, which I call 'streaming reaction'.

When the top seven or eight boys from each first-year house group are put into 2E, it is obvious that most of them will not be able to maintain a high position there. In fact, table 35 shows that only two were able to keep up their position; the rest were all placed lower than in their first-year classes. The tendency was not so marked in 2A, with only sixteen boys doing less well. It was reversed in 2B and 2C.

The depressing effect of streaming reaction on the Express form is unlikely to influence their estimates of the length of their school

TABLE 35

EXAMINATION PERFORMANCE BEFORE STREAMING COMPARED
WITH PERFORMANCES AFTER STREAMING

Form	*Number of boys who were placed* higher *in second year than first year*	*Number of boys who* maintained *same place in second and first years*	*Number of boys who were placed* lower *in second year than in first year*
2E	0	2	28
2A	7	4	16
2B	17	2	6
2C	15	0	2

careers to any great extent, because all the E stream are expected to go into the sixth form and they are reminded of this constantly throughout the year. 'All of you will be expected to go on into the sixth form and *many* of you will, I hope, go on to university,' would be a typical remark. Streaming reaction is very pronounced in the E stream, but it takes a different form (see below).

2C is also affected by its polar position. It is not much to a boy's credit to have got a higher place in class if the class is 2C. Masters discussing 2C with me put it bluntly. 'There's not one boy in the class who has any sort of academic ability. In fact, most of them shouldn't be in the school at all. It's not fair on them and it's not fair on the school.' Similar comments were frequently made to me in front of the class and were obviously audible to the front rows of boys. Hence the low prestige of 2C minimised the correcting effects of streaming reaction with respect to leaving age.

It was in 2A and 2B that the reaction had its maximum effect. The relative positions of the two forms were for a long while ambiguous, since the Head had not made it clear.[12] Some masters thought 2A and 2B were on the same level, others that 2A was better than 2B. Only one thought 2B was academically better than 2A, but it is significant that he was able to make the mistake and persist in it for a considerable length of time. In these two classes, then, streaming reaction was a major factor in affecting the length of time the boys wanted to stay at school.

Another instance of 'streaming reaction' is shown in the personal assessment of success (table 36). The boys were asked 'Do you consider that the past year at school has been a success?' The difference between 2A and 2B is not significant, but the difference between 2E

67

TABLE 36

PERSONAL ESTIMATE OF SUCCESS IN SECOND YEAR

Form	Regarded the past year as a success	Couldn't say	Regarded the past year as unsuccessful
2E	19	1	11
2A	24	–	7
2B	21	–	7
2C	24	2	4
Totals	88	3	29

and 2C is—especially when one considers the way the staff assess the 'success' of the two forms in tackling academic tasks. The difference can be accounted for only by the past experience of the two groups, the different sets of standards they have acquired and the way in which their new experiences measure up to those standards. This view is confirmed by an analysis of the experience of the eleven boys who regarded themselves as unsuccessful in 2E. On average, they dropped sixteen places in their second-year examinations compared with their first-year ones. The rest of the class dropped eight places on average. During the year two of these boys had been considerably disturbed emotionally, crying in lessons, crying before school and refusing to come to school. A third went through a similar period and his father wrote to the school complaining that 'the boy is utterly demoralised'. The only other category of boys to yield so large a number of disturbed cases in the second year was the bottom of 2C!

Finally, table 37 shows another area of activity that is affected by streaming. The boys were asked to estimate the average amount of time they spent on homework each evening. Streaming gave rise to

TABLE 37

ESTIMATED LENGTH OF TIME SPENT ON HOMEWORK BEFORE
AND AFTER STREAMING

Form	Estimated average time spent each night: first year	Estimated average time spent each night after streaming: second year
2E	1 hour 3 minutes	2 hours 0 minutes
2A	1 hour 4 minutes	1 hour 43 minutes
2B	1 hour 10 minutes	1 hour 18 minutes
2C	1 hour 1 minute	1 hour 7 minutes

distinctly different climates: 2E estimated spending almost twice as much time on their homework as 2C. Although there is considerable overlap in the estimates given by individual boys in the four classes (which, of course, deserves further analysis), the table does give a convincing demonstration of another aspect of the process of differentiation.

The third and fourth years

The study of the continuation of these processes in the third, fourth and fifth years could not be conducted in the same way. The school changed its policy with respect to streaming in 1964, so that although the E stream continued unchanged into 3E and 4E, the others were reorganised into sets. This meant that at the end of the second year 2A, 2B and 2C disappeared and the pupils were re-sorted into three unstreamed classes, 3P, 3Q and 3R. The new groups stayed together for some of the major academic subjects but were 'set' for a number of subjects that entailed specialisation or were difficult to teach to groups of mixed ability. The specialised options meant that pupils from all three classes could choose, or were directed to, various subjects. For example, they were able to take metalwork, physics or music, but not two of the three.

The second type of setting meant that pupils were sorted according to academic ability into 'sets' that came into being for that subject only, e.g. mathematics. Both types of set cross-cut the unstreamed classes P, Q and R, so that no one grouping contained the same pupils for more than a fraction of the timetable. The intense interaction restricted to a group of thirty boys, all with similar academic (and frequently social) characteristics and faced with similar problems by the school system, which had been the major feature of the old system, no longer existed. At this stage in the study it was impossible to launch the intensive period of field work that would have been required to tease out the effects of the reorganisation.[13]

The tables presented here are, therefore, constructed with the aim of showing how the processes described in the first and second years continue into the third and fourth. The change of organisation mentioned above makes the interpretation of the tables difficult, and they are given in an abbreviated form. More detailed analysis of these two years has had to be restricted to the E stream alone.

As expected, the choices made between 3P, 3Q and 3R were more numerous than those between 3E and 3P, 3Q and 3R. The 'setting'

TABLE 38

DISTRIBUTION OF FRIENDSHIP CHOICES ACCORDING TO
SCHOOL CLASS, THIRD YEAR, 1964 (1962 INTAKE,
END OF THIRD YEAR)

No.	Form	3E	3P	3Q	3R	Others	Total
30	3E	88	8	13	14	9	132
30	3P	14	67	29	27	12	149
27	3Q	13(14·4)	28(31·1)	76(84·5)	21(23·2)	2(2·2)	140(155·4)
27	3R	9(10)	14(15·6)	13(14·5)	82(91·1)	14(15·6)	132(146·8)
		124	117	131	144		

Note: numbers in brackets are corrected for number of pupils in the class; standard used 30 pupils/class.

TABLE 39

DISTRIBUTION OF FRIENDSHIP CHOICES, AS IN TABLE 38:
CLASS NUMBERS STANDARDISED AT 30 AND PERCENTAGED

Form	3E	3P	3Q	3R	Other	Total
3E	66·5	6·0	9·8	11·0	6·8	100·1
3P	9·4	45·5	19·5	18·0	8·1	100·0
3Q	9·3	20·0	54·5	15·0	1·4	100·2
3R	6·8	10·6	9·9	62·2	10·6	100·1
	92·0	82·1	93·7	106·2		

of 3P, 3Q and 3R meant that the chance of meeting and maintaining old second-year friends in subject sets was quite high. In addition, the formation of 3P, 3Q and 3R was more recent than the formation of 3E.

The proportions of choices made by pupils of classes 3P, 3Q and 3R into 3P, 3Q and 3R, discounting the choices made into their own classes, are: 19·5 per cent, 18·0 per cent, 20 per cent, 15 per cent, 10·6 per cent and 9·9 per cent. The average proportion, 15·5 per cent, is much higher than the average proportion of choices made by 3P, 3Q and 3R into 3E and vice versa—8·7 per cent. This is a dramatic reversal of the situation in the second year, when connections with 2E were more numerous (14 compared with 17·3).

There is evidence that the reversal was brought about by factors additional to those mentioned above. For example, the overall popularity of the E stream has also declined dramatically (see table 40).

Evidence from informal interviews, questionnaires and direct observation confirms the hypothesis that the reversal has a secondary

TABLE 40

AVERAGE NUMBER OF FRIENDSHIP CHOICES RECEIVED
PER BOY IN EACH THIRD-YEAR CLASS, 1962 INTAKE

3E	4·1
3P	3·9
3Q	4·9
3R	5·3

cause in the spread of elements of what has been termed the adolescent sub-culture. By the middle of the third year,[14] a large minority of boys in 3R had extended their activities from collecting pop records to sporting Beatle haircuts and attending coffee bars and dance clubs in the town centre at night. 'Adolescent culture' and 'pop culture' activities spread through the year group from this nucleus and a similar group in 3Q, and was more markedly associated with anti-group pupils than with pro-school pupils.[15] 3P and 3E were the last forms affected. Even by the end of the third year, only a small number of 3E and 3P boys could be termed sophisticated or fully initiated into the culture. By the fourth year, most of the boys could be termed relatively sophisticated and even those who did not attend the 'hard core' coffee bars and dance clubs in town went to youth clubs or held record sessions, where they kept in touch with the latest developments in fashion, music and style.

TABLE 41

AVERAGE NUMBER OF FRIENDSHIP CHOICES RECEIVED
PER BOY IN EACH FOURTH-YEAR CLASS, 1962 INTAKE

4E	4·6
4P	3·7
4Q	4·6
4R	5·0

The figures for the fourth year confirm this analysis, but point to a slight modification of the situation due to the much wider dispersion of the sub-culture (see Table 41). However, it is important to note that, although in the third year the spread of adolescent culture mores and activities modifies the effects of differentiation and polarisation, it is a *modification* and of fairly recent origin.[16] It represents a sphere of activity which has its centre of gravity outside the school and is free of school domination. Those that are least successful

71

within the school are most attracted to it. The spread of adolescent culture is examined further in chapter 5.

NOTES

[1] This chapter was first published as an article in the *British Journal of Sociology*, September 1966.

[2] The Technical High School has also been studied on a comparative basis, and a similar study has been made of a boys' secondary modern school using many of the ideas set out in this chapter. See D. Hargreaves, *Social relations in a secondary school*, London, Routledge & Kegan Paul, 1967.

[3] All the records from junior schools of the 1962 intake were burned in a fire in March 1963 which practically gutted the school office. At this time I had recorded notes for about half of them.

[4] Isolation in the sense that they are strangers to each other. They have shared no common experience and at this stage do not trust each other. For an extreme example of isolation caused by lack of trust and an uncertain external situation, see V. Pons, *Social relations among captive civilians in Kisangani* (forthcoming publication).

[5] The pattern holds good for other lessons I observed in this class. However, I do not wish to imply that such a relationship between seating, class position and interaction is typical of the school as a whole. Other classes had different patterns.

[6] There was a large minority of Jewish boys at the school—about one-ninth of the school population.

[7] Skills developed at one stage in the process—say junior school—are not necessarily appropriate at later stages (see page 140).

[8] E. L. Thorndike, 'Constant error in psychological ratings', *Jnl. of App. Psych.*, 1920, pages 24–29. Thorndike refers to this phenomenon as the 'halo effect'.

E. K. Wickman, *Children's behaviour and teachers' attitudes*, the Commonwealth Fund, New York, 1928, page 52: 'It is likely that a teacher's unfavourable impression of a pupil provoked by a single kind of distressing behaviour, would cause her to rate the child more rigidly on the other items of troublesome behaviour than she would another child concerning whom she had formed a favourable impression.'

[9] For a fuller exposition of this argument specifically related to delinquency, see A. Cohen, *Delinquent boys: the culture of the gang*, Free Press, 1955.

[10] Elton E. Jackson, 'Status consistency and symptoms of stress', *A.S.R.*, 27, No. 4, August 1962, page 469. Jackson finds that 'status inconsistency' (as measured on three ranks—education, occupation and race) is associated with symptoms of stress. The stress symptoms listed above refer to change in status over time rather than ongoing status inconsistency. However, there is an important similarity in the situations. The unsuccessful first year pupil experiences 'status inconsistency' in the sense that his internalised status (from 'best pupil' role at junior school) is not consistent with his new status at the grammar school.

[11] Approximately the top quarter of each first-year form went into 2E, the second quarter into 2A and so on. See Fig. 6.

[12] At the end of the first year there was a change of headmasters. The ambiguity existed for longer than would normally have been the case owing to the administrative disruption this caused.

72

[13] Data have been collected but they must await the chance of a second period of fieldwork and the development of new techniques.

[14] In the second year, only two or three boys had been to coffee bars and these were not regular visits.

[15] See B. Sugarman, 'Involvement in youth culture, academic achievement and conformity in school', *B.J.S.*, vol. XVIII, No. 2, June 1967, page 151.

[16] When I started the study at Hightown Grammar School, many of the activities now common in the fourth year were confined to relatively small groups in the fifth and sixth forms. Club-going and many of the attitudes that go with it were new phenomena which spread down the school to the fourth and third years.

5 Elaboration of the model of sub-cultural polarisation

In chapter 4 the model of differentiation and polarisation within the sub-cultural complex found in a grammar school was presented and substantiated. It is now important to take certain aspects of the model and subject them to closer scrutiny. This will be done in several ways. In the first section we shall examine the differing role perspectives of the teacher and the parent towards the process of polarisation. The second and third sections provide a further testing of some of the assumptions made in the construction of the theory, in particular, the effect of streaming on friendship choices and the relationship between academic performance and behaviour. The fourth section presents a further elaboration of the model and a refinement in its interpretation. The single purpose will be to establish both the power and the limitations of the model as an explanatory device. Once this is established it is possible to proceed to a more detailed understanding of the educational processes within one stream of the school.

Parent role and teacher role perspectives on polarisation

The organisational change from the division of the first year into house groups to the division of the second year into forms based on academic ability was designed to make the classes more homogeneous from the point of view of academic standards. This academic homogeneity was intended to make the next phase of teaching more efficient and to facilitate the learning process for all the boys, whether in the top, middle or bottom streams. For example, the masters emphasised the technical and diagnostic functions of the school examinations, in helping to forecast a boy's ability to take the academic course in four or five years, to take the arts or science version of the course, or to take a less academically orientated
74

course. Their approach led them to talk in terms of the 'best interests' of the individual pupil, even when relegating him to the bottom stream. They could point out that his examination results showed he was quite unable to profit from teaching intended for boys who would be moving ahead even faster over even more difficult ground in the next year and that, if he were to remain in their company, he would either hold them up or, more likely, become demoralised and fall further behind. In the company of his academic peers, however, he would be able to proceed at a more suitable pace and even make his way into the sixth form. He was not debarred from it simply because he was in the bottom stream.

However, most interested and ambitious parents are usually reluctant to accept this view in relation to their own child if he is allocated to a low stream. In the first place, they know the implications of the examinations at the end of the first year, and they exert strong pressure on their child to settle the issue beyond doubt by his performance in them. If this fails, they may visit the school to discuss their son's position and put a special case on his behalf. In my experience, success on such occasions depends first on objective considerations and second on the ability of the parents to manipulate[1] the official ideology outlined above. For example, they may argue that their boy has suffered from illness, that he has had difficulty at home through illness in the family, or that he is temporarily upset at school in a way that affects his performance.

I was able to record the details of several such cases.[2] The one described here has been selected from the 1962 intake and will be referred to again later. John Baker was tenth in 1D at the end of the spring term. During the parent–teacher evening, I discussed his progress with his mother and then with his father. (They each saw most members of staff separately—'We're sure to cover most of the teachers then.' In fact, they covered most of them twice.) I pointed out that John was obviously an intelligent, interested boy and his work was often very good. However, he was extremely slow—so slow that he rarely finished his classwork and often had to do both classwork and homework at home. As a result, he did not always finish his homework, or did it badly. I told them he was border-line for the E stream and that I thought he might be better off in 2A, where he would have five years until O level.

His mother retorted that she was worried about him. She felt sure he would be misplaced in 2A, since he was very intelligent and needed the stimulus of other intelligent boys. Without it, he could easily become bored and estranged from the school. After all, she had had quite a lot of experience in getting her children through grammar school. Her elder daughter was teaching and the younger was at university. She knew, she claimed, that her son was more intelligent than either of her daughters. It was only slowness that held him back. She felt he might be under a certain amount of psychological strain, which caused this slowness, and that it would be temporary. The worst thing that could happen would be for him to fail to get into the E stream. His cousin was in the school and top of the E stream in his year.

Several days later, I was approached by Mr Wilkins, Baker's English master. He too was anxious for Baker to get into the E stream. He felt he was obviously E stream material and had the sort of family background that would enable him to make full use of the opportunity. 'I know the family well. His father is a senior lecturer in a technical college, and they're a very cultured family.' I said the boy would probably make it without much difficulty, since he had been fourth in the Christmas examinations. He replied, 'It's his confounded slowness that's the trouble. I'm sure it's only a temporary psychological setback. It caused him to slump to tenth at Easter, and he has to come fifth or sixth to be sure of a place.' Wilkins had organised a group of staff prepared to petition the headmaster should Baker fail, on his own showing, to make the E stream. In the event, the precaution was unnecessary, as he came fourth in his class and went into it automatically.

This is only one of a number of cases I have recorded where articulate, ambitious, middle-class parents who were able to manipulate the ideology of the school interceded successfully on their child's behalf. It is significant because it shows how the middle-class parent, aware of the internal processes of the school, and alive to the dangers of the bottom streams, comes quite naturally to see her child as a special case which should not be allocated according to the normal objective criteria. In this instance, the parent was well versed and forceful enough to argue a case that was convincing to some of the teachers ('a very intelligent, cultured child'; 'temporary psychological difficulty'; 'needs E stream to bring him along'). The case was convincing because it was couched in educational terminology and because it came from an educated, middle-class woman.

In the presence of the teachers, many of the real fears cannot be expressed.[3] These fears recognise that streaming has unintended effects besides its intended technical functions. Unintended consequences (latent functions or dysfunctions) alter the situation for the boys selected for the bottom stream, since there they will be in the company of tough eggs and roughnecks who are not interested in academic work. One mother whose boy was put into the fourth or D stream of a nearby five-stream grammar school complained, 'It's all very well for the teacher to argue that Donald is not going to do well in the B or C stream, but I know my Donald has ability, though he's lazy and easily led. If he's not in a form where the boys are working, he'll slack. It's the devil's own job to keep him at it as it is, without having to compete with the influence of a few undesirables.'

This version would not have convinced any teacher of the need for special treatment. I have records of a case where a publican's wife instanced two or three boys in the C stream as a bad influence on her son. The master at once retaliated that she had no right to say such a thing. Her boy had been put in the same form as other boys of his educational standard. There were just as many good ones in the class who could influence her child for the better.

It is clear from the above that the teacher role and the parent role bring different elements of the streaming process to the fore.[4] This is especially true of ambitious parents whose boys are allocated to lower streams. They are faced with a dilemma: on the one hand, the school stresses that the allocation is on educational grounds and the stream is best suited to their boy; on the other, they may begin to see in their child (or fear in advance) a change of attitude to school work and a change of friends that seems to promise less, not more, educational progress. In the circumstances, it is understandable that the parent will attempt to intervene. In my experience, the chances of working-class parents wanting to intervene in this way are very low; their ability to do so successfully is even lower.[5]

In short, then, while the teacher has an interest[6] in stressing the purely diagnostic and pedagogic aspects of streaming, the parent is mainly concerned with its associated sub-cultural development. The sort of friends the boy makes and the attitude he develops to his work are radically affected by polarisation, and are matters that concern his parents far more directly than the technical pedagogical arguments. Parents' ability to interfere with this process on their children's behalf is related to their ability to present the problem in terms of the school's ideology, and is linked to social class

The effect of school organisation on friendship choices

Throughout this book the friends chosen by an individual have been used as an important index of behaviour and as a means of interpreting the informal social structure in its relations with the formal requirements of the normative system. It can be assumed that a person chooses for his friends those whom he respects and likes and those whom he perceives to be like himself in some significant respects.[7] If a person changes his friends, it is important to know whether the change denotes a conscious manipulation, in order to bring his friends more in line with his interests, likes and behaviour, or whether external forces constrain him. In both cases the effect may be that the person changes his own attitudes and behaviour in order to be more in line with his new friends. In the first case the organisation plays a passive or constraining role in that it places limits on the number of people a person can get to know or make friends with. In the second it plays an active part, sorting and perhaps separating those people who had previously been friends, and making new alliances possible, which are then conditioned by the principles on which the reorganisation has taken place. It is important to know to what extent the organisation plays this active role.

In the first year the house groups coincide with the academic classes and are the only organisational groups that affect the boys. Their friendship choices are overwhelmingly concentrated into the house group. Table 42 demonstrates this. Where friendship choice is outside the house group, it is still restricted to a very small universe within the total school population. For example, the two other groups from which boys chose friends were (1) boys who had gone to the

TABLE 42

NUMBER AND PERCENTAGE OF CHOICES INTO
OWN HOUSE GROUP OR FORM

First-year forms (also house groups)	Total number of friendship choices made by boys in the form	Friendship choices made into own form	Friendship choices into own form as percentage of total
1A	135	99	73·4
1B	132	94	70·5
1C	157	116	74·4
1D	122	95	77·8

same junior school as themselves, (2) Jewish boys, who tended to choose Jewish boys[8] (see table 43).

TABLE 43

(a) NUMBER AND PERCENTAGE OF CHOICES NOT ACCOUNTED FOR IN TABLE 42, BUT (1) BEING IN SAME HOUSE GROUP, (2) HAVING GONE TO SAME JUNIOR SCHOOL AND (3) BEING JEWISH

	1	2	3
House group	Friendship choice made to boys outside house group	Boys in column 1 who went to the same junior school as the boys chosen in 1	Jewish boys in column 1 choosing Jewish boys in 1
1A	36 (out of 135)	23	4
1B	38 (out of 132)	12	10
1C	41 (out of 157)	29	1
1D	27 (out of 122)	20	4

(b) NUMBER OF FRIENDSHIP CHOICES IN COLUMN 1 NOT ACCOUNTED FOR BY 2 OR 3

House group	Number	As a percentage
1A	10	7·4
1B	17	12·9
1C	11	7·0
1D	5	4·1
	43	

Some of the boys in column 1 are also included in column 3. When allowance is made for this overlap, table 43(b) emerges. That is, only 43 out of 546 choices (7·9 per cent) cannot be accounted for by at least one of these three variables. In fact, many of these 43 choices are to prominent senior boys, such as prefects, fifth formers, and even one member of staff. Most of them may be termed 'admiration' choices and do not denote friendship in the usual sense. If they are removed, the figure decreases to about 5 per cent. Finally, if reciprocal choices alone are considered, only one pair is left unexplained —the two captains of rival house soccer teams and key members of the first-year football team. The suggestion here is not that the organisation determines specific friends, but that it limits the group from which friends will be chosen and that it will increase the solidarity of a particular category of pupils if special organisational arrangements bring them together.[9]

These choices were made at the end of the first year at the Grammar School. It might be expected that by the second year the boys would have formed friendships on a more individual basis, cutting across organisation lines. Certainly, as we have seen, the reorganisation in line with academic ability cut across cliques and friendship pairs developed in the house groups. In considering this reorganisation, however, we must remember that from the second year the house group continues to exist for a number of purposes throughout an individual's school career, e.g. morning registration, Friday morning prayers, meals, milk distribution at break, and house sporting events. Despite these activities, it ceases to be the major parameter controlling friendship choice. In the second year its place is taken by the academic form (see table 44).

TABLE 44

THE NUMBER OF FRIENDSHIP CHOICES INTO (*a*) THE SAME ACADEMIC FORM AS THE CHOOSER AND (*b*) THE SAME HOUSE GROUP AS THE CHOOSER

(a) *Second year academic forms*		(b) *Second year house groups**	
2E	91	2α	84
2A	94	2β	79
2B	63	2γ	75
2C	92	2δ	60
Overall 340/589	= 57·7%	298/589	= 50·6%

* The house groups 1A, 1B, 1C and 1D become 2α, 2β, 2γ and 2δ in the second year. The change in notation signifies that although the groups are made up of the same pupils, they are no longer teaching units. The teaching units are the streamed classes, 2E, 2A, 2B and 2C.

When examined in greater detail, the data amply demonstrate the importance of the academic group. Nearly all the change in reciprocated friendship choices is controlled by this new parameter. Table 45 examines the change in friendship choices between the first and second years. Of the 124 first-year friendships that were curtailed in the second year, only fourteen (11 per cent) were curtailed if both boys moved into the same academic stream. Similarly, of the 64 new reciprocated friendships made in the second year, only six (9 per cent) were made outside the pupils' own second-year academic form.

The reciprocated choices that were renewed in the second year split fairly evenly between house and academic form. However, this does not mean that both house group and form are equally effective in maintaining friendships developed in the first year. On the con-

80

TABLE 45

BREAKDOWN OF NEW SECOND-YEAR RECIPROCATED CHOICES AND OLD FIRST-YEAR RECIPROCATED CHOICES NOT RENEWED INTO (1) THOSE MADE INTO THE SAME ACADEMIC STREAM AND (2) THOSE MADE INTO DIFFERENT ACADEMIC STREAMS

	New reciprocated choices in second year		*First year reciprocated choices not renewed in second year*	
Choice into	(1) same academic stream as chooser	(2) different academic stream	(1) same academic stream	(2) different academic stream
1A	14	2	2	16
1B	20	2	2	36
1C	18	2	0	40
1D	6	0	10	18
	58	6	14	110

or	(1) into same academic stream	(2) into different academic stream	*Totals*
Choices made for first time in second year	58	6	64
First-year choices curtailed in second year	14	110	124
Total	74	116	188

$$x^2 = 103 \cdot 44 \quad df\,1 \quad p < 0 \cdot 001$$

trary, there is a marked discrepancy between them. Only fourteen out of 74, or 18·9 per cent, in the same academic year were not renewed, while 110 out of 174, or 63·2 per cent, in different academic streams were not renewed.

These results lead us to conclude that in the second year the academic form largely replaces the house group as the unit within

TABLE 46

BREAKDOWN OF RECIPROCATED CHOICES THAT WERE MADE IN THE FIRST YEAR AND RENEWED IN THE SECOND YEAR

Choices **into**	*Same academic stream*	*Different academic stream*
1A	16	24
1B	8	18
1C	20	12
1D	16	10
Totals	60	64

which friendships are generated and maintained. One would expect a further erosion of the early friendships generated in the first year—especially the 64 friendship choices that still straddle academic streams—as the year group moves through the school.

The question posed initially was to what extent the boys in their second year had developed friendships across organisational lines in pursuit of individual or social class-generated interests and activities. The answer remains as before. The majority of friends are chosen within the primary organisational groups to which the pupils belong.

Friends are, therefore, chosen from the population the organisation makes available. Where this population is highly selected on the basis of sex,[10] academic ability and religion, the friendship networks of the pupils are endowed in these specific elements. The process of streaming further restricts the variation available and friendship networks become still more homogeneous and narrowly confined by social and academic characteristics. This finding gives strength to the model presented in chapter 4, because it emphasises the reliance of the individual on the streamed class, which is an organisational manifestation of the process of differentiation.

The relationship between academic performance and 'behaviour'

The model of sub-cultural differentiation presented in the previous chapter rests on an assumption that there is a positive relationship between academic performance and 'behaviour'.[11]

The reasoning behind this assumption may be presented in an abbreviated and simplified form as follows:[12]

1 *A boy who is good at work* tends to behave well because by doing so he supports the school system that gives him high status.
2 *A boy who is bad at work* tends to behave badly to dissociate himself from a system that gives him low status.
3 *Teachers well disposed towards a well behaved boy* tend to encourage, praise and even raise marks as a reward for trying hard ('halo' effect).
4 *Teachers ill disposed towards a badly behaved boy* tend to criticise, punish and reduce marks as a further method of punishment.

Several tests of this relationship were designed, and two of these are presented here.

The first was simply to ask teachers to rate their pupils according to behaviour and academic standard. This was most conveniently carried out while they were engaged in preparing estimates for the General Certificate of Education examinations (1964), and was confined to the three fifth forms taking the examinations, 5A, 5B and 5C (1959 intake). I had hoped to obtain estimates from masters taking English, French, mathematics and science, and one other subject (i.e. the five matriculation subjects) representing the academic core of the course. In the event, this only proved possible for one form, 5B, and results for the other two classes are based on four estimates.

Form	*Subjects*
5A	French, English, Mathematics, Chemistry
5B	French, English, Mathematics, Geography, History
5C	French, English, Geography, History

Teachers were asked to grade behaviour on a five-point scale (good, fairly good, average, poor, bad) and were requested to base their estimates on general classroom behaviour, politeness, helpfulness, and attitude to school. The estimates of performance were based on the GCE nine point scale[13] for which estimates were being prepared (grades 1–6 constitute a pass and 7–9 degrees of failure).

The grades of performance and of behaviour were calculated[14] separately for each boy, and all boys were ranked according to the results. The ranked lists were then divided, as nearly as possible, into three equal parts: good, medium and bad (see tables 47 and 48).

TABLE 47

'BEHAVIOUR' GRADES FOR FORMS 5A, 5B AND 5C

Behaviour

	Good		Medium		Bad		
Form	*Behaviour grades*	*Number of boys*	*Behaviour grades*	*Number of boys*	*Behaviour grades*	*Number of boys*	*Total*
5A	1·0 –1·8	13	2·0 –2·6	11	2·8–4·2	11	35
5B	1·25–2·0	10	2·25–2·75	12	3·0–4·5	9	31
5C	1·25–2·25	7	2·5 –3·25	7	3·5–4·5	10	24

As expected, different masters used the behaviour grades rather differently. Some used the full range, frequently giving a 1 or a 5, some used an optimistic scale, mainly 1–4, others a pessimistic scale, mainly 2–5. It was thus not possible to establish absolute criteria for good, medium and bad behaviour (or performance). Instead I assumed that the rank order of the various lists was accurate and

83

TABLE 48

'PERFORMANCE' GRADES FOR FORMS 5A, 5B AND 5C

	Performance					
	Good		Medium		Bad	
Form	*Performance grades*	*No. of boys*	*Performance grades*	*No. of boys*	*Performance grades*	*No. of boys*	*Total*
5A	2·8 –4·6	11	4·8 –5·4	13	5·6 –8·2	11	35
5B	1·75–4·5	11	4·75–6·0	10	6·0 –8·5	10	31
5C	3·75–5·75	6	6·0 –7·0	9	7·25–8·25	9	24

drew arbitrary boundaries in such a way that each category had approximately equal numbers and the boundaries did not clash with my experience of the forms. For example, 5C came out as being the worst behaved and the worst performers, even though the boundaries for good and medium were set lower than for the other forms. The most obvious inaccuracy of this method is that masters who used the full scale (1–5) influence the result more than those who used a restricted one. However, no master restricted himself to a three-point scale, so this source of error is probably not very great.

TABLE 49

CORRELATION BETWEEN BEHAVIOUR (ESTIMATED BY TEACHERS) AND PERFORMANCE (ESTIMATED PRIOR TO GCE)

Estimated performance	Estimated behaviour			
	Good	*Medium*	*Bad*	*Total*
5A				
Good	9	2	–	11
Medium	2	5	6	13
Bad	2	4	5	11
Totals	13	11	11	35
				$\gamma = 0·64$
5B				
Good	7	4	–	11
Medium	2	6	2	10
Bad	1	2	7	10
Totals	10	12	9	31
				$\gamma = 0·80$
5C				
Good	5	1	–	6
Medium	1	4	4	9
Bad	1	2	6	9
Totals	7	7	10	24
				$\gamma = 0·74$

TABLE 50

THE RELATION BETWEEN 'BEHAVIOUR' GRADES AND ACTUAL ACADEMIC
PERFORMANCES FOR FORM 5A

Actual performance at GCE	Estimated behaviour			
	Good	Medium	Bad	Total
Good (3·1–5·2)	7	4	–	11
Medium (5·3–6·2)	4	6	3	13
Bad (6·9–9)	2	1	8	11
Totals	13	11	11	35

$$\gamma = 0.69$$

It is significant that no individual with a 'bad' behaviour grade got a 'good' performance grade, while four out of 90 boys got a 'good' behaviour grade and were bad performers. The clear suggestion is that while there are quiet and well behaved boys who turn in poor work, there are no noisy and badly behaved boys who turn in good work. It occurred to me that this result might reflect a tendency for teachers to underestimate the performance of boys who behave badly. In order to check this, I substituted the actual GCE results for the estimates and repeated the tabulation (see table 50). Although the actual performances proved to be worse, on the whole, than the estimates, the same pattern prevailed: no boy with a 'bad' behaviour grade scored in the 'good' performer range.

Further considerations in the interpretation of the model of sub-cultural polarisation

We have seen that as a cohort of students moves through the school, a sub-cultural polarisation takes place. There is a strongly imposed system of values (school values), which orientate the individual towards academic achievement and a characteristically middle-class value complex emphasising the importance of 'good behaviour'. It is taken up most strongly, as we have seen, by those who are most successful in the academic competition within the cohort. However, this is not to say that all those competing have an equal chance. Other research[15] has shown that cultural factors emanating from home environment enter in. Those whose home encourages and instructs them in academic competition are predisposed to succeed more than others.

At the other pole, there is the system of values which develops as a reaction to the externally imposed system. In Hightown Grammar

School it took the form of a reversion to locally derived working-class values adapted to the new situation and opposed to the school values. It is important to stress that although a reactive sub-culture will be found in most competitive institutions of this sort[16] (e.g. schools, universities, Borstals, etc.) it need not take a form similar to that described in Hightown, and in institutions where class differences are negligible (e.g. public schools), it may well be unrecognisable as a 'class' phenomenon. Indeed, even in Hightown Grammar School, a boy's rejection of the school value system did not necessarily imply that he embraced the 'anti-group' culture. There were cases of boys who, like Priestley, failed to embrace either and remained isolates, or were befriended by other boys of low status, frequently younger than themselves.

There seems no reason to suppose that the values attaching to some of these minority 'solutions' to the problem of failure could not, in some situations, provide the basis of the major anti-group culture. However, on the available evidence it seems reasonable to postulate that in grammar schools in working-class areas of depopulation with residual core cultures, the dominant anti-group sub-culture will be similar to that found in Hightown Grammar School. Organisational differences in the school may, of course, be a second source of variation. In Hightown, for example, the streaming system accentuated sub-cultural polarisation.

Having presented this model of some of the major processes within the Grammar School, it is important not to reify it and see *all* the features of the school in terms of these categories.[17] The existence of the two opposed sub-cultures does not mean that every pupil can be neatly classified as an adherent of one or other. To be sure, some pupils will seem to have nearly all the characteristics of one of the 'types' but the behaviour of even the most representative boys is conditioned by the situation of the moment. Examples are contained in my observations on Short of 5C and Sherman of 5B.[18]

Short truanted for long periods during his last term at school in order to work as a petrol pump attendant, and he left before taking the GCE examinations. He sat in class with heavily nicotined fingers, adorned by thick gilt rings, and hair grown as long as possible. The only item of school uniform that he wore, his tie, was pulled and distorted until it resembled a piece of string. When detentions, or the threat of them, for unsatisfactory behaviour or performance were used in an attempt to get him to conform to the values of the school, he truanted or 'went sick' until the pressure died down. Letters explaining his absence were sometimes forged and sometimes written by his mother, who had for some time sympathised with him and thought he was being victimised at school.

However, in observing his behaviour over a period of time, I was struck by the amount of co-operation he gave the school and by his acquiescence in its values. He was usually reasonably courteous and, on some occasions, even competed in answering questions or showed enthusiasm and interest in the classwork. I am not here querying the overall assessment of Short's behaviour. He could be, and on other occasions was, difficult to control and unreliable at his work. I seek only to stress that membership of the anti-group did not entail defiance in every gesture and total dedication to upsetting the system every moment of the day.

A second example also illustrates the point. Sherman was frequently top in 5B. He rarely misbehaved in class and was prominent in co-operating with teachers during lessons. On one occasion, however, I observed that after a lesson in which he was conspicuous for his enthusiastic participation, he waited until the master had left the room, then immediately grabbed an innocuous classmate's satchel and in a few moments had organised a sort of piggy-in-the-middle game. He passed the bag across the room, while the owner stood helplessly by, occasionally trying to intercept or picking up a fallen book. The initiation of this activity so soon after the lesson seemed to be a conscious demonstration of his status within the informal structure of the class. He was indicating that, although he was good at work, he was not a swot and would not be excluded from groups based on other than academic values.

Both these boys found it necessary, in order to maintain their positions, to operate both sets of norms, even though by most criteria they stood at opposite ends of the scale. In fact, any boy unable to do this without at least a little facility would find his position difficult. Anyone consistently unwilling or unable to co-operate with the school in a wide variety of situations could not be retained (e.g. Badman in chapter 4). When the full quota of punishments and threats had been exhausted, he would have to go. On the other hand, a boy consistently unwilling or unable to operate the norms of the anti-group sub-culture would be bullied or pilloried by his peers beyond normal endurance (e.g. Russell in chapter 7).

It follows that a boy who exhibits extremes of pro-school or anti-school behaviour in an *inflexible* way will not be popular. Boys who truanted and were implacably anti-school were in most cases actively disliked by their fellows. For example, in the second year, no one chose Badman as a friend and he was actively disliked by eighteen boys in his own form. Yet he was not an isolate. He was characteristically with a companion and I frequently observed him at the centre of a jostling group. He was strong and forceful enough to impose his company on unwilling companions, and smaller boys who attempted to slight him were terrorised into accepting his company. On a few occasions he set upon such boys and beat them viciously. He was usually caned for these offences.

It is worth noting that a number of boys most persecuted by Badman did not choose him as an enemy. For example, Blundell was so badly beaten on one occasion that he was unable to come to school for several days, but he did not choose Badman as an enemy. A quiet, well behaved middle-class boy, he had worked his way up from fifteenth to fourth in 2C although rather unimaginative and shallow in his work (IQ 117). He was an isolate in 2C, where academic achievement was not valued. He chose six boys as friends, two of whom were first-formers. The only one to reciprocate was Simon of 2B, a new boy, very quiet and not yet really established in the school. After the beating, he had a badly cut lip and swollen eye. He refused to come to school and also refused to tell his parents who he had fought, unless they promised not to tell the school. His aunt, however, came to the school to complain without his knowledge, and gave the form master an account of the beating.

The incident illustrates the extent to which anti-group norms governed certain aspects of behaviour within 2C. Blundell's academic performance gave him but little status within the form (it was appreciated mainly by his parents). On the other hand, the norm that a boy should not squeal on another after being beaten in a fight was extremely well developed. Blundell recognised the extent to which it could damage his standing in the form, so he wanted the whole incident hushed up. He had before him the example of one Murdock, who made the mistake of complaining to teachers about persecution from Priestley. Murdock was the second most unpopular boy in the form (after Badman).

The isolation or active dislike of extreme deviants is supported by evidence obtained from research into delinquency. Croft and Grygier[19] found that, in most classes in a secondary modern school,

88

delinquent boys were 'rejected' (i.e. had many enemies) and that truants were isolated (had few friends or none at all). However, in backward classes the situation was different. Boys who were well behaved were not very popular and those with outstandingly bad behaviour were not rejected.

The difference between Croft and Grygier's findings and my own can be explained by the difference in the type of school. Boys of outstandingly bad behaviour were rejected in the Grammar School, even in the bottom stream. Badman, for example, earned more rejection choices than any other boy in the second year. However, he had many friends in Cornish Road Secondary Modern and had been asking for a transfer to that school for over a year.

The low status of extreme deviants needs some explanation,[20] for it is generally true that, within each stream, the boys who were extremely poor at work, outstandingly badly behaved, or very persistent truants eventually become isolates or were rejected. Those in this position in the Grammar School were usually on their way out of the system. Once their work or behaviour had deteriorated to a certain level, they started building friendships outside the school among boys who were already at work, or at secondary modern schools. Long periods of absence or truancy frequently preceded the eventual break, and during such periods, their friends within the school formed new alliances and developed new activities.[21] When they returned, they were frequently an embarrassment to their erstwhile friends. Work had to be explained to them, recent developments and current gossip had to be repeated, and old friends found themselves with divided responsibilities. After a few attempts to remake their position within the form, they frequently gave up while they waited for their release. In other words, the ability to operate both sets of sub-cultural values was as important to popular 'anti' group pupils as to popular 'pro' group pupils.

TABLE 51

AVERAGE NUMBER OF FRIENDSHIP CHOICES RECEIVED FROM ALL SOURCES BY THE TOP, MIDDLE AND BOTTOM THIRD OF EACH SECOND YEAR CLASS*

	2E	2A	2B	2C
Top	5·4	5·1	3·0	2·7
Middle	4·7	4·7	4·7	6·0
Bottom	4·3	3·9	4·1	3·3

* As defined by the main summer examinations

Table 51 shows how the distribution of popularity within each second-year form is affected by the academic ranking. In 2E and 2A, the academic forms, the top third of the class is also the most popular, and the popularity of each third grades smoothly down to the bottom. In 2B and 2C, the less academic forms, academic prominence is not rewarded by popularity within the form. In 2B the top third is least popular, and in 2C it is only slightly more popular than the bottom third. In both these forms, the most popular section is the middle third. These figures can be represented diagrammatically, as in Fig. 7.

These results confirm the analysis and point to the reason why an *extreme* 'anti' group rarely develops in a grammar school. The boys in the anti-group cliques can remain in the school only so long as their behaviour and academic performance are in some sort of balance

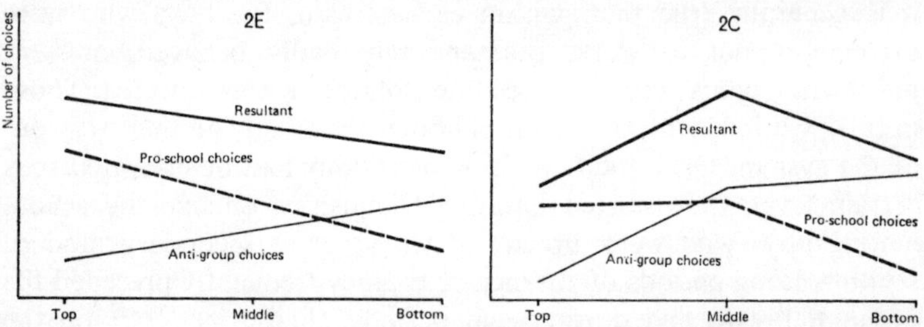

Fig. 7. How the distribution of popularity in each second-year form is affected by academic ranking.

with the demands of the school system. The demands of the system and the sanctions that can be imposed are sufficiently rigorous to ensure that a boy who does not offer a modicum of co-operation finds his position untenable. After a period of growing isolation and abortive attempts to reform, he invariably leaves.

The popular anti-group leaders[22] are boys who, to a large extent, 'get away with it'. They take their opposition so far and no further. They never completely destroy their basis for co-operation with the school: they may copy their homework but they do not usually fail to produce it unless they know the master is unlikely to check it or they have a water-tight excuse.

There is a second reason why the boys at the bottom of 2C are isolates. Those who were butts in their first-year forms—Priestley of 1C, 26th out of 30, Murdock of 1B, 28th out of 28, Roberts of 1D, 29th out of 29—were all placed very low in academic performance. This was, in fact, a major factor determining the attitude of their class-

90

mates towards them. In 2C, both Murdock and Priestley were still the targets for quite a lot of teasing. Very soon after their arrival in 2C, Priestley began a systematic persecution of Murdock. Murdock complained to me that Priestley sat next to him in lessons and criticised his work, frequently punched him, and got on his nerves. Murdock was soon an object of ridicule in the class, often in tears and complaining to staff about his persecution.

As with all models, the one discussed in the last two chapters is a simplification of reality. In this last section, an attempt has been made to modify some of the earlier simplifications. To this end, I have stressed that individuals operate with more than one set of norms, but further elaboration is required. We have to take account of the fact that individuals behave differently in different situations.

Attitudes and opinions expressed publicly in a classroom situation are very different from those expressed by the same pupils in a loosely supervised playground situation.[23] One rather unusual example of this came to light during a visit to a prominent Scottish public school (during the annual cricket tour). The boys of Hightown Grammar had received strict instructions about their behaviour. It was impressed on them that the standards expected at the school they were visiting were very high, and that if they saw a well-known celebrity they were not to comment too obviously.

After the visit—during which the boys behaved very well and obtained an honourable draw in the cricket match—I asked them their impressions. They said they had been struck by the correct behaviour of the public school boys on the cricket pitch and in the company of their masters. Equally, however, they were all horrified by their hosts' behaviour in the changing rooms and at tea, where there had been no supervision. There were complaints that the public school boys were foul-mouthed and unmannerly, and that they were two-faced because in the changing room they sneered at the masters they had been so polite to just a few moments before. When I pointed out that they too probably indulged in a certain amount of this behaviour, they retorted indignantly that while they did not pretend to be so well behaved to our faces they certainly did not run us down to such an extent behind our backs.

It is also important to note that both sets of values are given expression in the classroom. A teacher in a classroom situation tries to produce an atmosphere in which anti-school values are inappropriate and where, if they do appear, they can be clearly defined as inappropriate and dealt with as such. The new and inexperienced or ineffective teacher fails in this because he allows the distinction to become blurred and confused. It is basic to the art of teaching to be able to diagnose the meaning of an interruption or interjection. It might occur because the pupil has been carried away and has reached a deeper insight, or requires clarification, or it could be made with malice aforethought ('How much will he stand? Where will he draw the line?'). A new and enthusiastic teacher can quickly be drawn into a morass: he seems unable to stem the flow of interruptions, and sections of the class lose interest and start conversations on their own.

After repeated ineffectual warnings, the master attempts to bring the situation under control by using sanctions. But when confusion has already been established the pupils see sanctions as unfair and repressive (Why me? Why now? So much else has been allowed), whereas the master thinks them too mild because they are ineffective in restoring order. Further sanctioning (see chapter 8) merely creates an antagonistic atmosphere in which anti-school values are appropriate and the definition of them as inappropriate becomes more difficult. In these circumstances, the whole class will misbehave. The best boys commit misdemeanours that the worst would not be guilty of with an experienced teacher—shouting across the room, copying, causing a fracas by taking another boy's ruler, talking while the master addresses the whole class, and so on. When this develops, the whole class may behave according to anti-school norms. I once witnessed a situation where the entire form marched round the room stamping their feet and singing songs, while the master sat, his head in his hands, quite unable to stop them. This sort of situation rarely arises in grammar schools, and I was able to record only one incident so blatant at Hightown.

This section of chapter 5 represents a refinement in the interpretation of our polarisation model. Increased precision was obtained by considering two implications that were left undeveloped in chapter 4. First, the positions of *extreme* pro- and anti-group pupils were examined. It was found that unless a pupil is flexible in his attitude he runs the risk of ostracism from his fellow pupils. A highly uncompromising anti-group pupil cannot be kept in the grammar school. Second, the situational modifications of behaviour were examined. Appropriate behaviour in the classroom situation was seen to be dependent on the teacher. The really successful teacher can control the situation to such an extent that examples of anti-group behaviour rarely occur, and all the pupils are constrained to behave in accordance with the pro-school set of norms. Where the reverse happens, all except the most extreme pro-school pupils could misbehave.

It is important to realise that this situational modification is not a contradiction of the major structural argument. In the first place, exceptional teachers are so rare that in the normal school day the proportion of time in which their influence is felt is very small. Second, exceptional teachers are more likely to be successful in their careers and, as we shall see, these teachers move away from teaching the academically poorer streams. This unequal distribution of teaching talent intensifies polarisation.

NOTES

[1] The word 'manipulate' is used here (and throughout) to mean 'to handle', 'to manage', 'to turn to one's own purpose or advantage'. I am not using it to mean 'to give a false appearance'.

[2] I do not imply that interference by parents on this issue of streaming was widespread or necessarily unfair. Only one or two cases a year were recorded during the fieldwork period. Parental concern about sub-cultural polarisation also involved the sort of friends the boy was making and his or their standard of work. See A. Tropp and G. Baron, 'Teachers in England and America' in Halsey, Floud and Anderson, *Education, economy and society*, for a comparison between English and American school systems on this issue of parent participation.

[3] Many of the fears and opinions that could not be voiced in the school came to me *via* neighbourhood acquaintances and my wife. This illustrates an advantage of the participant–observer role.

[4] Some of the staff who had children in grammar schools combined the teacher role perspectives with parent role perspectives in interesting ways. The role set of teachers who are also parents would be a fruitful area of investigation which would throw much light upon the way tensions are dealt with in a role set.

[5] See the cases of Buttle and Docker in chapter 7.

[6] The word 'interest' is used here in the Marxian sense. It is not intended to imply that teachers are necessarily in favour of rigid streaming but that, given a streamed system, they have an interest in stressing certain aspects of it in order to safeguard their position with respect to parents and other outside bodies.

[7] See Theodore M. Newcomb, 'The prediction of interpersonal attraction', *American Psych.*, vol. II, 1956, pages 575–86, and subsequent research.

[8] Jewish boys had extra opportunities for meeting each other. At dinner time a coach called at the school and collected the boys, who went to the Jewish canteen for Kosher food. For those who brought sandwiches, a room was provided in the school. At morning prayers, a special Jewish assembly was held separately. During religious instruction lessons, Jewish boys were often allowed to work on their own in a spare room. Finally, before and after school, a special bus ran between Clearview and Brightside, where almost all the Jewish boys lived. The majority of boys using this bus were Jewish, and this provided an

added opportunity for Jewish boys to maintain friendship across house group boundaries.

[9] L. Festinger, S. Schachter and K. Back, *Social pressures in informal groups*, Harper, 1950, and Tavistock, 1959. See pages 33–59 for an analysis of the relationship between spatial ecology and group formation.

[10] Although the girls' grammar school is only a stone's throw from Hightown Grammar, the organisational segregation was almost complete. There were no formal arrangements for pupils from the school to meet each other, the girls were not allowed to meet boys during the lunch hour and the arranged times for going home were staggered. When I first entered the school, a number of sixth-formers came to me with the problem of how to meet and get to know girls. One or two of these boys were worried about the possible effects on their personality of never having had a real girl friend while at school. One of the reasons for the rapid spread of pop culture and its attendant club going was that it provided one of the few ways of meeting girls in a structured but relatively free atmosphere (see chapter 6).

[11] See, in particular, chapter 4, page 57.

[12] Each of the elements 1–4 can be tested separately. An investigation of points (1) and (2) has been carried out and will be prepared for future publication.

[13] This scale is a standard one used throughout the country for recording the estimates and the results of the GCE examination.

[14] Arithmetic means were used for both scales.

[15] See, for example, J. W. B. Douglas, *The home and the school*, MacGibbon & Kee, 1964, page 52.

[16] L. T. Wilkins, *Classification and contamination*, a Memorandum (Schools) from the Research Unit, Home Office, London, December 1955; J. L. Moreno and H. H. Jennings, 'Sociometric control studies' (prisons) of *Grouping and regrouping*, Sociometry monographs No. 7, 1947.

[17] For this reason, I have abandoned the usual procedure of presenting the evidence first and ending with a generalising model and am presenting the model earlier in the discussion, so that it is possible to use it as a backcloth for the description of more detailed material (chapter 6).

[18] These cases were recorded during my observation of the 1959 intake.

[19] I. J. Croft and T. G. Grygier, 'Social relations of truants and juvenile delinquents', *Human Relations*, 1956, 9, pages 439–66.

[20] At first glance, this finding would appear to contradict an aspect of the model presented in chapter 4.

[21] See W. F. Whyte, *Street corner society*, Chicago Press, 1954, page 50 ff. Whyte describes a similar situation when Doc returns to the gang after a long absence. Doc's presence imposes a strain on Angelo's leadership.

[22] I have not discussed the way in which popularity is related to power. A boy like Badman is frequently able to offer leadership in important situations, even though he remains unpopular.

[23] J. Webb, 'The sociology of a school', *B.J.S.*, vol. XIII, No. 3, September 1962.

6 The express stream: a developmental study

We have seen that the pattern of friendships within a year group is influenced by the social pressures affecting that group. The individual's response to these social pressures is conditioned, but not determined, by a number of his own social characteristics.[1] As this response is being worked out, it causes an alignment (and, as it proceeds, a realignment) of individuals within the year group. Those with a similar response to the dominant social pressures tend to coalesce, that is, choose each other as friends.

The classroom situation is complicated by a large number of factors. The simplified model being used here is that friendship patterns tend to realign under the pressures of twin forces towards

1 'Academic achievement.'
2 'Good behaviour.'

I have called the first part of the process 'differentiation' because a fairly homogeneous body of pupils is sorted and ranked with respect to the above criteria, that is, they are 'differentiated'. This initial process is therefore one which accentuates differences.[2] The good are rewarded and the bad are punished.[3] The good are frequently encouraged and the bad are frequently discouraged. Differentiation is therefore unstable, and it leads to a situation where the opposite ends of the differentiated group are faced with different problems: the problems of success and the problems of failure. It is the resolution of these problems that gives rise to polarisation.

Differentiation and polarisation are processes that take place at two levels: (1) over the whole year group, made up of four classes, and (2) within a single class or stream. This is implicit in the model described in chapter 4, but at that juncture it was possible to see the process only in a more general way, operating over the whole year group and affecting the relationships *between* forms. In this chapter

I shall describe these processes at work within one stream (the E stream), from the second year to the early part of the fourth.

We shall be looking in great detail at the way in which friendship patterns realign under the pressures imposed by the process of differentiation described above. As these new groups come into existence they provide the dynamism for the changes in norms and behaviour that produce sub-cultural polarisation.

Small social groups occupy a strategic position as determiners of the behaviour and attitudes of their members. Because attitudes and behaviour patterns are communicated or learned from other people, it is plausible to suppose that face to face communication among members of a social group would be a method through which much of the development of these attitudes and behaviour patterns would occur.[4]

Festinger *et al.* refer to 'Small groups . . . as determiners of behaviour and attitudes'. It is important to realise that attitudes and behaviour also 'determine' the composition of small groups. The two variables have a dialectic relationship. If one side of the equation is altered, then the other is also affected in some way. This assumption underlies the analysis in this chapter. Any allusion to some order of causal priority should, therefore, be regarded as an heuristic device adopted for the purpose of analysing the material.

Our approach in this chapter will follow three stages. A short introduction is followed by a detailed examination of the 2E sociomatrix. Changes in the friendship pattern are related to academic performance, 'behaviour' and social class in order to show how these factors influence the 'face to face' interaction of the pupils. The second stage is in two parts. The first outlines the construction of the 3E sociomatrix, which has been modified to fit the aims of the research. These modifications allowed the matrix to be used in developing quantitative indicators of the process of 'polarisation' in the friendship pattern. The second part is a detailed description of changes in the friendship pattern in 3E, a development of that presented for 2E. The third stage is a brief account of some developments which occurred during the fourth year and modified the effects of the processes under discussion.

The second year

We have seen that polarisation had begun in all classes of the second year. 2C was not only the least successful class academically, it was also widely regarded by staff as the worst behaved. The boys in 2C spent less time on homework than those in any other form and hoped to leave school earlier. Lack of success had not encouraged them to make more effort. They had for the most part lowered their targets (school leaving age from 17 to 16·7) and made relatively less effort to achieve them (they spent just over one hour on their homework compared with 2E's two hours). 2C boys were more likely to be late and absent from school, and nearly three times as likely to be punished by detention, as any other second-year class.

TABLE 52

AVERAGE NUMBER OF LATES, ABSENCES AND DETENTIONS PER BOY
PER YEAR IN THE SECOND-YEAR CLASSES

	Lates	Absences	Detentions
2E	2·5	15·5	0·5
2A	2·2	17·7	0·7
2B	1·1	19·6	0·4
2C	3·1	32·9	1·9

On the other hand, members of 2E were least likely to be absent and, apart from 2B, least likely to be put into detention. On the third index, lateness, they are quite high, but it will be seen that nearly half their average figure (1·1) was due to two boys, one of whom was put down from the E stream after two years.

Form 2E was formed by selection from the top boys of each of the four unstreamed first-year classes. It was thus very homogeneous. No boy had been lower than tenth in his first year. As a group 2E represented the most successful one per cent of all boys of their age in Hightown. They had emerged from a process of educational selection that had lasted five years (i.e. from the time they were first streamed in junior school at the age of 7+).

Despite this homogeneity, the 2E sociomatrix reveals that by the end of the second year differentiation and even polarisation had begun to affect the friendship structure of the form. However, the *dominant* influence in the 2E friendship structure was the history of past friendships brought over from the first-year classes and from junior schools. The strength of this influence must be understood before any subsequent change can be identified and interpreted as due to differentiation, polarisation or any other social force.

Many of the friendships recorded in the sociomatrix were developed in the first year or, even earlier, at the junior school. For example, of

97

the nineteen reciprocated choices made in 2E, in which at least one boy recognised the other as his 'best friend', twelve had some friendship relation in the first year and seven of these twelve had a relationship involving 'best friend' recognition. We have seen (chapter 5) that friendships made in the first year and separated by subsequent streaming tended to discontinue. On the other hand, those that were not separated in this way tended to continue. In addition, the friendships that were discontinued were replaced by friendship partners from within the new academic form, i.e. from a reservoir of boys who were even more alike socially and academically than the house groups of the initial intake, and who were faced by common problems. Thus it was argued that the *organisational* arrangements caused, in part, the developing anti-group sub-culture.

Within 2E no such organisational boundaries existed. The form was kept together for *all* academic activities. In addition, it must be remembered that friendships made in the first year had been formed in a differentiated situation, so that in the first year there were a large number of mutual choices between the top boys in each form available to feed into 2E. This was not the case in 2C, where fewer boys had already been friendly in the first year (see table 30, column (*a*)); in consequence, there was more room for development along new lines.

Nevertheless, not all the friendships made within the top boys of the first-year forms remained appropriate in the new situation. We shall be particularly interested in which friendships discontinue, which new friendships are generated, and why.

The 2E sociomatrix (Fig. 8)

The sociomatrix was constructed in the normal way, but it has a few additional refinements. The boys were asked to select their 'best friend' from among the friends they chose. These choices were then given preference over normal reciprocated choices. The boys were also asked 'which boys they did not get on with'. These choices are entered as negative signs and an attempt has been made to keep them as far from the central line as possible. Finally, where the evidence is ambiguous—for example, Done[5] chooses both Baker and Jeeves as his best friend, and Jeeves is chosen by Winston and Done— observational data were used to resolve the ambiguity. From observation data it appeared that Done was, in fact, more friendly with Baker and that Jeeves was more friendly with Winston.

For convenience the sociomatrix is divided into friendship areas

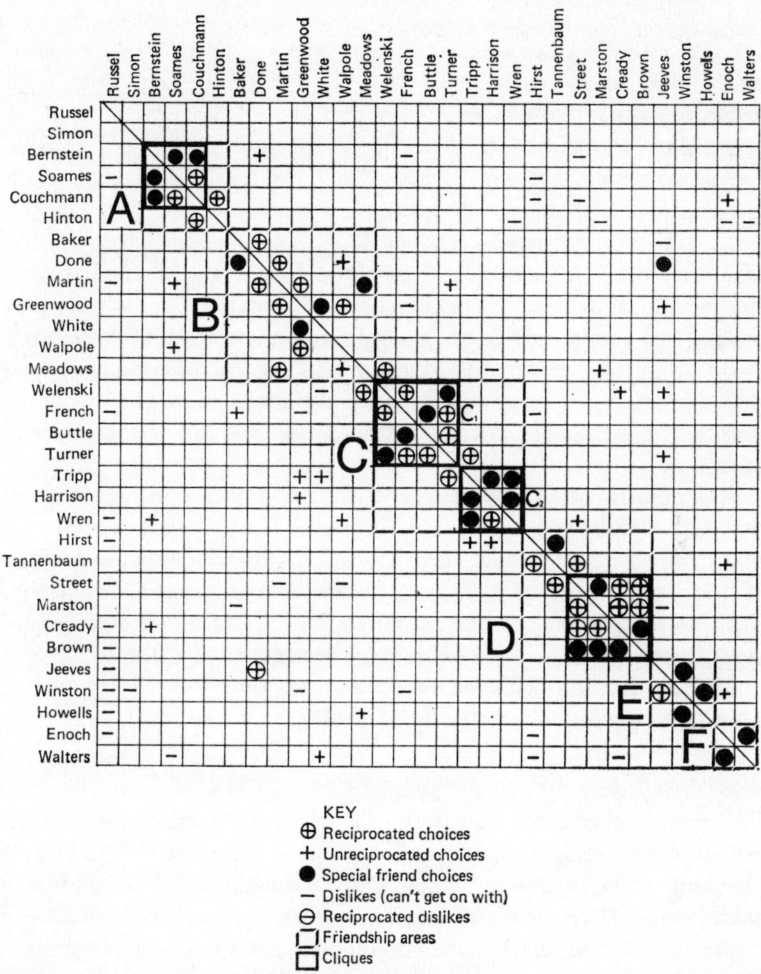

Fig. 8. Sociomatrix: friendship choices given and received within form 2E (1962 intake, second year).

and cliques. Cliques are shown by a solid line boundary and enclose groups of three or four pupils. A maximum of one incompleted reciprocal choice is allowed in the designation of a clique. Friendship areas are shown with a pecked boundary and are less rigorously defined. The intention is to divide the sociogram into natural areas in which the vast majority of friendship choices are located. Working down from the top of the sociomatrix:

Russell[6] and Simon

Both boys were isolates in 2E, and for similar reasons. Both were extremely quiet and shy and very proper and diligent. Russell, in particular, was prone to tears if teased and both were seldom reprimanded by teachers: neither had ever had a detention. Both represented an inflexible extension of pro-school values. They worked hard and never misbehaved—in Russell's case, not even in the smallest detail. Both were extremely isolated. Russell named only one boy in 2B as a friend (Boots, who reciprocated), and admitted to having one friend outside the school. Simon named only three boys, two in the first year and the other in 2A (Smythe, who reciprocated) and yet stated that most of his friends were in school. The boys they mentioned as friends were also extremely quiet, timid and liable to be teased.

Russell attracted twelve negative choices and Simon one Russell was actively disliked and teased. Simon was largely ignored. Russell was from an upper middle class Scottish family which had lost status in the world. Simon was from a 'respectable working class' family. It is interesting to note that although Russell did not choose Simon as a friend, he chose him as the boy he would most like to sit next to during lessons. This seems to indicate that Russell recognised that he had many characteristics in common with Simon.

Clique A

The core of clique A—Bernstein, Soames and Couchmann—formed a completely reciprocated triad. Hinton is linked with the clique, through a reciprocated choice with Couchmann. The clique is middle class (Bernstein's father was a sales representative, Soames's father a shipping clerk, Couchmann's a merchant and Hinton's a draughtsman). Soames was a lively boy but the others were all quiet, rather serious, and hardworking. They spent, on average, over two hours a night on homework and were very middle class and academic in their career choices—economist, historian, solicitor and surgeon respectively.

They formed a close-knit group. During the holidays Soames cycled over to play with Bernstein and Couchmann from the other side of Hightown. There were seven boys from his year group living within a few hundred yards, but he did not choose any of them as his friends. Both Soames and Couchmann chose Bernstein as their 'best friend' and he reciprocated 'best friend' choices to both. They both looked to him as being academically brighter than they were and expected help with problems about work and in realising their academic ambitions. On the other hand, he rested on them for companionship and support, particularly since he was a year younger than the rest of the form. For example, Soames was quite good at football and could have played with the main second-year game in the junior playground during dinner time. Instead, he helped organise a small game which included Bernstein.

The elements of this clique existed in the first year, but were brought together by the formation of 2E. Soames and Bernstein had been friendly in 1D where they had been members of a quiet, academically successful clique. Couchmann and Bernstein had been friendly at junior school and in the first year, where they were both members of an all-Jewish clique of first-year boys which cut across house group boundaries. Soames and Hinton were not Jewish.

The members of clique A were united by their interest in academic work. They complemented each other and formed a very tight-knit group which protected them from outside pressures (they disliked the members of clique D). At the end of the second year, I predicted that if the group stayed together, the performance of its members would improve.[7]

Friendship choices within area B

Area B has been drawn to include Baker, Done, Martin, Greenwood, White, Walpole and Meadows. It constitutes not a clique but rather a loose-knit network of friendship. This type of structure does not show up well in a matrix. It is, therefore, reproduced, with friendship area E, as a sociogram (Fig. 9). The sociogram reveals a three-tier friendship structure in which 'differentiation' is important. (The most successful are friendly with the moderately successful, who are friendly with the least successful.) For example, Done's reason for choosing Martin, which was a new friendship, was 'We are both clever. We have the same interests and the same ideas.' Similarly, Done's friendship with Jeeves was a new one and was undoubtedly connected with Jeeves's initial success in 2E. Jeeves and Done were both eighth after the first term. By the end of the year Jeeves was still eighth, while Done had worked his way up to fourth. In 3E, Jeeves's position deteriorated until he was fourteenth, and by that time the friendship had ended.

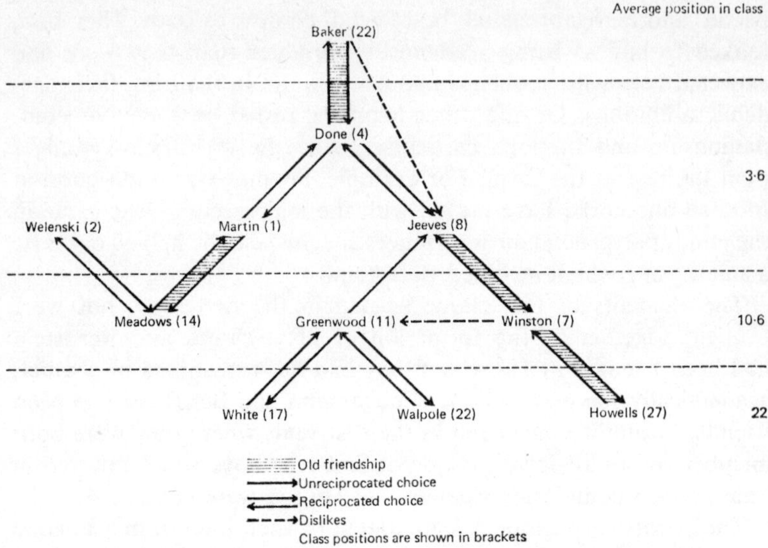

Fig. 9. Friendship areas B and E reproduced as a sociogram.

In contrast to area A, area B is loose-knit, containing many friendships which are new and affected by the new pattern of differentiation within 2E. The average difference between the class positions of boys making totally *new* friendships in this highly competitive network was only six. The difference for friendships that existed in the first year was thirteen. It is mixed from the point of view of social class.

Area C

Area C contains two fairly self-contained cliques. Tripp, Harrison and Wren (clique C_2) had been friendly at junior school and had been members of a similar clique in 1A which had included Jackson, who had gone into 2A. This time Wren, academically the most successful boy in the group (fifth), failed to choose Jackson (the academically least successful), although both Tripp and Harrison did. All the boys in the clique had a middle-class background and all lived in the new suburban part of Hightown. They were not particularly academically orientated, their major interest and out-of-school activity being rugby football. They were all middle class in their career orientation, however.

Clique C consisted of Welenski, French, Buttle and Turner—working-class boys (parents' occupations: bus conductor, police

102

constable, storekeeper and lorry driver). Although all the boys were together in 1C, only French and Turner and Welenski and Turner made reciprocated friendship choices.

Although these boys had neither the professional orientation of clique C_2 nor the academic orientation of clique A, they were all, with the exception of Buttle, in the top half of the form. The clique is an almost completely closed tetrad. The one choice missing is from Welenski, the most successful boy in the clique (second in 2E), who failed to choose Buttle, the least successful boy (21st in 2E).

Friendship area D

The boys in this area form a completely closed tetrad—Street, Marston, Cready and Brown—and two linked pairs—Tannenbaum and Hirst. They are mainly middle class and academically unsuccessful:

		Positions in 2E		
Name	*Father's occupation*	*Xmas*	*Spring*	*Summer*
Hirst	Company director	29	26	20
Tannenbaum	Owns barber shop	28	31	29
Street	Civil servant (Post Office clerk)	31	32	30
Marston	Owns butcher shop	19	22	9
Cready	Quality inspector	12	11	10
Brown	Office manager (dead)	24	19	16

The exceptions are Cready, who as we have seen (chapter 4) is working class and fairly successful academically, and Marston, who is middle class but fluctuates remarkably in his academic performance. Almost all the friendship choices in this area signify new friendship relationships and represent the beginnings of an 'anti-group' clique in 2E. However, at this stage, it must be emphasised that this represents a relatively mild beginning compared to the development in non-academic streams.[8]

Cready's rather anomalous position in the group is explained by his close friendship with Brown. It was the only reciprocated one in this area that dated from the first year. It was a 'best friend' relationship in both years, and they were also friends at junior school. This friendship therefore continued to exist in spite of the 'anti-group' development. Brown had performed very well in 1C (eighth, sixth and ninth), but during the *first* year his father had died and his form master had remarked to me on a deterioration in his attitude to the school. 'He's not trustworthy, he'll let you down. He seems to have become shiftless. He's not straightforward.'[9] As Brown's work and behaviour deteriorated, he moved into the incipient 'anti-group' clique, taking Cready with him. Even in the first year, Brown was fairly obviously the stronger character and dominated the friendship.

However, Cready never became a central member of the group. His friendship choice to Bernstein, the shy, scholarly Jewish boy in clique A, illustrates this, as does Welenski's choice of Cready (Bernstein was third and Welenski second in 2E). So do the hostile relationships between the quiet, generally well-behaved boys in area A and those in area D. All the boys in area A disliked at least one boy from area D, but no one disliked Cready. The only one to record a dislike for Cready—Walters—was, in fact, a candidate for the anti-group clique.

Of the other boys in area D, Marston, a cheerful extrovert with a deep booming voice, gained a reputation as a 'character' and a 'silly nuisance', but like Brown he still found it possible to make a special effort for the important summer examinations. He improved his position from twenty-second at Christmas to ninth in the summer examinations.

It is thus apparent that a wide variation of behaviour was possible, even within this incipient 'anti-group' clique. Cready hardly misbehaved at all, Brown and Marston sobered up near the examinations and even pupils like Street and Tannenbaum, whose performance held out little hope of improvement (31, 32 and 30; 28, 31 and 29, respectively), were not usually difficult to control with the normal classroom techniques (i.e. without resorting to punishment).

However, a number of indicators point to their non-academic orientation. Their choice of friends outside 2E reveals that they were more likely to choose friends from 2C (the bottom stream) than from any other group in the class:

Choice of friends outside 2E

	2A	2B	2C	Others
Clique D	2	2	5	3
Clique A	2	2	–	3
Clique B	10	3	1	2
Clique C	6	–	1	–
Others	6	7	–	4
Totals	26	14	7	12

Their classroom behaviour was also more likely to lead them into trouble. These six boys earned seven detentions in the whole of the second year, while the other 25 boys in the class earned only eight between them. During ten lessons which I observed they were repremanded three times as often as the rest of the class. The only boy in area D who was not put into detention during the year was Tannenbaum, and he shared the distinction of being late more often than any other boy in the form (seventeen times). The average number of house points gained by this clique (45·1) was also well below the average for the class as a whole (58·5)—as was the amount of time they spent on their homework (one hour as against two).

Friendship areas E and F

Friendship areas E and F are conveniently described together because they are small, because they are linked by Winston's choice of Enoch, and because both contain examples of incipient anti-group behaviour. Area E consists of two linked pairs, Jeeves–Winston and Winston–Howells (see Fig. 9). These three working-class boys (father's occupations: lorry driver, plasterer and fitter respectively) had been friendly in the first year. Winston and Howells had also attended the same junior school. Friendship area F contains only Enoch and Walters. Enoch's father was a partner in a plumbing business, while Walter's father was a turner.

The anti-group behaviour exhibited by Howells in friendship area E can be seen as withdrawal.[10] In 1D he had come sixth, seventh and third at the end of the Christmas, spring and summer terms respectively. He had been a member of the quiet, well-behaved group which included Soames and Bernstein, but after streaming he gradually severed all connection with it. He had been put in detention on one occasion in the first year for repeatedly failing to bring his notebook to woodwork class, but this was a relatively minor infringement. His absences had been high early in the year but by the summer term he had settled down to regular, punctual attendance. He had not been absent at all in his last term in 1D, and during the whole year he had been late only on two occasions. His reports for the year spoke of a good standard of work and behaviour and culminated with an excellent summer report. My general impression was of an intelligent (IQ 124), well behaved boy, perhaps slightly unimaginative and prosaic.

In the second year his behaviour and performance deteriorated abruptly. After regular, punctual attendance for five weeks, he began absenting himself on the slightest pretext and was frequently very late. His latenesses and absences for the Christmas term, after the initial five-week period of punctual and regular attendance, were as follows (L—late, A—absent; absences are recorded out of ten possible attendances a week, five mornings and five afternoons): 0 L, 2/10 A; 1 L, 8/10 A; 1 L, 2/10 A; 0 L, 0/10 A; 0 L, 10/10 A; 0 L, 10/10 A; 1 L, 0/10 A; 0 L, 1/10 A; 2 L, 0/10 A. There was only one week in which he was neither late nor absent. In this first term in 2E, he came twenty-fourth, but in the Easter and summer terms his position declined further to twenty-seventh. Associated with this decline was a further increase in absences, and his punctuality also suffered. He equalled Tannenbaum in being late seventeen times.[11] He also obtained the smallest number of house points in the form (23). By the end of the year, he had a reputation for not doing homework and for being away from school if there were tests. Over the year he was absent 68 times—by far the highest in the class (the average for class 2E was 15·5 times).

The broader implications of Howells's behaviour will be discussed in the next chapter. At this point we must concern ourselves with its effect on his position in the friendship structure of 2E. By the end of the year, he was excluded from friendship area A, where he had had two friendships in 1D. Instead, his only reciprocated friendship in 2E was with Winston, an old friend from junior school and the same neighbourhood. It is noticeable that Jeeves, who as we have seen was friendly with Done (a middle-class, high achiever), did not choose Howells.

Another boy displaying a similar though less pronounced behaviour pattern was Walters. His first-year positions in 1B were third, second and third. In 2E they deteriorated to twenty-ninth, twenty-third and twenty-eighth. His house point total (44) was below average and his absences (32) and 'lates' (4)[12] were above average. Walters's friendship with Enoch was a continuation of a first-year friendship. In 1B Enoch had been a 'star',[13] attracting eleven choices and reciprocating six of them. Even in 2E, both boys made all their choices into their house group, 2β, and in each case four out of the five were reciprocated. However, it is important to note that they had only one choice in common, and that whereas all Enoch's choices were to boys in 2A, two of Walters's four friends were in 2B:

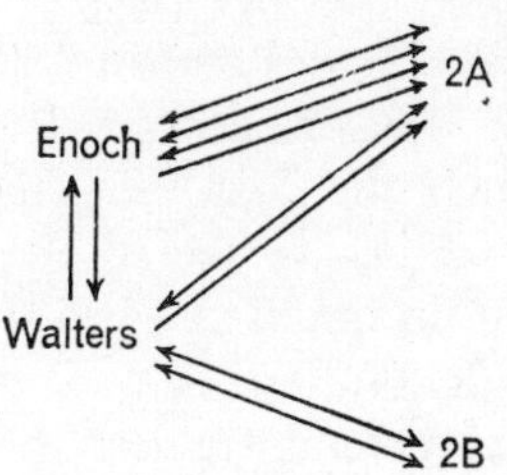

Enoch, whose start in 2E had not been much better than Walters's (eighteenth against twenty-ninth) and whose fall from his first-year position of first in 1B was almost as great (seventeenth against twenty-sixth), prepared to fight back. Some of the background factors that account for his resilience are listed below:

Enoch	*Walters*
Father middle-class: partner in plumbing and heating business—office work only.	Father working class—turner.
IQ 135, 127. Average: 131.	IQ 132, 131. Average: 131·5.
Traditional middle-class area.	Old working-class area.
Place in sibling order 2/2.	Place in sibling order 2/4
Brother in sixth form.	No siblings nor close relatives going to grammar school.
Majority of friends middle class and in A stream.	Majority of friends working class and split evenly between A and B streams.
Enthusiastic support of housemaster	Housemaster had always been surprised that he had done as well as he did in the first year.
Well thought of by most staff.	Not known by many staff.
Good at sport—excellent swimmer and runner.	Only average at all sports.

Although Enoch sometimes displayed a resentful and mischievous side in his classroom behaviour, he weathered the storm. He earned 97 house points (fifth highest), had no detentions or absences and was only once late. His position remained eighteenth in the spring term, but rose to twelfth in the summer.

It is apparent from the foregoing that the twin processes of differentiation and polarisation have begun to affect the friendship structure of the form. Many of the new friendships were obviously affected by the teachers' evaluation of the academic performance and 'behaviour' of the pupils. Done's reason for choosing Martin provides a direct illustration. In some cases, well established friendships, which continued through the first year and were perhaps even established in junior school, weathered the storm and have not broken up under the strain imposed by these forces—for example, Enoch's friendship with Walters and Cready's friendship with Brown (subsequent developments are described later). The processes have much further to go, however, and in 3E we can expect to find them imposing further changes.

The third year

3E: the sociomatrix, its construction and use in quantitative analysis

Many of the problems of presenting and analysing sociometric data have yet to be solved. However, a large number of hand sorting techniques are now available,[14] and the use of the sociomatrix instead of the sociogram means that the possibility of a large number of idiosyncratic arrangements being made from one set of data is reduced.[15] Moreover, computer techniques are finding their way into this field[16] and it may well be that we shall soon have a satisfactory method of constructing one unambiguous matrix from a set of data.

On the other hand, it must be remembered that the problem of eliminating alternative arrangements of the respondents is an artificial one. It stems from the assumption that the only data available are sociometric choices and that these data exactly represent some 'real' structure that is important to the researcher. In other words, the techniques for perfecting the sociomatrix have been pursued as if the perfect, unambiguous sociomatrix is an end in itself; the fact that it is a useful tool of analysis, to be used in conjunction with other data for a more general research purpose, has been overlooked. The use of the sociomatrix in conjunction with other data has been developed in this section, and the sociomatrix used is specifically tailored to fit the purpose of the research. Where the sociometric data are weak or ambiguous, data other than the pure friendship-choice criteria have been used to order the respondents in the matrix.

The procedure used in drawing up the matrix for 3E (Fig. 10) was as follows:

1 A disinterested person drew up the first sociomatrix, using a hand sorting system from an arbitrary starting point. He followed the rules enumerated below:[17]

108

(*a*) Special friends:[18] reciprocated choices of special friends normally took preference over reciprocated choices.

(*b*) Reciprocated choices took preference over unreciprocated choices.

(*c*) Where no choices remained unaccounted for, say with the last boy of a clique, other choices from the clique were examined.

(*d*) Where the sociogram closed prematurely, leaving no leads to other respondents, the volition of the manipulator was uninformed, but unbiased.

(*e*) Finally, the matrix was examined to make sure that reciprocated choices linking cliques were as near to the central line as possible. Where a boy's choices linked to well defined but widely separated cliques, his choices were arranged to be as nearly as possible symmetrical about the centre line.

2 The negative ('can't get on with') choices were then plotted on the sociomatrix. The order was again readjusted in an attempt to get the negative signs as far away from the central line as possible. The following guides were adhered to:

(*a*) Rearranging took place by altering the order within cliques, altering the position of cliques and by moving isolates and pairs.

(*b*) Cliques were not split up, nor were cliques without links juxtaposed. The rules formulated in the first phase took precedence over this rearrangement, so that rearrangement could only take place where the positive choices were not clearly unambiguous.

(*c*) It soon became clear that a natural polarity existed in the material—the good, well-behaved boys at one end and the less well behaved at the other. The arbitrary decision was taken to place the well-behaved boys at the top of the matrix and the bad ones at the bottom. This decision did not affect the internal order.

The resulting sociogram showed a distinct polarity. The boys at one end made no reciprocated friendship choices to the boys at the other, but they made a large number of negative choices, many of them reciprocated. This indicates no friendship structure between the ends of the sociogram, but a great deal of animosity. The extent to which this is true is shown in tables 53 and 54. Table 53 shows the

109

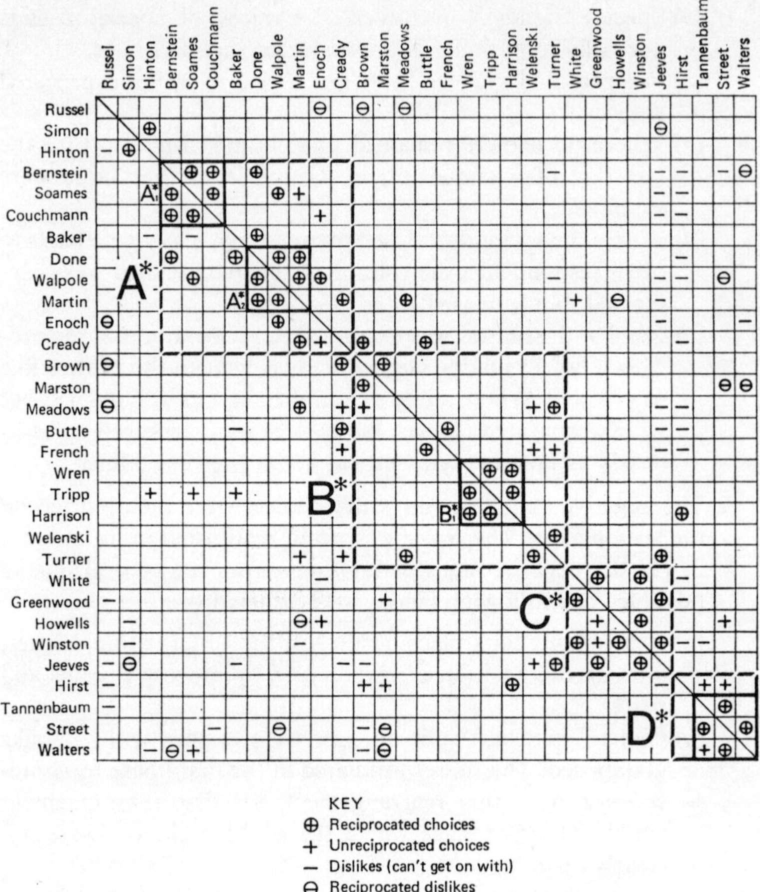

Fig. 10. Sociomatrix: friendship choices given and received within form 3E (1962 intake, third year).

extent to which the linear arrangement in the sociomatrix can concentrate friendship choices within a very limited range. For example, there are no reciprocated choices between the top third and bottom third. This in itself does not prove polarity. We must show that this linear arrangement also concentrates 'can't get on with' choices between the two ends.

Table 54 shows that this polarity does exist: nineteen 'animosity' choices were made by the top third into the bottom third, and fifteen

110

TABLE 53

FRIENDSHIP CHOICES BETWEEN THE THREE SECTIONS OF THE
SOCIOGRAM: TOP THIRD, MIDDLE THIRD AND BOTTOM THIRD*

		Friendship choices made into			
Friendship choices made by		*Top*	*Middle*	*Bottom*	*Total*
Top	Single	**25**	2	1	28
	Reciprocated†	**22**	2	–	24
Middle	Single	6	**19**	4	29
	Reciprocated	2	**14**	3	19
Bottom	Single	3	8	**22**	33
	Reciprocated	–	3	**16**	19
Totals:	Single	34	29	27	90
	Reciprocated	24	19	19	34

* Dividing lines were drawn between the top eleven, middle ten and bottom ten.
If the lines had been drawn in any other position, it would have accentuated the
difference between the three divisions.
† Reciprocated choices are counted each time they occur, i.e. not as pairs.

TABLE 54

'CAN'T GET ON WITH' CHOICES BETWEEN THE THREE
SECTIONS OF THE SOCIOGRAM: TOP THIRD, MIDDLE THIRD
AND BOTTOM THIRD

		'Can't get on with' choices made into			
Negative choices made by		*Top*	*Middle*	*Bottom*	*Total*
Top	Single	5	2	**19**	26
	Reciprocated	2	2	**4**	8
Middle	Single	3	1	9	13
	Reciprocated	2	–	2	4
Bottom	Single	**15**	6	5	26
	Reciprocated	**4**	2	–	6
Totals:	Single	23	9	33	65
	Reciprocated	8	4	6	18

were made by the bottom into the top. The next highest figure was
nine, made by the middle group into the bottom group. It is important that we examine the nature of this polarity and get some idea
of the qualities that are associated with the members of each of these
groups:[19] (1) academic performance, (2) social class, (3) outside
school activities.

1 *Academic performance.* The academic performances of the three
groups were distinctly different. The average position of the 'top
third' in the summer examinations was 12·2, while that of the 'middle
third' and 'bottom third' was 16·3 and 19·8 respectively.

2 *Social class*. The distribution of social class background between the three groups was also very different (see table 55). The table shows that boys in the 'top third' were predominantly middle class, while those in the 'bottom third' were predominantly working class.

TABLE 55

DISTRIBUTION OF MANUAL AND NON-MANUAL PARENTAL OCCUPATIONS IN THE TOP THIRD, MIDDLE THIRD AND BOTTOM THIRD OF THE 3E SOCIOMATRIX

	Top	Middle	Bottom	Total
Parents with non-manual occupation	9	5	3	17
Parents with manual occupation	2	5	7	14
Totals	11	10	10	31

3 *Club membership* can be used as one index of whether the boy is orientated towards the normative adult-dominated school culture or towards the anti-academic, adolescent-dominated culture. Clubs were divided in the following way:

1 *Pro-school, adult dominated*—school clubs, scouts, religious bodies and their youth clubs, libraries, golf and tennis clubs etc.
2 *Anti-school, adolescent dominated*—coffee bar clubs, snooker and billiards clubs.

Table 56 shows dramatically the extent to which the behaviour of the three groups differs on this issue.

4 *Estimation of time spent doing homework and age at which boy would like to leave school.* These indices similarly point to the marked differences in the values and behaviour of the three groups. The

TABLE 56

THE DISTRIBUTION OF CLUBS, CATEGORIES 1 AND 2, BETWEEN PUPILS IN THE TOP THIRD, MIDDLE THIRD AND BOTTOM THIRD OF THE 3E SOCIOMATRIX

	Club memberships			
	Top	Middle	Bottom	Total
Category 1 Pro-school, adult drommated	34	26	8	68
Category 2 Anti-school, adolescent dominated	1	1	14	16
Totals	35	27	22	84

analysis in table 57 demonstrates the existence of two opposed categories of pupil within 3E. On the one hand the well-behaved, predominantly middle-class, pro-school and academically-orientated group choose each other as friends and dislike many of the other group. At the other pole the anti-group are adolescent- rather than adult-orientated, spend less time on their homework and also choose each other as friends. The details of this structure are set out below.

TABLE 57

AVERAGE AGE AT WHICH BOYS WOULD LIKE TO LEAVE SCHOOL, AND AVERAGE TIME SPENT ON HOMEWORK EACH NIGHT IN THE TOP THIRD, MIDDLE THIRD AND BOTTOM THIRD OF THE 3E SOCIOMATRIX

	Average age (in years) at which boys would like to leave school	*Average time spent on homework each night (hours)*
Top	17·73	1·85
Middle	17·3	1·5
Bottom	16·55	0·97

The 3E sociomatrix (Fig. 10)

There is an obvious continuity between 2E and 3E, and a number of cliques remain virtually unchanged. This is true, for example, of the core of clique A—Bernstein, Soames and Couchmann—which becomes A^*_1 in the 3E sociomatrix. However, this is *not* true of other cliques, and in many cases the relationship between cliques has changed significantly. Large numbers of these changes[20] can be shown to illustrate the processes of differentiation and polarisation. Polarisation is now particularly distinct and, in some respects, has probably reached its maximum development.[21]

The major changes have resulted in a large number of interlocking friendships developing among the successful, largely middle-class, well-behaved pro-school group. The anti-groups have become more distinct and homogeneous and a middle transitional zone has developed, which straddles these two groups. This intermediate zone frequently contains successful working-class boys and less successful middle-class boys. The changes have necessitated a change in the labelling of friendship areas. The pro-school groups are included in area A*. The transitional zone is included in area B*, although it is so fragmented that it contains only one small clique. Finally, the areas C* and D* include the anti-group cliques.

113

The positions of Russell and Simon have undergone some change, although they still remain outside the major friendship areas. Both made minor concessions to their fellow pupils during the third year. The growing dominance of the pro-school clique both made this possible and rewarded it. For example, Russell stopped his practice of complaining to teachers when teased or bullied and Simon was able to make a friendship with Hinton, who no longer chose Couchmann. They therefore attracted fewer animosity choices, and such choices now come predominantly from the anti-group pupils in the form. No boy in the top third of the class chose them in this way. Both boys improved their class position and Russell won the class progress prize for his improvement.

The pro-school group: Area A*

Clique A remains intact as clique A*$_1$. Its pro-school orientation has paid off in that both Soames and Couchmann produce better academic results this year than last. Soames came tenth compared with twenty-fifth in 2E, and Couchmann fifteenth compared with twenty-sixth. Both Couchmann and Soames still choose Bernstein as their 'best' friend, but this time Bernstein reciprocates the 'best' friend choice only with Soames. Soames's close friendship with Bernstein was, he admitted to me, an important factor in his improved position in the form. This clique now makes three choices into the second pro-school clique of Done, Walpole and Martin. Two of them are reciprocated.

Clique A*$_2$ and its appendages are a modification of what was friendship area B in 2E. The two boys who have moved out, Greenwood and White, both had working-class backgrounds and did less well academically throughout the year (White marginally worse—twelfth, ninth and seventeenth, compared with tenth, seventh, seventeenth in 2E—and Greenwood rather dramatically worse—fourteenth, eleventh, eleventh, compared with fourth, fifth, eleventh in 2E). The two boys who have moved in, Enoch and Cready, have different characteristics. Both had rather anomalous friendship relationships in 2E, Enoch friendly with Walters and Cready involved with the anti-group clique, including Brown, Marston and Street. We saw that in 2E Enoch's behaviour and academic performance improved throughout the second year, while Walters's declined. This trend continued in the third year until the strain it imposed upon their friendship caused it to break up. In fact, by the end of the third

114

year Enoch chooses Walters as someone he dislikes. A similar development within clique D of 2E explains Cready's move into area A* (see below).

These changes concentrate in area A* the characteristics that were apparent in the second year. The average position of the boys in areas A and B in 2E (excluding Hinton) was 14·5; the average for area A* in 3E is 11·7—a remarkable improvement of nearly three places on average. The area is now made up amost entirely of well-behaved, middle-class high performers. Every boy in the group, except Baker, possesses at least two of these characteristics. Cready is the only working-class boy, but he is well behaved and hard working. Walpole was not a high performer (11, 16, 24),[22] but was hard working and middle class. Baker, the exception, was upper middle class (his father was a senior lecturer in a technical college) and owed his position to his cultural background and close friendship with Done. He was not in fact chosen by any other member of the group. The three key members of the group, Bernstein, Done and Martin, possessed all three characteristics (their class positions were 6, 4 and 1 respectively).

Clique A^*_2 within area A* contains two of the three key members, Done and Martin, and concentrates the qualities referred to above. They make all their choices, except one (to an ex-2A boy), within 3E, and thirteen out of their fifteen choices are reciprocated.

Cready's move into area A* and the break-up of clique D, the incipient 'anti-group' clique of 2E, was predictable on the basis of my observations of the group's classroom behaviour in 3E. In some lessons, Cready and Brown had moved away from Street and Marston and on a number of occasions Cready was exposed and tormented by the latter. For example, during a French lesson when each member of the form had the same short piece of French prose to learn and read, Marston ingeniously turned each reading into a teasing session without the master knowing. He started it during his reading, hesitating over the pronunciation of 'lorsque' and producing 'le Oscar' instead. The class dissolved into laughter. The master corrected Marston: 'Not "le Oscar", "lorsque".' The class burst into laughter again, while Cready went bright red and Street and Marston cried out 'Piggy, piggy, piggy,' from behind their textbooks.

One of the boys explained to me that Cready had been nicknamed Oscar because he was thought to resemble Oscar the pig, a cartoon character. He hated the nickname, but had not been able to prevent

115

its being spread about by Street and his friends. After Marston had spent some little time pretending to try and pronounce the word, he had set the shape of the lesson. Every boy who dared made the same mistake, while the class laughed and Cready grew more annoyed and embarrassed. His position was under strain because, as the socio-matrix reveals, he was on the point of moving away from the members of the old clique D of 2E towards clique A^*_2 in area A^*, where he chose Martin and Enoch. Here he no longer chooses Marston or Street as friends and his friendship with Brown is no longer a 'best friend' one.

Brown's continued friendship with Cready takes him and Marston (see Fig. 10) as a linked pair rather artificially onto the fringes of clique B. It is important to note that their downward movement in performance and their anti-group behaviour continued (they received nine of the eighteen detentions given).

Area B*

We have seen that one of the major developments in 3E has been the merging of friendship areas A and B of 2E to create a strong combination of cliques in area A^* of 3E. The attractiveness of this combination has caused the disintegration of clique C_1 of 2E (see Fig. 11)

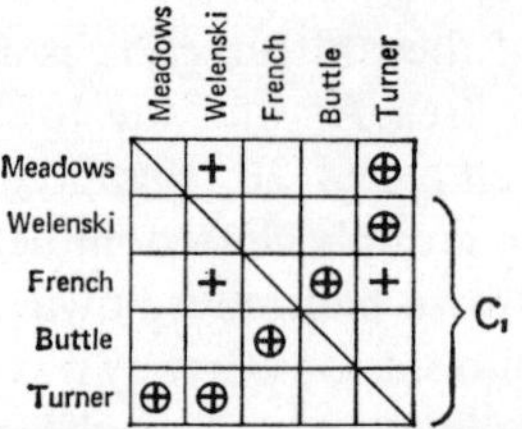

Fig. 11. Clique C_1 of 2E reconstructed but 3E choices plotted. In 2E this clique involved ten reciprocated and one single choice; in 3E it is reduced to three reciprocated and three single choices.

Martin and Cready, in area A, attract six choices from these boys (clique C), but reciprocate only two. On the other hand, Turner has moved closer to area C^*. He has a reciprocated friendship choice with Jeeves in area C^*, while his choices to Cready and Martin are not reciprocated. In fact, Walpole in clique A^*_2 dislikes him and Meadows, Buttle and French dislike his friend Jeeves. The choices of this clique, therefore, now straddle areas A^* and C^*, and this has led to its disintegration.

116

Before leaving this group, it is important to note the case of Buttle. In the second year, his performance declined rapidly: tenth, twelfth, twenty-first in 2E. He was a small, bespectacled boy with a respectable working-class background (father: storekeeper; mother: machinist). With this decline in performance there was no compensating deterioration in attitude to the school, nor in behaviour. In 3E the decline continued almost as precipitously (20, 22, 27), with again very little deterioration in behaviour. By the fourth year, he was unable to come to school.[23]

Clique C_2 remained almost unchanged in 3E as B^*_1; Tripp, Harrison and Wren continued their close association and non-academic, middle-class interests. Their other choices also straddle areas A* and D*. Tripp chooses the least academic middle-class boys in area A*, while Harrison reciprocates with Hirst from the predominantly middle-class anti-group clique D*.

*Area C**

The friendships within area C* represent a new development in 3E. The comparable association in 2E was no more than a couple of linked pairs, Jeeves–Winston and Winston–Howells. In 2E they had made seven choices outside the class (each chose Michael, 2B, and the other choices went to old junior school friends). In 3E these links have been reduced to four and the group is strengthened by the addition of Greenwood and White. It is linked with Welenski and Turner through Jeeves's choice of Welenski and his reciprocated choice with Turner.

This new combination is the result of class factors and school-imposed polarisation. They represent a group of working-class boys whose performance has deteriorated, slightly but noticeably, in every case (average deterioration of 4·6 places between summer 1964 and summer 1965).

	Average IQ	Father's occupation	2E exams			3E exams		
White	116	Pipe fitter and welder	10	7	17	12	9	17
Greenwood	140	Hoffman presser	4	5	11	14	11	19
Winston	127	Plasterer	3	9	7	7	10	13
Howells	122	Fitter	27	24	27	23	31	30
Jeeves	113	Driver	8	8	8	13	13	14

Coupled with the decline in performance is a commensurate decline in attitude to work and school, and in behaviour. Not one desires to be remembered at school as a brilliant scholar. They spend far less time on homework than the class average. They want to leave school earlier and only two desire a sixth-form career. Within the group, the boy whose performance has declined most steeply, Greenwood, has the worst attitude, while the two boys who still scrape into the top half of the class retain some of their ambition and pro-school values. Jeeves, the more successful of these two, is the boy who links with Turner and White (successful working-class boys). They can be described as the working-class anti-group, surprisingly more successful and less militant than the predominantly middle-class anti-group D*.

In its external relations with other cliques, area C* is characterised by a great deal of hostility. It gives or receives animosity choices from practically every other clique or grouping in the class. Only area D* is involved in more hostility (C* gives fifteen and receives twelve, D* gives eleven and receives nineteen). They are separated from the other unsuccessful working-class boys, Meadows, Buttle and to a lesser extent French, by being more mature and more militantly anti-school; and from the other anti-group clique by class-linked characteristics.

*Area D**

Hirst, Tannenbaum and Street were part of the incipient anti-group clique in 2E. In 3E, they combine with Walters, who showed anti-group tendencies in 2E and whose friendship with Enoch has ended. This clique has, therefore, resulted from the purged (of high performers) remnants of cliques D and F of 2E. There is one complication to the interpretation of area D*. Brown and Marston have not in fact improved their behaviour or performance, yet they have also apparently been 'purged'. Street and Walters now dislike Marston and Brown, while Marston reciprocates by disliking Street and Walters. When I asked Street why he and Walters had fallen out with Brown and Marston, he confessed that he still liked Marston quite a lot. 'He's a good lad. It's just that we can't get on.' They had had quite a lot of petty quarrels recently, partly over Cready, and at the moment 'We hate one another.'

This last remark was made with a sort of mock hostility. It was apparent that Street and Marston had periods of quite intense friendship, followed by quarrels and periods of hostility. The break between Cready and the boys of area D was therefore of a rather different sort. It was part of a gradual but irreversible trend. Cready no longer had anything in common with them. The break between Marston and the others was likely to be repaired when the immediate cause of the quarrel was forgotten. They remained 'potential' friends. In fact, in 4E the friendship between Marston and Street was renewed.

Thus we see that processes of differentiation and polarisation have developed markedly within 3E. The indices I have developed to demonstrate this unambiguously and the detailed examination of changes in clique membership bear the assertion out. I expected a modification of this extreme development in 4E, mainly because during my observation of the 4E class in the 1959 intake I had witnessed the levelling and concentrating effects of the impending GCE examinations. In this case, the mock exams after Christmas, and the subsequent official ones, had produced an atmosphere of purpose and dedication that inhibited anti-group development. In the 1962 intake this feature was present again but it was masked by a new development for a 4E class in Hightown Grammar School: the spread of features of the adolescent sub-culture.

The fourth year and the adolescent sub-culture: 4E

The sociogram formed from friendship choices recorded at the end of the fourth year confirmed my hypothesis at the end of the third year that in many respects the third-year sociogram marked an extreme point in differentiation and polarisation of the Express form. In the fourth year the spread of what has been termed an 'adolescent sub-culture' softened the animosities within the class and provided a common interest which to some extent cut them off from, and united them against, the staff. Elements of this sub-culture included hair styles, dress, interest in records and 'pop' stars, and activities such as dancing and frequenting coffee bars.

Even Russell, the boy with the most outlandishly pro-middle class adult culture orientation, recorded in his diary after a particularly bad spell of teasing that his dress needed some attention:

White shirt, school tie—OK.
School blazer—OK.
Required: new trousers, without turn-ups, new shoes and dark socks and new mackintosh.

Within a few weeks his appearance was transformed. He sported slim-fitting trousers, suede shoes with fashionably shaped toes and a hair-cut that enabled his hair to be brushed back at school and forward at night (a sort of semi-Beatle). He exchanged his old navy gabardine school mac for a stylish new white, three-quarter length poplin one.

During the year he began attending a local dance club and was soon going regularly two or three times a week. After a period of regular and persistent attendance,[24] he earned the job of disc jockey, which he held for well over a year. He was eventually able to translate the status he had gained in these adolescent activities into the school situation. This occurred naturally as the elements of the adolescent pop culture spread and became important in the class. He was able to converse on the latest records, giving his opinion not only on their merit but also on technical details relating to their 'sound', production and 'backing'. He shared in the fairly widespread borrowing and lending of records, and got to know and like a wide variety of people in and outside the school whom he would otherwise never have met. It was important that many of these new friends were girls, for this also enhanced his status at school. The process took place over two years (see case study, chapter 7) and it enabled me to gauge the growing importance of the teenage pop culture within 4E.

The development of the adolescent sub-culture within the fourth, fifth and sixth forms can be expected to modify the process of polarisation which is so markedly a feature of the third year. A detailed analysis of this process cannot be presented here but the degree and direction of this modification can be indicated.

Coleman[25] has argued that the adolescent sub-culture in American high schools stems from economic changes in society, which have affected American upper middle class schools more than the working-class schools. He sees the adolescent being 'released' from his or her family's demands into the adolescent culture, and feels that the traditional academic elite of American society is most threatened by the emergence of the sub-culture.

Neither of these trends—the complete release of the child into the adolescent sub-culture nor the threat to the middle-class academic elite—is easily recognisable at Hightown Grammar School. Considering first the idea of 'release' into the adolescent sub-culture, the data reveal that for adolescents of comparable age to the American high school students (16, 17 and 18 years) two developments in the

120

students' relations with the staff are apparent. These developments are in opposite directions. On the one hand, students in the fifth and sixth forms[26] acted with increasing enthusiasm and responsibility in extra-curricular activities and academic matters. For example, they provided leadership in school clubs (see Appendix 5), house teams and dramatic productions and in doing so made close personal relationships with the staff.

On the other hand there were developing areas of behaviour that escaped the supervision of teachers and sometimes of parents. During the fifth year many boys took up smoking[27] and going to social clubs where they could meet girls. A few would occasionally go out drinking. Such activities were hardly, if ever, discussed with teachers. Pupils assumed the staff would think badly of them if they knew they 'went out at night'. Teachers were constrained not to question them because of the embarrassment it would cause in the classroom and because it could be construed as prying and unnecessary.

The picture that emerges from the data is of a developing discreteness of roles and a disjunction between the world of the school and the adolescent peer group.[28] The model can be represented diagrammatically, as in Fig. 12. This picture contrasts with Coleman's

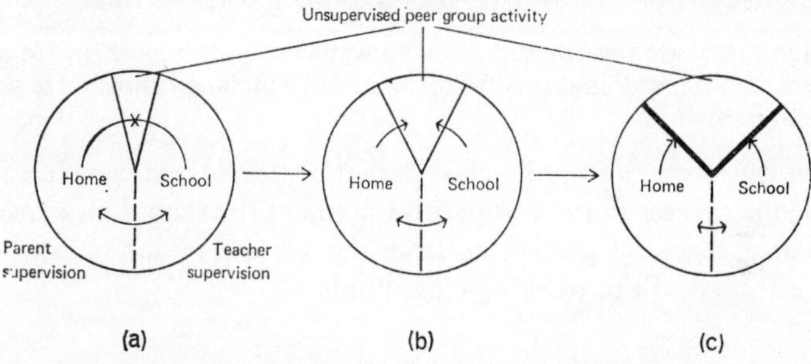

Fig. 12. The developing discreteness of roles and disjunction between the world of the school and the adolescent peer group: (*a*) junior school, (*b*) early grammar school, (*c*) late grammar school. Circles represent the total activity area of the pupils. The segments become more discrete and roles in each area more specialised.

analysis, in which he says that changes in society 'have taken not only job training out of the parent's hands, but have quite effectively taken away the whole adolescent himself'.[29] But it is similar to that proposed by Remmers and Radler,[30] who claim that the American teenager recognises the standards set by his peer group in some activities—for example, dress—and the standards of his parents in others—for example, political issues. I would add that for some of the teenagers at Hightown Grammar the school values also became increasingly important.

The model presented here does not imply that each of these areas is independent of the other. Precisely the opposite is true. The culture of the school is differentiated and polarised, and this is related to differentiation within the adolescent sub-culture.[31] This is clear from table 56, where a pupil's sociomatrix position within the classroom is shown to be closely related to his involvement in adolescent-dominated clubs. It is also apparent from my enquiries within the fourth and fifth years that the clubs themselves were differentiated. Those situated in middle-class areas were regarded as respectable but some of the clubs 'in town' were thought to be unsavoury[32] and even dangerous (one or two had been raided for drugs).

Although the non-academic orientation of the adolescent sub-culture poses a problem to middle-class academically-orientated families, there was little evidence that it posed a threat to their elite position. Middle-class parents typically relaxed control only in certain areas as they became aware that the boy was 'responsible'—that is, had internalised their own middle-class values. A quotation from a middle-class parent of a 12-year-old boy illustrates this.

> I don't regulate the amount of TV he watches. I don't have to. He much prefers reading or doing something himself to watching rubbish. He selects what interests him.

The resources the middle-class parent possessed and used to ensure academic success in the competitive arena of the school also ensured a greater degree of protection from the adolescent sub-culture than that afforded to the working-class pupil.

NOTES

[1] For example, the influence of the home, the education or social class of the individual's parents. A. Cohen, *Delinquent boys*, page 51, puts the problem in a similar way. 'As a first step, it is important to recognise that all the multifarious factors and circumstances that conspire to produce a problem come from one or the other of two sources, the actor's *'frame of reference'* and the *'situation* he confronts' (my italics).

[2] See T. Grygier, 'The concept of social progression' in *Criminology in transition*, ed. T. Grygier, H. Jones and J. C. Spencer, Tavistock, 1965, page 155. 'The mere process of sorting and labelling cannot, of itself, improve the effectiveness of treatment. On the contrary . . . it contains inherent dangers and unleashes powerful forces which are likely to work against, rather than for, the therapeutic goal.'

122

[3] Durkheim argues that punishment reinforces norms: '. . . "punishment" is due to the intensity of the collective sentiments which the crime offends; but, from another angle, it has the useful function of maintaining these sentiments at the same degree of intensity . . .' *Rules of sociological method*, page 96; also *Division du travail social*, book II, chapter ii, page 105 ff. He overlooks the fact that positive and negative sanctions flow in a predictable way to certain groups and that this produces a dynamic situation.

[4] L. Festinger, S. Schachter and K. Back, *Social pressures in informal groups*, Tavistock, 1965, page 3.

[5] Done's friendship with Jeeves was largely confined to after school, for example, they walked home together. It explains Baker's dislike of Jeeves. In the same way, Greenwood's friendship with Jeeves explains Winston's dislike of Greenwood (see Fig. 9).

[6] For a fuller description of this case, see chapter 7.

[7] As mentioned later, this happened. Soames improved from twenty-fifth to tenth, Couchmann from twenty-sixth to fifteenth, and Bernstein retained his position near the top of the form.

[8] It was pointed out in chapter 4 that many of the difficulties in 2E leading to the violation of 'best pupil' expectations were emotional problems. Baker, Walpole, Russell and later Buttle all experienced problems of this type.

[9] It is important to note that, although this change in the boy's attitude was related to his father's death, the house tutor merely reported the change in attitude. I noticed no measures taken by the school (other than recording the fact of his father's death) to help the boy over this difficult period and the ensuing years; in fact, there was little provision in the school to meet such a need. The boy was extremely intelligent (IQ 139), and close to his father. For example, his junior school reported, 'Home good. Helped by his father.' It is doubtful whether more than a few of the staff realised at the time that his father had died, and by the time the boy had reached the second year many of his teachers were new and quite unaware of the fact. His behaviour, which had initially been the symptom of an upset in family relationships, became transformed into a problem *per se*. His first- and second-year reports illustrate this. First year: 'Progressing satisfactorily; work well within his grasp. Has worked keenly.' Second year: 'Good in subjects which appeal to him. Must work hard all round. Far too inconsistent; needs discipline and concentration and better behaviour.'

[10] In contrast to the relatively exuberant, extrovert and aggressive pattern exhibited by the anti-group clique D—in particular, Hirst, Marston and Brown.

[11] The figure of seventeen is obtained from his end-of-term report, which is recorded from prefects' records. 'Lates' are also recorded by the form master. According to the form register, he was late 28 times. The school secretary reported that he sometimes arrived half-way through the morning. This sometimes enabled him to avoid detection because the prefect was no longer on duty.

[12] Average number of lates, 2·4; mode, 0.

[13] The term is used in its sociometric sense of attracting a large number of choices.

[14] Beum and Brundage; 'A method for analysing the sociomatrix', *Sociometry*, 13, pages 141–5, 1950.

[15] Forsyth and Katz, 'A matrix approach to the analysis of sociometric data'. *Sociometry*, 9, pages 340–7, 1950.

[16] J. S. Coleman, *Mathematical sociology*, Free Press, 1964.

[17] See K. M. Evans, *Society and education*, Routledge & Kegan Paul, page 25, for a method of drawing up a sociomatrix.

[18] After the boys had been asked to name the boys they had been friendly with

during the past year, they were asked to underline the name of the boy whom they considered their 'special' friend.

[19] These groups are arbitrarily defined as 'top third', 'middle third' and 'bottom third'. Though rough, they are *realistic* groupings. The positive and negative choices could not be *forced* into this pattern if they were randomly distributed throughout the class.

[20] The continuing effects of differences in home background are also much in evidence.

[21] The E stream takes the GCE O level examinations after four years. The third year is, therefore, the year before the end of the O level course.

[22] Walpole's class position shows this declining pattern consistently. 1D: 2, 2, 8; 2E: 16, 17, 22; 3E: 11, 16, 24. Enquiries confirmed that this was because term work was taken into account in the assessments of the first two terms. He always obtained high marks in homework and classwork because he was conscientious and was helped by Done. The summer term mark was a pure examination mark and could not be improved in this way.

[23] It would seem from this case that a change in values protects the individual from the tension implicit in Buttle's position. Holding on to his pro-academic values, while failing academically, exposed Buttle to tension. He found himself eventually unable to come to school (see chapter 7).

[24] His early attendances required a deal of persistence. He was nervous, shy and sometimes teased and dispirited.

[25] J. S. Coleman, *The adolescent society*, Free Press, 1961, page 288.

[26] The selection that takes place between the fifth and sixth forms undoubtedly affects the process. This is a complication that cannot be dealt with here.

[27] Same 40 per cent had 'taken up' smoking but only 25 per cent smoked 'frequently'.

[28] Although all students were informed before they filled in their questionnaires that the answered schedules would not be available to teachers, many asked for confirmation when they started to answer the sections concerning out-of-school activities. 'Sir, are you sure the teachers won't see this?'

[29] J. S. Coleman, *op. cit.*, page 4.

[30] H. H. Remmers and D. H. Radler, *The American teenager*, Bobbs Merrill, 1957.

[31] B. Sugarman, 'Youth culture, academic achievement and conformity', *Brit. J. Soc.*, vol. XVIII, No. 2, June 1967. Sugarman makes a similar point in his study of four London schools. He shows that 'achievement' and 'conduct ratings' are negatively correlated with 'teenage commitment'.

[32] Or more 'interesting', depending on one's point of view.

7 The home and the school: some case studies

The case studies in this chapter have been selected to illustrate the nature of the relationship between a number of the major social factors relevant to this book—academic achievement, social class and parental encouragement. The cases have been selected with the aid of the paradigm below to cover the full range of possible combinations of these factors.

Parental interest and encouragement	Middle class		Working class	
	High achiever	*Low achiever*	*High achiever*	*Low achiever*
	A	B	C	D
High	Martin	Baker	Welenski	Buttle
	E	F	G	H
Low	French	Russell	King	Howells, Docker

The paradigm includes two factors emanating from the home, 'social class' and 'parental interest and encouragement', and therefore shifts the emphasis in this chapter away from the school and peer group influences to the influence of the home. The school as a social system is here looked at from the outside (exoscopic as opposed to endoscopic)[1] and is seen as an arena for competing teams. Each team is composed of a pupil and his parents,[2] with the pupil filling the role of competitor and the parents that of coach.

The resources of each team will be discussed qualitatively under the following headings:

1 *Psychological.* In addition to the pupil's IQ, this variable includes the emotional resources of the family unit.
2 *Social.* Includes all the resources which stem from the social position of the family unit. Indicative of this variable are occupation and income.

3 *Cultural.* Includes the parents' ability to understand and manipulate an 'academic' or 'school' culture. An important indicator of this is their educational background.

The model will be used in the interpretation of the case study material and in a critical analysis of the concept of deferred gratification in chapter 9.

The case studies were selected to cover the full range of possibilities mentioned above. However, a number of precautions were taken in their selection to safeguard against possible intervening factors. As far as possible, all the cases have an IQ of 120 or over and are selected from the 1962 intake. All the parents were reported as providing their children with a good home and being interested in their children's education at the junior school level (junior school reports). As far as possible, all the cases were selected from the E stream. I have inserted two cases in categories G and H which do not fulfil the above criteria absolutely, but which do provide rich case material. In category G, King came from the 1959 intake and was in the Modern stream instead of the Express. In category H, Docker came from the 1963 intake and did not have an IQ of 120. There are two cases in category H, and the other case, Howells, fulfils the requirements.

Not all the cases will be dealt with in the same degree of detail. The reason is partly that my own collection of data[3] has necessarily been uneven, but it is also due to the conviction that certain combinations of these factors are more important to the understanding of the processes within the school than others. For example, category H occurs very frequently—especially if the whole year group is taken into account—as does category A. On the other hand, category E is rare, as is category G.

The variables of 'achievement' and 'parental interest and encouragement' need a little explanation:

1 *Achievement.* High achievers were selected from those pupils who generally performed in the top one-third of their class. Low achievers were selected from those who frequently fell into the bottom one-third of the class.

2 *The estimation of parental interest* is based on two sources of information, (*a*) a questionnaire given to the boys and (*b*) unstructured interviews with parents. (Interview material was collected when I attended first- and second-year parents' evenings as a teacher or visited their homes as a research worker.)

126

Cases of high and low parental interest were initially selected according to responses to the question on parental interest in the questionnaire. Cases of high parental interest were selected from those boys who answered 'Very interested and helped a great deal' to the question on parental interest, whilst the cases of low parental interest were selected from the boys who answered either 'Low interest and some help' or 'Very little interest and help'.[4] These responses were then checked against notes taken at the parents' evening.[5]

For the cases in categories G and H, I had full notes from interviews with teachers and the boys themselves, and they were easily classified.

The case studies

(*A*) *Middle-class high achiever; high level of parental encouragement: Adam Martin, IQ 128*

Adam came from a lower middle class family. His father was a salesman for a credit clothing concern; the family lived in an owner-occupied 'semi' in suburbia. He was the only child of careful, intelligent and interested parents. Adam had been top overall in every examination in the school (except for one minor examination in the first year, when he was second). His reports consistently contained remarks like 'An outstanding year of progress', 'He has every reason to feel proud of himself', 'An excellent report'. In four years he had been absent only once, for half a day, and had been late only once. He had never been in detention and each term (three times a year) he had gained more house points than any other pupil in his year. He frequently gained more house points per week than any other person in his house, and for this achievement his name was read out in house prayers. After a few words of praise he would be applauded by the whole house. Once a year he was applauded by the whole school as he received the prize he never failed to win. His classwork was impeccable; he was often top of class tests and frequently received praise for excellent homework.

His demeanour in class reflected his success. He was alert, enthusiastic, clean and well dressed. He seemed to radiate well-being and self-confidence. It is difficult with the data available to gauge the relative support from home and school in the case of so outstandingly successful a pupil. It is true to say that he had ample support from both. At school he was popular with the staff and never lacked a large number of friends among the pupils (to some extent they competed for his friendship). At home his parents provided an example of careful, capable management of social pressures. They were immensely proud of his success and never stinted their support. (However, the psycho-socio-cultural resources of the family were never put to test—cf. Buttle.)

(B) Middle-class low achiever; high level of parental encouragement: John Baker, IQ 129

A middle-class family (father: senior lecturer in a technical college) living in a fairly large semi-detached house in a more exclusive part of Hightown suburbia. His father and uncle were both old boys of the school and both had attended university. His sisters and cousins had all been academically successful and had attended universities and colleges of further education. The socio-cultural resources of the family were extremely high, but so were the acceptable standards of performance.

Baker was the boy whose parents had successfully put pressure on the school to make sure he got into the E stream (see chapter 5). In the event he made it by his own efforts. However, once in the E stream the characteristic that had most marred his performance in the first year—his slowness—increased rather than decreased. There was no doubt in my mind that this deterioration was brought on by the fiercer academic competition and his inability to meet it.

His parents complained that he had developed a sort of other-worldliness, taking himself off on his own for hours on end. To the teachers it appeared a dreamy nonchalance, irritating and, at its worst (forgetting homework and books), punishable by detention. To the boys it looked more like a superiority complex. They complained of his snobbish, off-hand behaviour.

This withdrawal, and his own belief in his superiority, are illustrated by his attitude to the school sports in the second year. He did not take part in the heats for the sprint races but on sports day he 'competed' by running alongside the official competitors on the opposite side of the track to the spectators, far enough away to avoid notice and comment. When he got home in the evening he boasted to his father that he could have won easily, had he competed.

During this second year his enthusiasm and interest in school work declined and after a period during which the family underwent some strain through the illness of an elder sister, he began to show signs

128

of 'school phobia'. His parents found it difficult to get him to remember what homework he had been set and almost impossible to get him up to go to school in the morning. He complained of vague maladies and on a number of occasions actually persuaded them he was ill. When it grew worse they took him to the family doctor, who failed to find any diagnosable complaint and referred them to the local authority's child psychiatrist.

The parents visited the school and had several long interviews with the headmaster, the deputy head and several teachers, explaining the symptoms and asking for advice. Various masters as well as myself saw the boy and talked to him. They tried to put him at ease, explained that they were available to help at any time and attempted to encourage him with praise and helpful suggestions. The psychiatrist gave the boy a weekly appointment.

In a very short time, the parents, the school and the local authority services had begun to co-operate fairly successfully on the case. Over the next few years of his school career the parents were able to keep in close contact with the school, partly through official channels but mainly through the links of personal friendship that existed between them and members of the staff. At the time of writing (the beginning of the fifth year), Baker's problems are still only partially solved. However, he has retained his place in the E stream and has remained friendly with Done, a middle-class academically orientated boy, despite a fair amount of hostility from the rest of the group with whom Done associates.[6]

A number of masters still regard Baker as one of the most promising boys in the E stream, despite his low position in the form. 'He's one of the most widely read boys in the form' and 'It's only his difficulty in exams that stops him being top of that form' are two comments I recorded. Baker is well placed to be a 'late developer'.

A diary he kept in the second year illustrates better than any description the continual tension that affects a middle-class boy in Baker's position:

Monday 12th. Getting up later than usual after feeling half dead, I convinced my unbelieving parents I was unfit to go to school

I rode to school feeling a lot better after a good dose of T.N.Tea.[7]

Afternoon school boring as expected.

Going home took me five minutes and the rest of the time I spent at home in a chair feeling cut off from decent enjoyable life. Tea I spent eating in front of the television taking little in but TV acts as a good

129

tranquilliser for the work before me. Homework has to be done but it seems like making articles not wanted any more.

I went to bed about 10.45 feeling thoroughly depressed at the thought of Tuesday, Wednesday, Thursday and Friday. But it is never different with me.

Tuesday 13th. Awoke about 8.00 a.m. Got up about 8.25 because of the barrage of threats I had got since waking. Got to school late: whether I got away with it or not I do not know as I am usually late or at least arriving just in the nick of time.[8] Morning school crawled past at the usual depressing crab-like pace. When dinner did save me from the crush of Latin and the boredom of English and French, I had to race down to the dining room like a scalded cat.

I spent the dinner playing football.

Games is the most depressing and boring and the most dead-lostiest of all. Having to change then run round on a $\frac{1}{2}$ inch carpet of mud getting yourself dirty so that you have to spend more time getting the dirt off. There is no point to it in my mind. Running after an odd-shaped ball getting bruised and kicked, barracked and told that 'he was just behind me', and 'what did you have to do that for'.

I managed to get home to face the grim task of the evening. The idea of having to do even a little bit of homework when you're befuzzled with boredom, hate, tiredness, anger and headaches just about made my day. On top of this I had to do an essay on Nelson for forgetting my book for one reason or another. On top of that I had to catch up with the work I missed.

Wednesday 14th. I awoke at about 8.15 a.m. I had a scant breakfast and cycled to school with minutes to spare. Morning school ended with Physics which is always drab, unlively and boring. Spent dinner playing football as usual. Scripture is spent doing learning for the expected Biology test. Biology test never appeared. Straight after school I went to the clinic. Tired and exhausted after a dash through rush-hour traffic I sit down for tea. Homework was slack tonight. Went to bed after watching a little television.

Thursday 15th. Awoke about 8.10 a.m., spent longer over toast and coffee before packing my bag for school. Cycled to school uphill as I have to, arriving 'fagged out' at school. Chemistry is first period. This period was quite interesting.[9] This is sometimes not so. The break is spent learning for the following French test.

The dinner break I spent playing football.

Afternoon school was tiring and I was glad to get home. The homework dragged on too long. After homework I watched TV until eleven then went to bed.

Friday 16th. Awoke 8.05 a.m. Spent morning not bothering much about the General Election, and I did not hear any news until I was at school. The first two periods were tiring. Biology was terrible as I was accused of a crime I had not committed but still I was given an essay. After dinner

130

break the afternoon dragged on because of the boring Physics. Once home I stayed in doing very little.

I have recorded a week of the diary in full because it illustrates the uniformly depressed state in which he finds himself. Adjectives like 'tiring', 'boring', 'terrible' and 'drab' abound. 'Interesting' is used only once. This is in marked contrast to the majority of diaries.[10]

Baker's position can be summarised diagrammatically as in Fig.13. The situation has developed through stages 1–6. Any additional

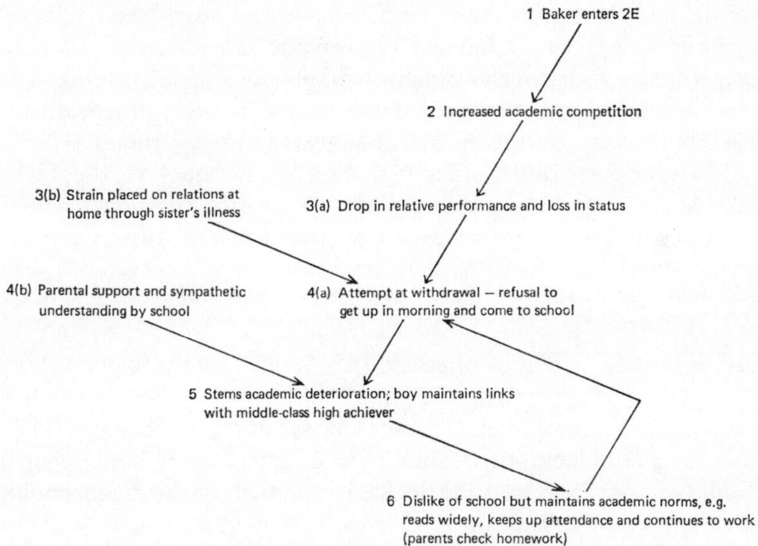

Fig. 13. John Baker's position, represented diagrammatically.

strain through illness, family upsets or problems at school is likely to cause a move back to stage 4(a).[11] Once this happens, however, 4(b) is activated and his behaviour again oscillates between stages 5 and 6. The problem is contained but not solved. Only an improvement in his school performance can solve it.

(C) Working-class high achiever; high level of parental encouragement: Pierre Welenski, IQ 124

Pierre was the third son in a working-class family of four boys (father a bus conductor) who were buying a fairly large terraced house in a working-class district of Hightown. The father was Polish by origin and had passed on to his children a high regard for scholar-

131

ship and academic achievement. Pierre was the second son to attend grammar school. Both exhibited the same serious dedication to their school work. However, their energies were narrowly applied and neither had shown any interest in the broader field of grammar school life. Pierre's only concession to this aspect was to act as secretary to the entomological society during its brief existence in his second year.

His parents were extremely interested in his school work but lacked the socio-cultural resources of the Bakers. They substituted for them a firm, disciplined respect for hard work and achievement. In his second and third years Pierre spent, on average, nearly three hours a night at his homework (50 and 100 per cent more than the average in his forms respectively). Such a combination of intelligence and disciplined, focused effort gained him second place in practically all his school exams during his first four years at the Grammar School.

Pierre's eldest brother did not go to grammar school. He did, however, supplement his secondary modern education with night school achievement and is now successful as a salesman in Australia.

(D) Working-class low achiever; high level of parental encouragement: Jeffrey Buttle, IQ 120

Jeffrey was the eldest of three children; he had two younger sisters, the elder of whom went to Brightside Grammar School. His father was for some time a dock labourer but was now a storekeeper. They lived in a tall block of flats built near Brightside to re-house people from the slum areas near the docks. His mother, an energetic, intelligent and vocal woman, worked 'part time' (9.00 a.m.–4.00 p.m.) as a machinist.

Jeffrey always received encouragement from his parents. His junior school report recorded that he had a good home and his work was 'consistently good'. In the first year at Hightown Grammar he was in the top half of his form (twelfth, fifteenth and seventh respectively). However, neither parent had had any experience of grammar school education. There were few books in the home. His parents had the desire and ambition, without the necessary skills, to assist during difficult periods. After gaining a position in the E stream, his class position deteriorated to twenty-first in the first and second terms.

After an absence at the end of the spring term in 2E with pains in the back and legs (suspected grumbling appendix), his father had to bring him to school. He was upset because he 'feared he can't cope with the work'. On the following day his father brought him again,

132

but he was in floods of tears throughout the first lesson. On Wednesday his father was back at the school and by this time was showing signs of exasperation. 'I don't know . . . If he goes on like this he'll have me in a mental home. I've brought him but he won't stay.' Jeffrey settled down for a short time but in June he was absent again. The school secretary reported that his mother sounded almost hysterical on the phone. 'She was almost shouting at me—"I can't possibly bring him in".'

The trouble that caused this absence apparently flared up in Mr Frank's lesson. It was explained to me by the secretary. 'Buttle complained of hay fever. George got a bit fed up with him not doing any work and said sharply, "Come on, hay fever doesn't make you stop work." He burst into tears and later he left the classroom. Mother and Father came in and saw Mr Lawless. The parents are thinking of psychiatric treatment and if necessary transferring him. They say he has nervous hay fever. They kept saying "He was always brilliant in primary school but he is not doing well here."'

It was clear even at this stage that Buttle's parents and the school were at loggerheads. The family resources were being stretched to the limit by his behaviour. Each time his mother or father brought him to school they lost a morning's work. Then there was the strain of living with the boy in his depressed and sometimes hysterical state. Finally there was the humiliation of having to escort him across Hightown[12] to school and have long, embarrassing conversations with members of staff that did not seem to result in any improvement in his condition.

His parents felt they were doing all they could and that the school was doing little to help *them* in a situation for which it should bear most of the blame. (They kept insisting 'He was always brilliant in primary school.') When the boy arrived home again, thoroughly upset by the incident in Mr Frank's lesson, they were near the end of their tether. The mother's phone call was really a frantic appeal for help, so that when the school secretary asked in a rather routine way 'Can you bring him into school?' she became 'almost hysterical'. It seemed to her that the school was once more refusing to come to her aid.

From the school's point of view, on the other hand, it seemed that they were doing all they could to accommodate her and her son's strange behaviour. Members of staff had given up their time to talk to her and encourage the boy. He had really nothing to worry about if only he would get down to work and behave normally. They could see no explanation for his behaviour. It was not a case of bullying or victimisation. If there were problems, then they must emanate from the home, and having seen the parents and heard of their behaviour it was clear that that was where they did arise.

This conflict situation was in sharp contrast to that involving Baker, where there was an atmosphere of co-operation, and the school matron could—and did—phone his parents quite frequently to find out how he was getting on.

The long summer holidays brought temporary relief to Buttle's problems but in the third year his position deteriorated further until he was twenty-seventh in class.[13] Just before Christmas in the fourth year he was away from school nearly five weeks with appendicitis. While he was away he was constantly worried by the work he was missing but when he got back he found it difficult to catch up and after absenting himself on several occasions refused to return. This time he was adamant and there was nothing his parents could do to persuade him.

The following résumé of an interview illustrates the parents' view of events.

Mother: The start of it was the appendicitis he had. He was off for five weeks and all the time he was worrying about the work he was missing. When the time came for him to go back it was too much for him to catch up.

I went to the headmaster but I got no satisfaction; he just wanted me to get him back to school. He said to me he would kill hisself rather than go back.

He wanted to get out of that E stream. He would have gone back if he could have gone into a different class. But the headmaster just wanted him back.

We didn't know where to turn. We took him to the psychologist and he said we were not to force him to school. Then we tried to arrange some sort of help from the school but nothing came of it.[14] In the end we took him to the social welfare. He used to promise to go back to get out of the room; then as soon as he was back home he said 'I'm not going back to that school'.

Father [*who came into the room at this point*]*:* I took him to school three times but each time he was back here before me.

Mother: The headmaster told me he could do it. He said he had a
134

brilliant mind. But what use is it if it affects your health? If your health goes you've got nothing. I had to live with him, I saw how it was affecting him. I couldn't force him to go to school if it was making him ill. Anyway, he was 14. You can't force a 14 year old boy all that way.

Father: He practically killed hisself getting into the E stream and then when he got there he found it was too much.

Mother: Mind you, he never did like the school much. Well, that is, he liked the first year but after that he didn't like it.

Father: We warned him the E stream would be difficult but he would go for it.

Me [*to Jeffrey, who had just entered*]: Was it mainly the work that worried you?

Jeffrey: Yes.

Me: Did you have plenty of friends?

Jeffrey: Yes.

Me: Do you see French[15] or any of those boys now?

Jeffrey: No.

Mother: He got terribly worked up in his inside—you could see him. It was terrible . . .

In the end the welfare people said if you don't want to go back to school will you go to college. He said 'yes' so they arranged for him to go to Moston [*technical college*]. He likes it there now and is doing very well.

The picture of this episode and of the Buttles' behaviour that I obtained from the school (from the headmaster and Mr Black) was in direct contrast with this. In addition, there was a great deal of confusion about the issues involved. The Buttles had wanted Jeffrey to be transferred from the E stream. The headmaster had not refused; he had mistaken the nature of the request. He had explained that the E stream was to be abolished and the boys would be taking five years over the GCE course, so there was no point in transferring him. The Buttles had wanted a master to visit Jeffrey to give him some tuition at home. However, the local authority refused to pay for this and since the Buttles lived a long way from the school or any of the masters' homes the idea had fallen through.

In the school's view the Buttles made unreasonable demands, were

135

unco-operative and to some extent incomprehensible. The teachers tended to characterise the boy as strange and lazy or lacking in moral fibre. When he left, and the office was no longer bothered by reports from the child psychiatrist, there was 'considerable relief'.

The school cannot be faulted on its treatment of the Buttles. Technically, it did more than was required. One master had given up some of his own time to go and visit them. However, it was apparent soon after the start of the case that there was very little sympathy for Jeffrey. The contrast with Baker's position—where several masters believed Baker had a problem which was understandable and which they should help him solve—was marked. I am arguing that the reason Baker was seen in this light was that his parents could interfere effectively with the normal processes of the school. They were able to legitimate his position by manipulating the ideologies accepted by the masters. Their status in the general social structure also helped to make this manipulation acceptable.

(E) Lower middle-class high achiever; low level of parental encouragement: Donald French, IQ 129

Donald's father was a policeman, a brusque, rather aggressive man. His mother, a mild and retiring person, was often preoccupied with the five children in the family. Although they lived in a middle-class area, his parents had rather slender socio-cultural resources and the family's psychological resources were under pressure from the five children and the long hours their father worked. It was probably for this reason that Donald felt he received hardly any help or encouragement from his parents. In addition, the father had rather ambiguous views about his son's education. He wanted him to continue at school and was proud of his success. On the other hand, he had reservations about a university career—'I don't care for the long-haired breed'—and often 'got at' Donald because he worked long hours in the evening. At the same time it is apparent that Donald had been the subject of a careful, disciplined upbringing. His parents knew his friends, approved of them and were in close touch with the way he spent his leisure time. They kept a much closer check on his behaviour than, for example, Howell's parents did on their son's. French, therefore, enjoyed far less leeway. If he was in trouble at school for fighting, his father promptly went along to sort things out and the matter was quickly settled.

Donald's disciplined application to work was successful. He came seventh in his first-year class and was put in the E stream, where he generally managed to keep in the top third of the class. As the academic pressure increased, he devoted more time and energy to warding off the challenge. He estimated that he usually spent two hours a night on homework. Towards the examinations at the end of the fifth year, his parents estimated that he had often spent three and a half hours a night revising. French was, in fact, in a very similar position to the other successful working-class boys in the E stream, Cready, Turner and Welenski. It is interesting to note that at school he maintained a friendship with these boys over the full course of his school career. When at home, he was more friendly with local middle-class boys. It was in relation to the latter that Donald felt the relative poverty of the social and cultural resources of his home and the lack of interest and support from his parents.

(F) Middle-class low achiever; low level of parental encouragement: Jerome Russell, IQ 122

A lower middle-class family (father a physiotherapist with his own private practice) living in a large terraced house in Clearview. Jerome was the only child, but his mother's mother and his great-aunt were also living with them, as well as his maternal great-grandmother until her death in his second year at school. On his mother's side the family had been upper middle class (his grandfather had been a dentist and his grandmother preserved much of the Victorian gentility—middle-class values—in her way of life). In order to preserve middle-class standards of living his father toiled long hours at two jobs and was frequently working from early in the morning to late at night.

Early in his first year at Grammar School Russell had been an unexceptional pupil and went largely unnoticed (undifferentiated middle). He was quiet and well behaved and very rarely said anything in lessons. On two occasions while I was teaching his class in the first year he submitted extra pieces of work. But although his work was always careful, neat and handed in on time it was not outstanding. Good behaviour and consistent application to work brought their reward, and during the year he improved his class position from fifteenth to tenth and finally to seventh. From 1D he moved into the Express stream, 2E. There was, however, one other element in his behaviour during the first year that was worthy of note. He was prone to burst into tears if reprimanded by a teacher and

137

already had the reputation of a 'cry-baby'. At this stage there was little evidence that he was teased about this, and it was probably a relatively unimportant aspect of his behaviour.

After he had been in 2E just two months, Mrs Russell phoned up the housemaster and complained that Jerome would not come to school because he was afraid of being bullied. When I visited the family his mother said they had only been aware of the difficulty a few weeks and had tried to help him without mentioning it to the school. However, it had become too much for him and he had refused point-blank to go to school. He had struggled, cried and refused to go out of the door.

In a separate conversation with his father I got quite another picture. His father felt sure the problem had started much earlier. Jerome had been under the influence of elderly women for a long time. When he returned from the army the father had attempted to lessen the boy's association with elderly females in the family but the attempt had failed and led to a row with his wife. Although he frequently did not finish work until 10.00 p.m. he had tried to interest the boy in football and rugby, buying him a ball and taking him to matches, but he had an aversion to sports. He said that Jerome had few friends, or even acquaintances, and made little contact with people his own age. The split in the family meant that he received less support from it than would have been normal in a family with these socio-cultural resources. In the fifth year, Russell was one of the two middle-class boys in 2E who recorded only 'some help and support' from his family. All the others recorded 'a great deal of help and support'.

Jerome's own version of his problems was closer to his mother's. He did not feel that either the work or any of the teachers gave rise to his difficulty. Instead he named seven or eight boys who had been teasing, punching and tripping him. They often pretended he was going to get into trouble from a teacher or prefect and generally tried to upset him. The boys he named were all from 2δ (his own house group) and from predictable sections of the differentiated and polarising second year. Malman, Badman and Warrington were from 2C, Watson, Corn, Fink and Westley were a working-class clique from 2A and Marston was from the incipient anti-group clique of 2E.

However, after the housemaster had warned 2δ about bullying in general and persecuting Russell in particular, his complaints about specific boys ceased, though the problems associated with the school

138

increased. The housemaster's intervention was sufficient to prevent any deliberate, organised persecution but it certainly did not increase his standing among the boys. I even saw Murdock[16] torment him myself. The others were aware of their superior ability and developed more subtle ways of demonstrating it. Games periods, for example, became a nightmare for him. He normally played football, but moved about the field so as to minimise his contact with the ball. It was now apparent that some of the boys purposely kicked the ball in his direction, or even at him. This usually reduced him to tears but, as the master refereeing the game pointed out, 'You can't punish a boy for kicking a football to another boy just because his name is Russell.'

In order to relieve this source of pressure I suggested that he be excused games for a short period until he could gain some sort of self-control. The idea was agreed to by his form master and housemaster but the head of the PE department vetoed it: 'Oh no! I'm much too old for that one to work.' He felt that if one boy was excused games, others would follow. Eventually it was agreed he could do cross-country running instead of football.

By this time (mid-November) the school had made a number of concessions to ensure Russell's continued attendance:

1 The housemaster called at the Russells' house on the way to school and for several weeks brought him to school in his car.
2 He was under the personal supervision of the head of the PE department during games periods and was transferred from playing football.
3 He was allowed in school during break so as to limit even further the possibility of persecution in the largely unsupervised playground.
4 A group of masters including the headmaster, housemaster and house tutor were alerted to the nature of his problems, talked to him and helped him on a number of occasions.[17]

These concessions represented an unusual amount of help and support for an individual pupil. It is doubtful whether his parents, unaided, would have been able to obtain this amount of special attention for him.[18] Nevertheless a number of incidents recurred that perpetuated the crisis and made it seem unlikely that an acceptable solution would be found.

The symptoms of Russell's school phobia typically started to build up on Sunday evenings. He began to feel tense, then sick and ill and could not sleep. By Monday morning he usually felt even worse. If he started crying he soon became hysterical, and would sometimes go on crying for the whole morning.

At first, as I have mentioned, Russell's version of his troubles was close to his mother's: he had been bullied and teased by other boys. But as these difficulties were removed it became clear there had been a second, underlying reason and his complaints began to include problems over work. Moreover, the incidents that made him cry and leave lessons began to be more directly the result of the action of a member of staff. Thus, he complained of being frightened of Latin with Mr Pitt because Pitt had threatened a detention for those who got less than five out of ten in a weekly test.[19] Mr Pitt agreed to stop this arrangement because of the effect it had on Russell.

At the end of the Christmas term Russell came thirtieth in a class of 32, and it was very clear that one of the reasons he became upset was that his relatively low standard of work interfered with the sort of relationship he was used to having with the teacher. Because his work was poor he lived under constant threat of detention or verbal reprimands. When he received a reprimand he was unconsolable. On one occasion he was rebuked by the French master, who drove home the point he was making by tapping him on the hand with a ruler. Russell left the room in floods of tears and missed all the rest of morning school.

Periods of strain in which a number of similar incidents occurred began to affect his opinion of the school and staff. He became highly critical, but the critical posture he developed was very different from that of the anti-group. He wrote that Hightown Grammar School was not worthy of the name of grammar school because the pupils were noisy, the staff did not control them properly and failed to recognise true excellence when they saw it. He reckoned his junior school was more like a grammar school. There the staff were more in control, he got 'excellent' for all his work and 'excellent' for his behaviour.[20]

He also developed a whole range of extra-mural interests.[21] Many of them were unusual hobbies, and he became most interested in the most unusual. They included astronomy, chess, philately, collecting dry cell batteries (he called this chlorology), reading (particularly Greek and Roman classics and advanced sciences such as nuclear physics), locks and keys, diary writing, gardening and an almost complete set of filed records and recordings of the 'Doctor Who' television serial.

In January, after a temporary abatement in the sort of incidents described above, another series occurred involving gym lessons, Latin and Biology. By this time a number of the staff were obviously fed up with the situation. His house tutor felt 'We were getting nowhere with Russell' and confessed himself to be of the opinion that there was something peculiar about him: 'Surely he'll never be a normal boy, there'll always be something queer about him.'

Mr Lawless was another of the four or five members of staff who let me know that they felt that Russell needed stricter handling. Lawless pointed it out while discussing another case:

Lawless: The Head is gradually coming round to the view that Murdock will have to go. I put him on report last week and he only got five periods signed up. He brought it to me on Monday instead of Friday. I've put him on report again . . . He just won't stand up for himself like the majority of boys. He's all tears.

Me: Did you do anything about him sitting next to Priestley in most lessons? [Murdock had told me that one of the major difficulties he experienced was sitting next to Priestley, who was constantly criticising him, punching him and making him cry. I had explained this to Lawless earlier in the week.]

Lawless: No, I turned a blind eye to it. He's got to stand on his own two feet. It's like that chap Russell, he'll never learn if people run around doing things for him. Too much is done—it doesn't help in the long run.

In fact the support the school was able to give Russell (including that which I was able to contribute through my research role) proved decisive. He weathered a series of disturbed periods, the last of which occurred in the fourth year, and as we saw in chapter 6, settled down to a successful and enjoyable school career. The following extracts from entries recorded during the last week of his diary illustrate this. They refer to his fifth year in the school.

At school a much better day. And at last all day was enjoyable. Perhaps showing a loss of tension and nervousness, I overslept until past 8 o'clock.
Excellent all day. Allan came round in evening.
Out of this universe! Baker called round and lent me . . .
Probably . . . the last entry in diary. I am seriously considering giving it up entirely. It is a bad thing now. It has outgrown its usefulness as a

companion and thus becomes tradition . . . conditions for us are on the upward surge. There is still a long way to go, but there is no room for any link with the past. This diary is a link with the past. That merits its death.

Russell's recovery had been very gradual. First a gradual gain in self-confidence was linked with an improvement in academic standards. By the end of the second year he had worked his way up to nineteenth in the form. After a relapse in the third year to twenty-ninth he again improved, this time to eleventh in the form.

In the third year he began to make friendly contacts with other boys, mainly outside the school. By the fourth year he was sufficiently sure of himself to adopt many of the characteristics of the adolescent culture which paved the way for his almost full integration in the fifth year.

(G) Working-class high achiever; low level of parental encouragement: Richard King, IQ 126

The family lived in a small terraced house in Old Hightown. Richard's father was a wood-cutting machinist and his mother left home when he was six years old, leaving his father to look after him and his sister (two years younger). His father, an intelligent, strong-minded, obstinate man, had been to elementary school. He supported his son and encouraged him in his education at junior school: 'I was deprived of a grammar school education myself because my dad told me to go to the wrong place for the examinations.'

But as the boy progressed through grammar school they quarrelled frequently and the father withdrew his support. As he withdrew, so the school stepped in. When he refused to pay the boy's fares to away matches the school paid them from the school fund. When the boy's clothes became scruffy and were not replaced, the school supplied new or second-hand ones. By the fifth year the boy spent hardly any time in his father's house. He was out after breakfast and returned only for an evening meal and to sleep. He spent no evenings at home. When his father eventually 'threw him out' the school was able to facilitate his being put into care and lodging with a neighbour. During practically the whole of his sixth form career he lived independently at a Toc H hostel on funds provided by the local authority.

King was successful at his work and in some subjects (e.g. English) outstanding. It was success and recognition of his exceptional talent, broadening into a structure of expectation and support in several fields, that carried him through his school career despite his father's mounting opposition. The following extract from his 'auto-

142

biography'[22] illustrates some of the difficulties and adjustments he had to make at the Grammar School:

> On the first day there I had only a rucksack whilst everyone else had smart shining leather satchels. A small boy pointed me out and everyone laughed. I felt like kicking his teeth down his throat but restrained myself because I couldn't forget what Burkey[23] had told me.
>
> When it became known that I had passed, all day my friends' parents' attitudes towards me changed to repulsion. I was treated as a 'puff' and was a 'brainy soft-arsed mardy'. That attitude got me into many fights with anti-grammarians.
>
> At home I fight, swear, give cheek, and talk rougher slang than I do at school. I do not exercise my knowledge when arguing but even so my friends still ask me to settle arguments and prove facts. All my mates think that I am a 'hard man' and all think it is hard luck for me to go to Grammar School because of the side of my attitude that they see. But at school I am compelled to wear baggy trousers and green blazer. I quieten down and have been embarrassed very easily since I have been here. The way I sometimes am called 'scruffy' would at home make me kick that person in his teeth but at school I let it pass. The people who laugh at me at school I would like them to laugh at me at home.
>
> In my first two years I have had a few fights and because I have won I am labelled a bully. Also through fooling about with a younger boy and making him cry I have been caned severely and am a 'bully whose bad behaviour will cease, as will detentions'. Now I do not feel the urge so much to knock someone down. The school is alright apart from homework. Outside temptations are distracting. Because of this homework I sometimes feel like giving it all up. I want to live on an island and be self sufficient. I think I have the knowledge to be so. In one of my depressed moods I went to my Uncle Fred and he talked me out of it. I still get depressed attitudes and don't do my homework. (Why should that human body order me what to do with my living time?) They are not as violent now as one extra violent one that I had last term. 'All his anti-social activities must cease!'

A number of problems are graphically illustrated here. In the first place, the clash between the school culture and the peer and neighbourhood cultures to which he was deeply committed led to ambivalence in his attitude to the school. It is this ambivalence that predisposes working-class boys towards the anti-group culture within the school. A period of bad behaviour and failure to do homework can in some cases damage their reputation or position with respect to work to such an extent that an accumulation of problems may result in the situation getting out of hand. (Bad behaviour → punishment and damaged reputation → low motivation → poor work and no homework → more punishment → eventually inability to do the work.)

King mentions two occasions when he was in fact on the threshold of such deterioration: once in the second year through bullying, when he was caned by the headmaster, and again in the third year, when bad behaviour again brought him to the headmaster's notice. ('All his anti-social behaviour must cease' was a quotation from the headmaster's remark on his report.) The second occasion was potentially far more serious as a threat to his school career but was checked by the interest and foresight of the English master, Mr Wilkins.

Whilst outlining to a staff meeting the criteria for judging to whom the 'progress prizes'[24] should be awarded, the headmaster cited King as the sort of boy who should never be chosen. He stressed that he did not want the prizes going to smart Alecs or slick layabouts who were clever but always near the bottom of the class at Christmas and Easter —the ones who were lazy and worked only for the summer exams because they were the most important of the year, and because they wanted the progress prize. He felt he could rely on the professional judgment of the staff to eliminate such types, mentioning King as a well-known example who was also a bully and a thoroughly bad character.

Mr Wilkins, however, was convinced otherwise[25] and for some months had been campaigning on King's behalf among the other masters who taught him. After the Head's pronouncement he arranged for some members of staff, myself included, to see the Head individually and ask him to reconsider his verdict on King. The intervention proved so successful that at the next staff meeting the headmaster made a long statement, apologising for misjudging the boy and putting the record straight with respect to his standard of work and character. The result of this timely intervention and the continuation of Wilkins's campaign was that King became known as a talented boy overcoming considerable handicaps in his home background. This reputation, with the help and encouragement he continued to receive from influential members of staff, ensured his later success at the O and A level examinations. Had Wilkins not mounted the campaign on his behalf, he would almost certainly have left school at 16 after a modest performance at O level.[26]

(H) Working-class low achiever; low level of parental encouragement: Peter Howells, IQ 124

Peter's parents were working-class (father a turbine blade miller) and were living in a large, rather scruffy terraced house in a dingy urban area. He had two sisters, both younger than himself. At junior school Peter had been an excellent pupil, nearly always top of the class. During his first year at Hightown Grammar he maintained this standard and at the end of it came third in his form. His report was excellent and he went automatically into the E stream. His parents were proud of his achievement and anxious for him to do well. However, the family's psycho-socio-cultural resources were low, and after the first year they found they could no longer supervise his work —it was 'a bit above us'.

In the second year the academic competition increased and Peter found it difficult to keep up. His parents explained his subsequent failure in the following way: 'He caught scarlet fever and was away from school for six weeks. When he returned he was a long way behind the others and he never really caught up.' His parents reported that around this time he sometimes spent four hours a night on his homework, but to little effect. He came twenty-seventh at the end of the year.

His school record shows a different sequence of events (see chapter 6). After five weeks in 2E he started to be frequently absent or late[27] in a haphazard way; his longest period of continuous illness was two weeks. His behaviour deteriorated, he truanted, broke off friendships with a number of high achievers and by the third year was a member of the working class anti-group in 3E. In the fourth year he reported that he wanted to leave school at 16 and spent only 25 minutes a night on homework. He passed the lunch hours smoking in the park with two low achievers from the form to which he had been demoted.

The difference between the parents' version of the cause of his decline—illness followed by unavailing hard work, followed by a 'soured personality'—and the sequence recorded in my field notes and in school records, is explained by what I call the 'leeway' experienced by boys whose parents are unable to interpret what is happening within the school (i.e. have low cultural resources). A boy in this position soon realises that his parents are extremely dependent on *him* for information and interpretation of what is going on at the school. He can withhold or even fabricate information and soon builds a slanted picture of his position. An interview with Peter's parents made it clear they were unaware of his truancy during the second and third years (as was the school). The truancy was reported to the headmaster by his mother only in the fourth year, and even after this his father was still unaware of it. In an extreme case this

145

'leeway' can result in the parents taking the boy's side, characterising the school's attitude as persecution and writing absence notes to cover up the default.

(I) Working-class low achiever; low level of parental encouragement: Paul Docker, IQ 110

Docker's case has been included because it demonstrates how limited psycho-socio-cultural resources can be rapidly exhausted and lead to the termination of a child's grammar school career. Paul arrived at Hightown Grammar in September and left in October. He was transferred to a secondary modern. He was still ten years old on his arrival and he left less than two weeks after his eleventh birthday. His grammar school career can be summarised as follows:

Week	1	2	3	4	5	6	7	8	*Total*
Attendances	4	8	8	0	4	6	5	0	35
Possible attendances	4	10	10	10	10	10	10	10	74

The Docker family lived in a new flat in a rebuilt slum-clearance area. The father worked in a tool room as a cutter grinder. Paul had four brothers and sisters. The eldest sibling, a boy, was in the fourth year at Hightown Grammar School when Paul arrived there. His elder sister was at Brightside High School and his younger sister was top of her class at junior school. A baby was born only a few weeks before Paul started at the Grammar School.

At the beginning of October I heard that Paul Docker was probably going to leave. The headmaster told me that 'it appeared to be a straightforward case'. The mother had five children who were proving too much for her; the boy was apparently not coping with the work and wanted to leave, and she was going to withdraw him. I expressed surprise at the diagnosis. The five weeks Paul had been at the school were not enough for him to appreciate what grammar school life was going to be like.

I spoke to his eldest brother, Brian, in the fourth form. He pointed out that Paul had been absent on a number of occasions early in the term and had a lot of homework to catch up. He was finding it impossible to cope with the backlog as well as the fresh work being set, and this was worrying him. According to Brian, Paul thought it was going to be very hard and wanted to leave. His mother was under considerable strain with the five of them. She herself had passed the scholarship when she was young but had been unable to go to grammar school because her family had been too poor. However,

146

she had encouraged the children and they had all done very well at school. Brian admitted that he himself had been a problem at the Grammar School, and had taken a long time to settle down. He had found the homework difficult, and this had upset him, leading to sleeplessness, a great deal of absence and even truancy. He had eventually settled down in the fourth year and was doing well—he was extremely good at maths. His sister had been no trouble but was not doing particularly well at Brightside High School.

Paul's version was slightly different. When I asked him why he was leaving, he replied, 'Mum is very worried. She dropped the baby the other day and said "I've never done that before, in all the years I've had children I've never done that." She thinks it's too much. She says she's not going through it all again with me.' He said he was happy at the school now, although it had frightened him at first. But he could not do the homework. He felt that if he could be helped with that he would like to stay.

I took both brothers to their home in my car and suggested I called to see their mother. However, the elder boy dissuaded me. 'She wouldn't like that, it would upset her. She would like to be prepared before you come, as she finds it difficult with the baby.' He suggested she should visit the school, and I agreed. I saw the elder boy several times during the next few days and he gave me to understand that things were much better. The headmaster arranged for Paul to see him each day at four o'clock to discuss the homework he had been set and how to tackle it. But at the end of October I heard that Paul was to be officially transferred to Brightside Modern. Mrs Docker had apparently written to the education office:

. . . Paul is unable to settle down, crying at night and always complaining of not feeling well. I have been to see his headmaster and also the Welfare Officer and though they have been very considerate, trying to sort out his problems, I'm afraid it is too much for Paul, although he has tried his best, all this trouble is beginning to get on top of me and I'm afraid that if he can't be moved either him or I will have a nervous breakdown.

Her letter had been sent to the school accompanied by a note from the Chief Education Officer requesting information on the pupil.

The head replied that he had consulted members of staff but they had little acquaintance with the boy. There was no evidence of unsuitability. Written work was adequate. English and maths were satisfactory. However, he had missed so much school time that unless there was some hope of improvement in his attendance he would not

147

be able to make up for lost time. He had found Paul a likeable boy and would be sorry to see his grammar school career abandoned so easily. Yet he knew he was a very marginal entrant and that his family circumstances were difficult. Regrettably, the latter, rather than his innate ability, would probably be the deciding factor.

The headmaster thought that the qualified plea for a longer period of investigation would be sufficient to get a decision on the matter postponed. He was therefore surprised and a little annoyed by the Education Officer's subsequent letter. The Chief Education Officer replied that he had gone into the circumstances carefully and had studied the reports from the boy's primary school head teacher and the school welfare section. Taking all these into consideration, he felt that the boy was a border-line entrant to Hightown Grammar School and a transfer to Brightside Secondary Modern might well prove educationally justified as well as socially reasonable. In view of this, arrangements were being made for Paul's admission to Brightside Secondary Modern at his parents' request.

In this case Paul Docker was transferred almost before the school was aware of his existence or the problems he was facing. However, the Head was probably correct in his pessimistic assessment that family circumstances would be the deciding factor. For Paul, the problem had been the unplanned arrival of the fifth child a few months before he was due to start his grammar school career. His mother, on the testimony of the children and the staff who had met her in connection with her eldest son, had been the sustaining force, but she could no longer cope. The boy had seen his mother in tears on several occasions and heard her proclaim that she could not go through with it all again (meaning his grammar school education), or the strains she felt it would impose on her. He was in fact predisposed to find the school uncongenial (there was no evidence from the school that he was a problem). His position can be contrasted with Baker's.

Analyses and conclusion

It is implicit in the arguments presented in this book that in order to achieve a stable performance, a pupil requires a flow of short-term gratifications[28] (received through his activities within the school) which are in line with the expectations built up during his past performances.[29] The same idea lies behind much of the material in this chapter, and is documented in some detail in the cases of Baker,

Buttle, Russell, Howells and Docker. These cases are used to take the analysis further, the outcome of the divergence between expectations and actual experience being related to family resources.

The school is regarded as a competitive arena in which the flow of rewards is limited. The competing units are presented as family units, competing on the basis of nominal equality but in fact differing markedly in the resources relevant to the process of education. The effects of these differences in resources are seen most clearly when the 'failure' cases of Russell and Baker are compared with Howells, Docker and Buttle. All these cases put a severe strain on the family resources and where they were not strong enough to sustain it (Howells, Docker and Buttle) an adjustment, leading to a lower-grade educational career, had to be made.

Docker's case is unusually abrupt and spectacular because the family's slender resources were threatened from two directions at once. His entry to grammar school was not an immediate success, and the problem (i.e. his subsequent distress and need for encouragement and practical help) was thrown back onto the parents. At the same time the family resources were being stretched to the limit by the unplanned arrival of a baby. Their financial means were not great. The expense of the new baby and new, high-cost rented accommodation had been added to that of providing for four children and two adults. The financial problem could only be alleviated by the father's working overtime and thus adding to the pressures on the mother and further eroding the psychological resources,[30] endangering the family's stability.

The cultural resources were low, but in any case could not be brought to bear on the problem of Paul's work because of the overwhelming pressure from other directions. Had they been greater— had the family had more understanding of the help available from the school and welfare services—they could have been used to alleviate most of the pressure from Paul's initial failure. As it was, these resources consisted largely of the mother's willingness to help and encourage her children. She lacked the self-confidence and understanding necessary to visit the school or call on outside help: although orientated towards educational achievement, she was not part of an educated sub-culture.

The cases of Buttle and Howells are in many ways more typical of failure cases. Their family units had resources comparable to Docker's, but were not threatened with the same internal crisis. These boys failed to maintain their position in the school despite the advantage of a high IQ and initial success. Their problems stemmed from the more intense competition of the E stream and the demoralisation which followed from inability to secure the expected flow of short-term gratifications to which they had become accustomed. They differ from each other in that Buttle's parents maintained a close and effective supervision of his work and progress, while Howells' removed themselves from the area of conflict. Howells' parents felt unable to apply pressure in case it did more harm than good. This leeway enabled him to mislead them, and led to an anti-group accommodation for his failure.

Buttle, on the other hand, had no such leeway. His parents could offer no tangible assistance (i.e. with his homework or in obtaining help from the school; in common with Howells's parents, they lacked the cultural resources), but they maintained a generalised pressure through insisting that he had a 'brilliant mind' and through close supervision. An anti-group solution was not possible unless he was prepared to risk losing the support and affection of his parents. In this situation Buttle was faced with no alternative to complete collapse (see Fig. 14).

The leeway Howells exploited, and his ability to adopt an anti-group solution to his failure problem, was characteristic of many

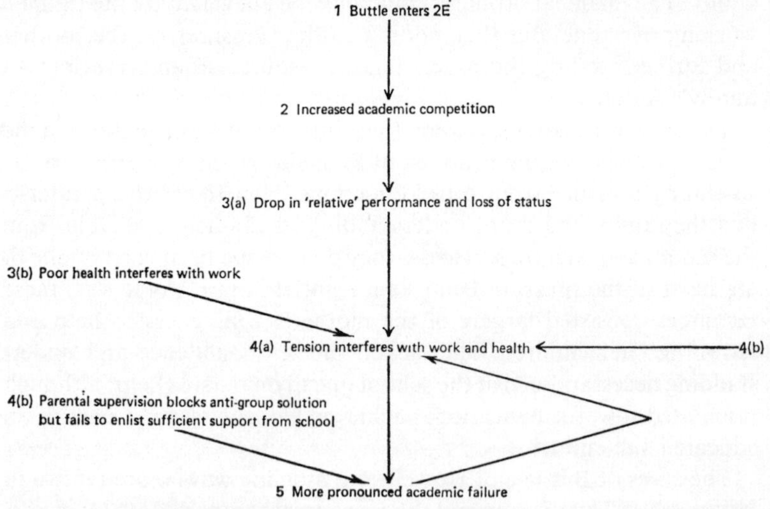

Fig. 14. Paul Buttle's position, represented diagrammatically. Buttle oscillated between stages 4 and 5 until he could no longer endure the tensions involved.

150

working-class boys. After a year or so at the Grammar School many working-class parents were already largely dependent on their son's interpretation of his position at school.[31] This development effectively undermined the parents' role as *coach* in the competing unit. As long as the flow of short-term gratifications from a relatively successful school performance continues, this change in the family unit may pass unnoticed. When the flow is impeded through failure, the boy's change in attitude to school work can go undetected by his parents. In extreme cases an anti-group solution can be adopted without the parents realising the extent and direction of the boy's changed position in the school.

Most parents of 'anti-group' pupils will admit to realising that something was going wrong. Few are as straightforwardly honest as one Mrs Peabody:

I blame myself. I used to ask if he had done his homework and he used to say, 'Yes, I did it at school,' or 'We didn't have much tonight.' I sometimes felt that he wasn't telling me the truth but I used to believe him. I wouldn't have known how to check his homework even if I had looked at his books, but I thought that he would have done it for my sake. Not for my sake really but because he knew I wanted him to get on—for his sake, really.

Mrs Peabody did not find out to what extent her son had been misleading her until she heard from the education office that he had been truanting. He denied it to his mother until the last possible moment —until they were both confronted with proof by an official committee. He had created two separate worlds. A change had been forced on him in one situation and he had used the leeway inherent in his position to seal it off from the other. At school he was regarded as a waster, totally unreliable and without much talent, while at home his mother still regarded him as a respectful, perhaps lazy, but intelligent and promising boy.

For most parents in this position it is impossible to take the school's point of view. They have known their children since birth and for eight years have received nothing but praise from the school. Then, in the space of a few years, sometimes a few months, they get reports that contradict everything that has gone before. When the socio-cultural resources of the family are inadequate to absorb and counter this development, the blame is frequently put on the school. The parents' positive orientation to education may remain, but they become hostile to the school: 'The grammar school has soured him.' 'There were some masters who had it in for him.'

The role of the parent can change in such circumstances from encouraging the boy to co-operate with the school to protecting him from it. While maintaining their commitment to education in general, they may encourage their own child to leave.[32]

We have now broadened our perspective to include the influence of the home. The school is seen as a competitive arena in which teams consisting of the pupil and his parents compete for scarce rewards such as examination success. This view underlines the source of inequality in the educational system. It is important to realise that as society becomes increasingly stratified by educational achievement this source of inequality will become more and more important. Sir John Newson (among others) has suggested that 'as the working class comes to realise the opportunities that education has to offer it will increasingly make use of them'.

There is nothing in the 'failure' cases discussed in this chapter to suggest that inability to realise the importance of education was the cause of 'defeat'. I use the term *defeat* advisedly, because in a very real sense the families described here played for high stakes and lost. They were defeated by the system and by the achievement of their competitors. This analysis ties in closely with the conclusions drawn from the historical data in chapter 2. The 'professionalising' period was associated with rising educational standards and an increase in class differentiation. In this chapter we have seen in detail the process by which this comes about, and it is clear that pious hopes about a relative improvement in working-class achievement are dangerous as well as wrong.

NOTES

[1] N. Raynes, *The analysis of organisations as social systems*, unpublished M.A. thesis, Manchester, 1963.

[2] Parents are considered as the representatives of the kin group who have most to do with influencing the child. If in some cases other members of this group have considerable influence, they will be included in the discussion.

[3] Much of the data presented in this chapter was collected during a survey, which was financed by a grant from the Social Science Research Council.

[4] The response was skewed, with very few answering 'very little interest and help'.

[5] Despite this precaution, it is important to note that the variable 'parental interest' is only a subjective estimation. It is probably unlikely that a low level of parental interest in the case of, say, French means the same thing objectively as for,

say, Howells. This limitation of the paradigm has been borne in mind whilst writing the case studies.

[6] Baker was in all probability one of the reasons for Done's break with Martin in 4E.

[7] He arrived at school very late, missing some of morning school. His mother phoned and explained.

[8] He had in fact very few 'lates' recorded.

[9] This is the first mention of something interesting. Later on he again records chemistry as interesting, and 'I am very good at this'. He recorded one of his highest marks in chemistry at the end of the year.

[10] Over eighty diaries were collected.

[11] This in fact happened two or three times during his school career.

[12] The Buttles did not possess a car. The bus journey involved changing buses.

[13] I have no notes of disturbed behaviour during this period, but this may be due to my research role, changing from participator to visitor.

[14] Buttle's parents wanted a master from the school to call at their home and tutor Jeffrey in the major subjects. This sort of arrangement had occasionally been made in the past. In Buttle's case there were two obstacles that could not be overcome: he lived a long way from the school, and his parents could not pay for private tuition.

[15] He was also very friendly with Buttle. But they have not seen each other since Buttle left the school. It is important to note that it was the close supervision by the parents that prevented Buttle from adopting the anti-group solution to his 'failure' problem.

[16] Murdock himself was frequently teased and upset by other boys.

[17] In addition he was given an open invitation to visit my home to discuss his problem whenever he felt the need. He became one of several boys who visited me fairly regularly during the period of the research (four years). He also wrote a daily diary through which he communicated his feelings and opinions in a way he found difficult in conversation.

[18] Some of this special treatment was undoubtedly due to my interest in the case. I was directly responsible for arranging some of the concessions, others were suggested by me, and in addition the fact that it was known that I was interested supported the effects of others. The situation contrasts with the case of Buttle, where I did not intervene except to collect information.

[19] It is interesting to note that when I checked this with Mr Pitt he denied it rather indignantly. Then, when I pressed the point, he admitted that for the last few weeks he had put those with less than 5/10 in detention. However, Russell, who was poor at Latin, had not yet been put in detention.

[20] Even in his fourth year at the Grammar School he revisited his junior school.

[21] Cf. Priestley in chapter 4. In his second and third years Priestley developed an interest in stocks and shares, and stresssed the real importance of this knowledge for his career after school. Russell several times pointed out almost contemptuously that the so-called 'top' boys at the Grammar School knew nothing about important matters in science and literature, whereas he knew more about some subjects than even the masters.

[22] In 1963 all the fourth-year pupils wrote autobiographies as a project in connection with the research.

[23] Burkey—Mr Burke, his ex-junior school master—had warned him that he would be expelled if he behaved badly at the Grammar School.

[24] Progress prizes were given to boys who made most progress during the year. They were often given fairly mechanically to the boy who had pulled up most class positions between the Christmas and summer exams.

[25] He felt that King had exceptional talent and was potentially first-class university material.

[26] In a similar case which occurred soon after Mr Wilkins joined the school, the campaign failed because the boy, who had truanted ('taken the afternoon off'), met the headmaster in a local park when he should have been at school. In the resulting argument both took up uncompromising positions and the boy never returned. Wilkins felt that had he explained the boy's position to the Head before the incident the outcome would have been different.

[27] The school secretary told me that when he was late he sometimes came in half-way through the morning.

[28] They include for example, verbal praise, complimentary remarks on written work, high marks and selection for minor responsibilities.

[29] This has been shown to be of importance to the performance of pupils entering the school. In some cases, the 'best pupil' role expectations developed in junior school are not fulfilled by a flow of short-term gratifications in the grammar school. This is linked in chapter 4 with emotional disturbance and also with the anti-group sub-culture formation.

[30] It is important to note that the problem was not a direct result of financial straits.

[31] This was very apparent at the first year's parents' meeting. Many were worried about their ability to supervise their boy's homework.

[32] The correlation between success and encouragement is also documented in the Plowden report C.A.C.E. *Children and their primary schools*, pages 33–34: 'The most striking feature of both these sets of comparisons is the large part played by parental attitudes and the fact that it tends to be greater among the older than the younger children. . . By that time (top of the junior school) the *child's very success or failure in school work may increase or weaken parental aspiration*.' See the table below, also from the Plowden report:

	Infants	Lower junior	Top junior	All pupils
		Between schools		
Parents' attitudes	24	20	*39*	28
Home circumstances	16	25	17	20
State of school	20	22	12	17
Unexplained	40	33	32	35
	100	100	100	100

Courtesy H.M.S.O.

The percentage contribution of parental attitudes rises to 39 in the top junior classes. This is almost twice the figure for parental attitudes in the early junior classes. This is also true for the within-school variation.

8 The staff and staff–pupil relationships

This chapter completes the description of the major sub-systems within the school. The aim is to lay bare the most important elements of the school's internal organisation and to show how they affect the teachers in their relationships with each other and with their pupils. The first half discusses the major factors affecting the staff and their relations with each other, and sets the scene for an analysis, in the second half, of the factors that impinge more directly on their relationship with the pupils. I conclude with an examination of staff–pupil relations, which is related to the processes of differentiation and polarisation.

The Staff

In April 1963 the staff of Hightown Grammar School comprised 39 teachers. This included the headmaster, who taught only six periods, and the senior master, who taught half the usual teaching load of 30 out of the 35 periods in a week. The academic background of the staff was as follows:

Graduates of the nearest provincial university	15
Colleges of education, colleges of art and design, etc.	11
Graduates of Cambridge	6
Graduates of other universities	7
Total	39

The staffing position in the school reflected the strengths and weaknesses of the position in the country as a whole. The science staff were poorer qualified in terms of (1) the number of degrees, (2) the quality of the degrees and (3) post-graduate training (see table 58). On the other hand, the science staff had a higher proportion of responsibility allowances, although the actual monetary value of their posts tended to be lower than on the arts side.

TABLE 58

COMPARISON OF THE ACADEMIC QUALIFICATIONS OF THE
MODERN AND SCIENCE STAFF OF HIGHTOWN GRAMMAR SCHOOL, 1963

	Staff			
	Modern (arts)		Science	
	Number	*Percent*	*Number*	*Percent*
Good honours degree	13	65	3	25
Other degrees	6	30	6	50
Without degrees	1	5	3	25
Totals	*20*	*100*	*12*	*100*
Post-graduate certificate in education	16	80	6	50
Responsibility posts	13	65	9	75

Note: only 32 of the staff were classifiable as 'arts' or 'science'.

The disparity between the qualifications of the staff on the modern and science sides was consistent with the examination successes achieved by the various departments.[1] In the GCE examinations of 1963, the total number of passes achieved by the three fifth forms in each subject taken by all three forms was:

Modern (arts)		Science	
History	50	Mathematics	25
English	38	Physics	11
Geography	47	Chemistry (two forms)	12 (18)
French	32	Biology (two forms)	3 (5)
Total	*167*	*Total*	*51 (59)**

* The numbers in brackets are increased because only two of the three forms took chemistry and biology.

The discrepancy between the modern and science results was frequently discussed. Staff on the modern side often used the adjective 'disgusting' to describe the science results. One history master remarked, 'Let's face it, most of the staff on the science side could not hold down a job on our side.'

The distinction between the graduate and non-graduate teachers requires some elucidation. Non-graduates were typically recruited to teach the non-academic subjects such as art, handicrafts, music, physical education, etc. There were, however, three non-graduates teaching on the science side and one on the modern side. Although the average age of the non-graduate teachers was about the same as that of the graduates—35·9 years compared with 36·25 years—they received, on average, a salary of £1,072 a year, while the average for

156

graduates was £1,380 a year. The difference of £308 was made up of £179 earned through being graduates and £129 earned through higher responsibility allowances.

The recruitment and subsequent mobility of the staff can be described as locally bounded. The number of graduates from the local university only partially indicates the degree to which the staff were connected locally. In 1963 the vast majority (71 per cent) had some local connections before coming to the Grammar School. Thirteen went to a local grammar school (i.e. within ten miles' radius)—four were 'old boys' of Hightown Grammar; nine went to a local grammar school and to the local university, while six came from outside the area but went to the local university (total: 28). Of the eleven others, only three could really be called newcomers to the area, that is, had moved in during the last five years. On the other hand, the staff was not Hightown-centred. Only six out of 39 actually lived in Hightown, and all six lived in the middle-class fringes of the city. The staff's places of residence formed an arc within the middle-class suburbs of the conurbation and its satellite towns. Their local connection was, therefore, primarily with a particular section of the conurbation.

By the summer of 1967, nineteen of the original 39 had left.[2] Three had retired, ten moved to new appointments within the same general area (within ten miles of the school), and five had moved well outside the district.[3] Nearly all the moves entailed a promotion or change of job with a rise in salary. For most of the leavers, the promotion prospects within the school had been slight, and if they wanted promotion they had to leave.

Some left regretfully and one or two welcomed their departure as a release; for most, however, it was fairly predictable in terms of their experience, qualifications and the opportunities presented. Of the sixteen moves, three moved to take up responsibility allowances, two to take up deputy headships of departments, five to take up headships of departments, three to technical colleges and colleges of education, one into educational administration, and one to a university. Investigation of the careers of all the teachers who worked at Hightown Grammar School since the war shows these moves to be typical of the more general pattern of spiralism within a locality. Very few grammar school teachers, it seems, move out of the State system into public schools (or vice versa). Rather more move out into technical colleges and colleges of education. Some move into secondary moderns, but usually only for a headship or deputy headship. The majority spiral within the local community and stay in grammar schools.

Early work in the sociological study of schools has emphasised the power of the community in the control of school staffs. This is particularly true of the early American classics by Waller and Hollingshead. In *Elmtown's youth* Hollingshead describes some of the controls a local American community exerted over its teachers:

Teachers were not expected to hold parties or dinners and thereby attempt to further their interests by inviting townspeople to them. If they did, the local people criticised them for putting on airs. The Superintendent warned his teachers, on orders from the Board, not to smoke in public, or to be seen in a tavern or at a public dance.[4]

And again:

The ministers of these churches systematically question young people about statements teachers made in class relative to the Bible and religion. If the teacher is reported for 'radical' or 'irreligious' statements, this teacher is watched, and, if two or three unfavourable reports are brought in, the matter is taken up with the Board of Education.[5]

In Hightown there was no comparable degree of community control. Teachers were free to behave as they wished, as free as any other professional person living and working there. Equally, they were free to teach their subjects according to the dictates of conscience. If parents had complaints about the school, they were expected to direct them to the headmaster, and this they normally did. The only notable exceptions were the parents of Jewish boys who sometimes telephoned their complaint to a Jewish member of the education committee, who in turn relayed it to the Director of Education. The complaint would then be passed down to the school from the education office with far more authority than a single parent could have mustered. But even in these circumstances there was seldom, if ever, any need for the headmaster or the staff to kow-tow or conform in the way Hollingshead describes. In fact, it was on occasions of this sort that the real freedom of action of the grammar school head master and his staff was demonstrated.[6]

The organisation of the school
The formal organisational structure of Hightown Grammar School was designed to control two spheres; the academic, or primary, sphere and the social, or secondary, sphere. The same staff were
158

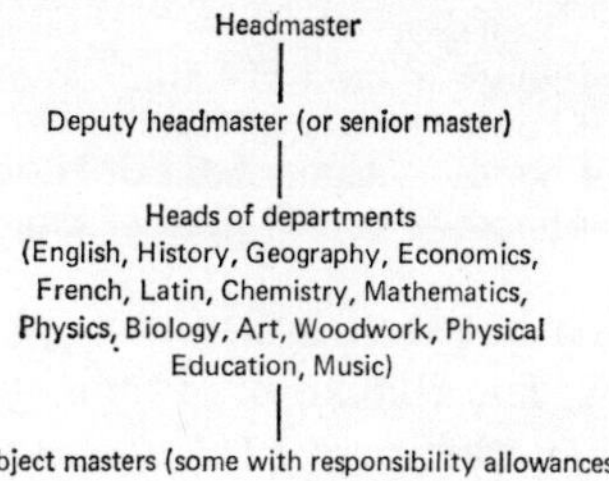

Fig. 15. Academic organisation of Hightown Grammar School.

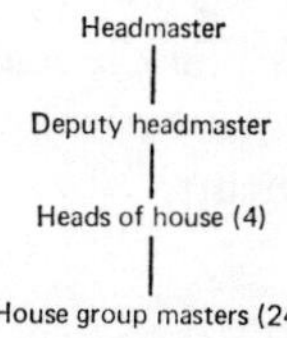

Fig. 16. Social, or house, organisation of Hightown Grammar School.

involved in both spheres and, with a few exceptions, all appear in different capacities in the charts in Figs. 15 and 16. The headmaster and deputy headmaster retained an overall responsibility in both systems, but heads of departments frequently acted as ordinary house group masters within the house system.

Housemasters were usually chosen from among the deputy heads of the large departments, or the heads of the small departments, for example Woodwork, Metalwork and Latin. It was thus theoretically possible for a head of a department to serve as a house tutor under his own deputy, but in practice this did not occur.[7]

The allocation of cash allowances to the positions of responsibility in the two systems illustrates the degree to which the academic system predominated:

Cash allowances per annum	Heads of academic departments	Deputy heads	Other responsibility allowances
£450	English, Maths		
£355	History, Geography French, Chemistry		
£260	Biology, Physics		
£165	Art, Music, Handicrafts	English, History, French, Maths	
£100	Physical Education, Economics	Geography	Third English, Chemistry, Physics, Biology, Physical Education

Heads of houses

  £260: (1) Head of house + head of Latin
      (2) Head of house + head of Handicrafts
  £230: (3) Head of house + deputy head of History
      (4) Head of house + deputy head of English

The figures show that heads of house were paid very little for their work in this capacity. The allocation of their extra allowances breaks down as follows. They were paid £165 a year for their departmental responsibilities and only £65 or £95 a year for their responsibilities as heads of house.[8] The top job in the house system was, therefore, worth less than the bottom job in the academic system. Yet the heads of houses were involved in a great deal more work and responsibility than most heads of departments.

The subject department system

Figs. 15 and 16 give the impression that Hightown Grammar had a predominantly bureaucratic form of organisation. The school had a number of bureaucratic features—for example, sets of formal rules, a hierarchy of officers, division of labour (departments) and a career structure based on ability and seniority—but to conceive of it entirely in these terms is misleading. The main task of the school, teaching, was performed equally by heads of departments, heads of houses and assistant masters. For some purposes the staff are best looked upon as a professional group, differentiated on the basis of seniority, whose activities were controlled by professional and traditional norms. Within the classroom and in his relation with the pupils, the teacher at Hightown Grammar had a broad area of professional autonomy which is not usually a feature of bureaucracies. This factor must be borne in mind while interpreting the remainder of this section.

Heads of departments had a formal responsibility to the headmaster for the teaching of their subjects. In practice this was a relatively minor consideration, since the staff were all adequately qualified in the subjects they taught and shouldered most of the responsibility themselves. In general, it boiled down to a number of 'chores'.[9] For example, the head of department was responsible for organising the syllabus, ordering textbooks and equipment, and for stocktaking. Some of these 'chores' had their compensations; the head of department also distributed the work load within his department and thus had the power to allocate coveted teaching, such as the top

160

stream taking the GCE and the sixth form. Traditionally, heads of departments kept a large proportion of the sixth form teaching to themselves, except where the second-in-command was well established in the school or exceptionally well qualified.

TABLE 59

ANALYSIS OF TIMETABLE FOR THE EIGHT ACADEMIC DEPARTMENTS WITH THREE OR MORE MEMBERS OF STAFF, 1962–63

	Heads of department (8)	*Deputy heads (8)*	*Others in department (12)*
Non-teaching period	6·4	5·4	5·4
Sixth forms	17·3	8·3	2·6
Express streams	4·1	3·3	1·6
Fifth forms (not C streams)	2·3	5·0	3·1
Middle school third and fourth (not E or C)	3·0	5·0	5·4
First and second year (not E or C)	1·9	4·4	7·5
Bottom stream (C)[10]	–	2·3	6·7
Games	–	1·3	2·7
Total	35·0	35·0	35·0

Note: numbers represent the average number of teaching periods in each type of teaching.

The extent to which heads of departments retained control of the most coveted teaching is demonstrated by table 59. The categories of teaching are arranged roughly in order of desirability and prestige. It can be seen that heads of departments commonly kept most of the sixth form teaching and a large part of the express stream teaching for themselves, while the deputy heads usually did most of the teaching in the fifth forms as well as the balance of teaching in the E stream.

It can also be seen that 65 per cent of the teaching in the first and second years, and 83 per cent of the bottom stream teaching, was done by masters who were neither heads nor deputy heads of departments. Moreover the table tends, if anything, to under-estimate the differential allocations because much of the sixth form teaching allocated to the 'others' was, in fact, O level teaching, and much of the genuine prestige teaching was in the hands of one or two of the most senior 'others'. The six most junior 'others' taught the sixth form for only one period a week and, similarly, did little teaching in the express stream.

The 'allowance' system, with its graded posts and responsibility allowances, was more a formal recognition of seniority and qualification (status-confirming) than the authority structure. Heads of departments rarely called departmental meetings, and most departmental business was done over coffee or during odd breaks in the teaching timetable. In some cases, the heads of departments were expected to perform duties outside their immediate departments. For example, the head of English was expected to run the senior library, and the head of Physical Education was expected to arrange sports fixtures for the school teams, though he did not necessarily supervise matches himself.

In the larger departments—those with three to five staff—the 'second-in-command', or deputy head of department, was formally recognised and also frequently had extra duties. For example, the deputy head of English was expected to edit the school magazine, and the second geography master organised the sixth form field work each year. However, most teachers carried out some extra duties, which ranged from running school teams, organising the cricket kit and producing the school play to routine administrative duties, such as controlling the school savings bank, organising the distribution of stationery and report books, and arranging the timetable. The significance of these jobs varied for the individuals concerned. Some regarded them as chores, while others sought them and used them to build up a portfolio of minor responsibilities that would stand them well in the event of future opportunities of advancement becoming available.

The house system

The house system was designed to co-ordinate social as distinct from academic activities. It was introduced to replace the form teacher system in 1956 and broaden the basis for social and community activity. I am not concerned here with the developmental aspects of the house system, but with outlining its main organisational functions and relating them to the academic system. For this purpose, I use data collected mainly in 1963 and 1964.

The house system in British schools originated in public schools, which were boarding establishments. Its adaptation to day schools inevitably involved a considerable amount of distortion. However, at Hightown Grammar School a great deal of effort had been devoted to the development of the system and every activity that could meaningfully be organised on a house basis was worked into the framework.

As we have already seen, the intake of pupils in the first year was allocated at random to the four houses. In the first year, the four house groups coincided with the academic forms. In the second year, the house groups remained, but their academic functions were removed. They now formed the basis for registration, for the distribution of free milk at morning break, and for dinners at mid-day. In addition, one morning assembly a week was given over to house prayers, conducted by the housemaster, and various games, scholastic competitions (debates, declamations) and charity activities were organised on a house basis. Finally, rewards and punishments (house points and detentions) were organised on a house basis too.

House points could be awarded by any member of staff for meritorious effort during the normal school day. Generally, they were given for good work, and most teachers developed informal rules for their allocation ('anyone getting 8/10 gets a house point' was a typical principle applied to set pieces of work). The house point, a scrap of paper signed by the member of staff, was usually handed to the house group master, who recorded it and passed it on to the housemaster. The housemaster then kept the grand total to announce in house prayers, so that the boys could compare the relative positions of the houses in the inter-house competition when they met members of other houses in their forms afterwards. The boys' individual totals were also recorded on their reports.[11]

Detentions

The detention system constituted the major official punishment system, and in some ways provided heads of houses with their major burdens and responsibilities. A master usually awarded a detention as a last-resort punishment, after a protracted tussle with a pupil or group of pupils. He entered it in the house detention book, along with the date and the formal reason. He was also required to set the work for the hour's detention. This detention was then usually vetted by the head of house to check on the seriousness of the offence and to decide whether it was necessary to deduct a house point. Housemasters were frequently of the opinion that ineffectual teachers used the system to slough off their responsibilities,[12] and would sometimes take the opportunity to suggest other methods of dealing with the offence. Another reason why the housemaster kept the detention book under surveillance was the rule[13] that a boy who appeared in it two or three times the same week was to be caned. In addition, the

163

housemaster presided over and was responsible for a group of house prefects, who helped him in the running and supervision of the house.

It will be seen that the housemasters' duties and responsibilities pervaded most aspects of school life. They were responsible for the boys in their house in a way heads of department were not. This wide range of responsibility and heavy work load, with the low rate of pay for the job,[14] inevitably caused a certain amount of disillusionment among them. One remarked that what he received for the job did not pay his fares to school. He viewed it as 'hard work with little reward, responsibility with no power'.[15] It was certainly true that housemasters found it difficult to get much 'co-operation' from the older members of staff who were their seniors in the departmental system. These staff, who pre-dated the house system at the school, were the ones most opposed to it and they did least to make it work. They tended to regard their responsibilities as beginning and ending with the registration of their pupils and were described to me by one head of house as 'nine-to-fourers'.

The headmaster always supported heads of houses in their attempts to awaken enthusiasm and organise the perennial house activities. But his support was of a generalised nature and normally consisted of remarks to the whole staff about the importance of the house system and how he felt sure they would 'give wholehearted support as they always had done in the past'. There was never any question of outspoken criticism of the system on such public occasions, but there was much muted criticism in discussion afterwards. Sometimes a large amount of the responsibility for getting the particular activity 'off the ground' fell back onto the housemaster. After one such meeting, a head of house remarked that I would hear a great deal about the educational and social advantages of the house system while at the school, but that I should not overlook the fact that it removed a lot of work from the headmaster's shoulders.

Staff relationships and career pressures

We have seen that the problems facing the house system resulted from the fact that, to some extent, it violated the 'seniority principle'.[16] In general, it was understood that as a person rose in seniority within the school his voice carried more weight, and he was accepted as a person with an opinion that mattered and needed consulting. I noticed that when the senior master first introduced me to the staff, he took great care to introduce me to the more senior

164

members first. In addition, if I was going to observe a lesson, he almost invariably explained the situation well beforehand to the senior men, but often felt free to catch the junior staff just before the lesson started.

The departmental system, on the other hand, tended to confirm and add status to seniority. There were two instances in Hightown Grammar School where this was not the case and a junior, but more highly qualified, man held a responsibility allowance. Both gave rise to tension within the department, and on several occasions, to incidents that owed a great deal of their intensity to the older man's violated status aspirations.

Seniority also affected the staff's informal associations. An analysis of cliques through the observation of seating and association patterns during break and lunch-time revealed that the two most important criteria on which these associations were based were seniority and department. It was noticeable that the only senior member of staff to associate with the new members was one of the senior men who had been by-passed in favour of a more qualified junior man (that is, one whose seniority had not been recognised by the system). The other teacher in this position was very much an isolate and left for a promotion soon after my arrival.

The development of seniority was marked by the accumulation of a number of minor chores and responsibilities that were also, to some extent, status-enhancing. The degree to which a member of staff aspired after such jobs depended on his qualifications and the direction of his ambitions but, whatever the latter, some minor responsibilities nearly always had to be incurred. The examples described below are intended to illustrate the way they grew and became important to the member of staff.

A new member of staff was most likely to be approached first of all to help in the training and supervision of one of the football teams. These were numerous, since the school played rugby and soccer during the long winter season and would often field eight or more teams on one weekend. Each team required two members of staff, but in the first instance he would probably be called in to assist the master in charge. The teams themselves had something of a status hierarchy, so that after the new member has been promoted to and proved himself capable of running a minor team, he could aspire eventually to run the first XI or first XV. During his first and second years, he might also be asked to take on a minor clerical or administrative job—issuing stationery, running the school savings bank or obtaining advertisements for the magazine. In the following years the activities undertaken might include putting on a house play, staging an inter-house declamation or debate, taking teams on tour, organising a visit abroad, running school and inter-school debates, or running the junior library. Eventually, they might culminate in a considerable portfolio of responsibilities. Three fairly typical examples were as follows:

1 *Classics master—head of house:* first XI cricket and football, cricket kit (responsible master). Visits to Italy. Responsible for report books. Represented school on local authority committees and area sports committee.
2 *Deputy head of English—head of house:* first XI cricket, editor of school magazine, football and cricket tours at home and abroad. Certificated referee. School debates and inter-house debating competitions. Organised theatre visits.
3 *Science master—careers master:* very active—conferences and local contacts. Duke of Edinburgh Award Scheme (responsible master). Senior Scouts, camps, sports teams—had run first XI football.

The jobs available within the school were open to innovation and enlargement. A keen new member of staff might start a judo club or resuscitate a moribund cross-country running or canoeing club. Activities of this sort could bring an aspiring teacher into the limelight. The activity would be mentioned by the headmaster in prayers, the member of staff praised for his initiative, and once the activity was established it became a regular and public part of school life. As it became established, so the name of the master responsible became associated with it and gained acceptance.

Hence at certain stages in a schoolteacher's career, these activities are extremely important. An application for a senior post, especially a headship, must include a wide variety of them, and be supported by a substantial number of community activities. Active participation in organisations such as the Church, Scouting, local choirs, local government, local societies (e.g. history, drama, etc.), the Workers' Educational Association, the YMCA and other youth clubs; attending a wide variety of courses; interests of a liberal and cultural nature, are essential. Their importance is exaggerated in teaching because of the nature of the work and the classroom situation. It is very difficult for a selection committee to obtain information on the applicant's teaching ability—even if it could be obtained, it would be extremely difficult to assess. It is therefore usual to assume (unless there is evidence to the contrary) that, at a certain stage, a person is a competent teacher. The appointment is made on 'other grounds', i.e. the variety of his teaching experience and the interests and activities mentioned above.

So the career pressures in grammar school teaching are not very strong in the direction of innovation in the classroom or attempts to improve pupil–teacher relationships in the teaching situation. From the career point of view, it is important merely to have a competence within the classroom, to obtain good examination results and to be seen to be in control.

The career pressures and the process of establishing oneself as a teacher structure the staff into easily recognisable categories. This was remarked by a number of members of staff. One described the situation in a particularly graphic manner. 'This school is like a sandwich with a soft top, a soft bottom and a hard core or filling. On the top, you've got the Head and Mr Price wanting to be loved,[17] Mr Tonkins—he's all talk—and Mr Wright, a very nice man but too soft. [All the teachers mentioned here were in their fifties or sixties.] You can't carry on like a benevolent, pipe-smoking Mr Chips. He's much too soft, his Chemistry results are terrible. You've got to be prepared to drive them like Mr Wood, thumping them through History. Wright has let many a boy down in this way. The hard filling contains people like Mr Wood, Mr Lawless, Mr Werk, Mr Stevens and myself [all, including himself, were in their thirties] and the soft bottom is made up of people like Mr Cook, Mr Harris and Mr Robin, where all hell breaks loose in the classroom.' [These three teachers were all in their first or second year of teaching.]

This diagnosis came from the deputy head of a department, a young, ambitious man, shortly before he moved to become head of department in another grammar school. It accords quite well with the view expressed by other members of the staff from the 'hard core', who thought the younger men were not of the high calibre of former generations either with regard to their dedication to the school or their academic qualifications.

It also accords fairly well with the view expressed by some members of the 'soft top'. Wright, the benevolent pipe smoker, reckoned that the moral and character-building aspects of grammar school education were far more important than the academic discipline of Mr Wood. He would tell stories, purported to be true, of the academically brilliant scholar who became over-ambitious and arrogant, and eventually went to prison for trying to embezzle from his firm. Mr Price, another from the 'soft top', said on one occasion that whenever there was a dispute between a boy and a master he was always inclined to give the boy the benefit of the doubt.

The 'soft bottom' were conspicuous in a number of ways besides their lack of discipline. They tended to dress rather informally and fashionably, with tight fitting trousers and pointed shoes. They attempted an informal and closer relationship with their pupils, and were the masters who could most frequently be seen joking and talking with pupils in their spare time. On the other hand, their classes tended to be noisy and after a few months at the school they were giving large numbers of detentions and other minor impositions. The staff with one or two years' experience gave an average of nearly fifty detentions in one year—far more than any other category. Heads of house gave, on average, only seven in the same year.

It is worth noting that while members of the hard core were not necessarily the most popular members of the staff, they were very noticeably the least easily criticised, whereas criticism of members of the top or bottom could be overt and sweeping. For example, 'Poor old Johnny, he's been a good teacher in his time and nobody could deny that, but he's just given up.' Or 'I've just caught two boys in the quad, copying homework. It's incredible they should feel they can get away with it. That young chap Robin really is the end. They know they can get away with it with him. He really must be thick.'

Criticism of members of the hard core could never be so outspoken. For example, I was once told, 'Some members of staff seek to disguise their discipline problem by holding private detentions instead of recording them in the detention book.' I knew who was being referred to but was left to draw my own conclusion. The man in question could not easily be faulted for poor discipline. It was the way he maintained it that came under fire. On other occasions, I heard 'hard core' teachers being criticised for lack of tact, over-enthusiasm and overbearance, but rarely for inefficiency or lack of discipline.

It is clear that as well as portraying an aspect of the staff structure at Hightown Grammar, this description can be seen to coincide roughly with the stages in a teacher's career. A new master quickly
168

becomes part of the 'soft bottom'. As he masters the techniques of teaching and his classroom control improves, he can begin to think in terms of taking on extra responsibilities. Eventually he is experienced enough to contemplate promotion and it is at this stage that he moves into the 'hard core' and becomes a prominent, forceful member of the staff. During this stage some are promoted into higher teaching posts and others are promoted out of grammar schools (into colleges of education or further education). The characteristics of the 'soft top' are developed most markedly in the last few years of teaching, when promotion is no longer a possibility and the teacher's energies may be sapped through illness.

In the foregoing analysis I have described the major factors influencing staff relationships at Hightown Grammar School and the way in which the social forces that teachers encounter channel their socialisation and subsequent development. In the next section I shall attempt to relate these developments to relationships in the classroom and to the major processes of differentiation and polarisation within the student body.

Staff–pupil relationships

Willard Waller's classic work *The sociology of teaching* summarises succinctly the problems of the teacher in the authority structure of the school:

The one-room country school must have a different social structure from the city high school with five thousand students, but the basic fact of authority, of dominance and subordination, remains in fact in both . . .

It is a despotism resting upon children, at once the most intractable and the most unstable members of the community . . .

A school may in fact maintain a high morale through a period of years, so that its record in the eyes of the community is marred by no untoward incident. But how many schools are there with a teaching body of more than—let us say—ten teachers, in which there is not one teacher who is in imminent danger of losing his position because of poor discipline? How many such schools in which no teacher's discipline has broken down within the last three years?

To understand the political structure of the school we must know that the school is organised on the authority principle and that the *authority is constantly threatened* [my italics]. The authority of the . . . teachers is in unremitting danger from (1) the students, (2) the parents, (3) the school board, (4) each other, (5) hangers-on and marginal members of the group, (6) alumni.[18]

This aspect of teaching is little understood and little remarked on by recent works in the sociology of education,[19] yet is fundamental to the understanding of the teaching situation and teacher–pupil relationships. Educationalists and even sociologists frequently use gardening analogies when talking about the process of education,[20] e.g. 'cultivating' pupils. The metaphor is totally misleading. I have yet to hear of a gardener being reduced to a nervous wreck by errant plants, but I have not taught nor done research in a school where at least one member of staff did not have chronic discipline problems. In some difficult secondary modern schools, the proportion of staff thus affected was 25–30 per cent. In Hightown Grammar the figure fluctuated between 5 and 10 per cent which, in my experience, is normal for a school of its type.

Such teachers are an important reference group[21] in any staff room. Their latest 'exploits' are talked about and widely disseminated. They influence the attitudes of the rest of the staff profoundly, because they illustrate what could lie in store for any of them should they fail to control their pupils in the classroom situation. At the beginning of this analysis, then, it is important to examine some of the major factors that affect the classroom situation from the teacher's point of view.

The somewhat exhaustive list of danger points Waller sets out is not appropriate to our discussion, and is highly coloured by the American position. The higher status of teachers in Britain and the differently constituted administrative structure mean that categories 2, 3, 5 and 6 (the parents, the school board, hangers-on and marginal members of the group, and alumni) are far less important in the British situation,[22] especially in grammar schools. Exceptions may occur at time of change and educational reorganisation, when these groups can become very important, but normally they fade into insignificance alongside the pressures from the pupils (1) and from each other (4). Aspects of the career pressures on teachers have already been discussed. In this section I shall deal with the pressures from the pupils.

The classroom situation

At Hightown there were seven teaching periods of forty minutes each, giving a total of 4 hours 40 minutes' teaching time a day. Thus the classroom situation existed for 66 per cent of the time from 9 a.m. to 4 p.m. The rest was taken up with morning registration, prayers,

170

morning break, lunch time and afternoon registration, in that order.

A member of staff was normally expected to teach thirty out of the thirty-five teaching periods. Depending on the subject he taught, he would see between six and nine different forms each week (180–270 children). Efforts were made to limit the number of forms any one master taught to a reasonable level. This was done by including a certain amount of games, sixth form teaching or even (say) religious instruction in the timetable. Also, during the first year, house tutors were expected to teach their house groups in at least one subject. Another way in which the problem of 'getting to know' the children was combated was allocating the same form to the same master, year after year, as the form moved through the school. Even this was difficult to ensure for more than a few years in most subjects, however, because of streaming and staff and timetable changes.

Not surprisingly, I recorded a large number of occasions when even quite experienced teachers made mistakes of identity, or were unable to remember who a boy was when confronted with his blank report card.[23] One experienced member of staff who prided himself on his knowledge of his pupils and their background called a boy by the wrong name for over a year.

A second difficulty confronting the specialist subject teacher in Hightown Grammar School was the constant flow (as opposed to numbers) of pupils. Typically, a master would be confronted with 120 to 180 different faces in one day in four to six groups at different stages in the syllabus, and capable of different rates of progress through a complex subject-matter. It is under this considerable pressure that some grammar school masters gradually regress to being textbook guides who dictate notes, read from textbooks and assign a minimum of time to more stimulating activities that make heavy demands on the teacher's physical and emotional resources.[24]

It was noticeable at Hightown that some of the most varied and interesting teaching was done in the English department. English was allocated five periods a week, but because the head of the department thought the English Literature examination was not a suitable or necessary one for fifth-year boys, the English staff were freed from a large amount of syllabus and examination pressure.[25]

The third, and perhaps most important, pressure I wish to discuss here derives from what I will call the asymmetry of the teaching situation. The relationship between teacher and pupil in the classroom is asymmetrical in the sense that the pupils form a group (normally about thirty at Hightown Grammar), while the teacher is an individual. Even when the teacher addresses an individual pupil, it is normally a public event in the sense that the rest of the class hear the interchange, and it is frequently an interchange related to a common academic task. It was, in fact, relatively rare for an individual member of staff and an individual pupil to be seen together in private conversation outside the classroom.[26] When it did occur, the most common reason was that the boy was receiving a reprimand or, if he was a more senior pupil, instructions about an activity for which he shared a responsibility.

This rarity of the individual relationship underlines the relative importance in reality of the asymmetrical nature of the pupil–teacher relationship. The teacher *must* be concerned with the academic progress and behaviour of the whole group. Unless he sub-divides the the class in some way (which was rare at Hightown), he cannot give too much leeway to individuals without endangering the standards set for the whole group. The boy who talks to his neighbour when he should be listening is not just a nuisance, he is threatening the whole system of teacher authority. If he can talk unchecked, so can the next boy; in a short time, everyone is talking and the classroom would be in chaos. Quite obviously a teacher cannot check every minor interruption. He draws the line on the basis of personal experience.[27]

Some of the factors involved in this process are illustrated schematically in Fig. 17. The emerging teaching performance is

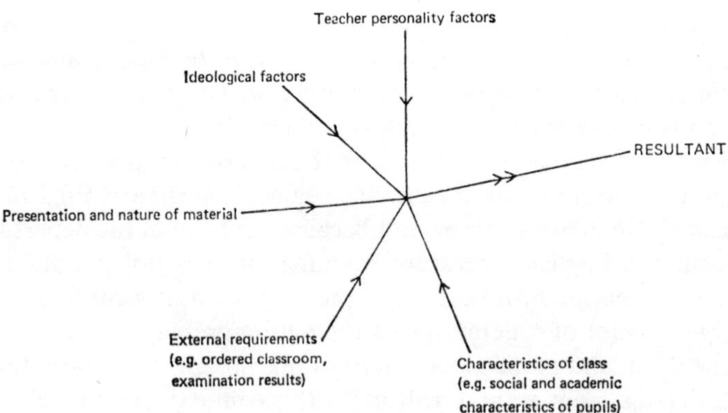

Fig. 17. Emerging teacher performance as the resultant of five complex factors.

172

shown as the resultant of five complex factors. These have been defined fairly arbitrarily but serve to show the complexity of the process and to explain why no *objective* method has yet been devised to assess the classroom performance of a teacher. The successful teacher achieves a *personal* solution, which is a balance between the major opposing interests. To give too much leeway invites chaos; not to give enough would be to turn his lessons into dreary episodes of instruction and rote learning.

To achieve this balance, he is constantly involved in a complex sequence of 'on the spot' decisions. Every action he initiates invokes some sort of response from his pupils and necessitates a decision to modify or not to modify the initial approach. It is futile for a teacher starting with a new class to lay down a formal set of rules governing his interaction with the pupils and expect simply to supervise these rules, or his pupils to adhere to them. The balance, the result he desires, has to be engineered through the process of interaction. It cannot be legislated for. It is the mark of the successful teacher that the expectations his pupils develop about the classroom situation, through the process of interaction, are close to his own.

The ability to control this process has to be learnt. The young, inexperienced master who has yet to develop the necessary techniques finds teaching an emotionally demanding and physically exhausting performance. But even the experienced teacher has to contend with the problem. He finds it less exhausting because he has developed the means of control,[28] but the pressures imposed by the asymmetry of the teaching situation are ever present, and the experienced teacher too forgets it at his peril.

At Hightown Grammar, the fate of an experienced and well qualified teacher from a college of further education exemplifies this. Mr Wimble's lessons with the fifth year were described to me by another member of staff. 'He tries to get round the problem by arriving at lessons late and leaving early. He also fortifies himself at a pub during the dinner break. He's usually about ten minutes late for the lesson, so by the time he arrives there's quite a lot of noise. Before he goes in the din is terrible, but it gets *worse* when he goes in. Poor Mr Wood underneath says he's relieved when Wimble goes five minutes early, because the noise dies down again.'

Another master who had recurrent discipline problems with certain forms found himself persecuted outside the classroom as well as inside it. He was one of the few who lived near the school. I once saw him being followed through the local park by a group of boys, who hid behind trees and bushes, jeering and chanting after him. The tortured look of embarrassment on the man's face painfully revealed the extent of his public humiliation.

The teacher persona

The method by which the young schoolteacher solves or avoids the problems outlined above can be described as the development of a teacher persona. The essential elements in this development are:

1 The establishment of role distance between teacher and taught; the establishment of a more formal atmosphere, where the teacher does not become personally and emotionally involved. He manipulates or manages from a distance.
2 The teacher develops a presence which is associated in the minds of the pupils with a set of appropriate behaviour patterns.

The secret of the successful teacher is that he is rarely challenged (none, in my experience, was never challenged). It is not that the anti-group is violently suppressed[29] but that anti-group behaviour is seen to be inappropriate. 'Why is it that when Mr Black comes into the room everyone automatically behaves themselves and gets down to work?' a puzzled third-year boy once asked me. 'He never canes anybody, or loses his temper.'

A more extreme example—which, nevertheless, catches an essential truth—is expressed by Waller:

The mask which the teacher wears in study hall is characterised by impassivity and imperturbability. This, then, is the reason for those peculiar set expressions which one observes on teachers' faces, for those expressions which enemies call wooden and friends call granite-like; these men are *forced* to pose much as symbols of authority, and they have chiselled their faces into the pattern of authority. *Fear*, after all, is a great teacher, and one learns, under duress, to obviate the possibility of the entry of anything personal when that might detract from our validity as a symbol.[30]

Many teachers at Hightown Grammar School recognised this persona as part of their teaching equipment. At the beginning of a new term one remarked, 'Oh well, don the old mask and walk in like the Lord of Creation.' Another explained in conversation that any teacher must be able to lose his temper just at the right moment. He must never *really* lose it, though, otherwise he would lose control of the situation. To some extent, the teacher is a Wizard-of-Oz character.

174

His control rests on bluff and his skill at manipulating the awesome mask of authority.[31]

A number of ritualistic elements in the organisation of the school supported the persona and increased the role distance between teacher and pupil. At Hightown Grammar, pupils stood up when a teacher entered the room. The masters sat on the platform during prayers and the school stood when they walked out. Pupils addressed teachers as 'Sir', and teachers were expected to wear gowns on a number of public occasions.

In the course of a sixth-form revue[32] the prefects 'took off' various members of the staff, mainly the senior ones. When I saw these imitations, with their characteristic facial expressions, modes of gait, catch phrases and so on, I assumed that some of the masters would be a little upset. A blow to their dignity? Not at all. Most of them were delighted with the mimicry. To be imitated in this way was to be recognised as an established 'character', a personality on a school level. The development of the teacher persona can, therefore, be looked upon as progressive and linked with the concomitants of the development of seniority described in the first section of this chapter.

Teacher–pupil relationships: some structural aspects

To some extent, the development of the teacher persona and the concomitants of seniority are the result of socialisation into an on-going system of social relations. To the observer there are within a grammar school two distinct spheres characterised by interconnected networks of informal relationships—the staff and the pupils. Relationships of an informal kind rarely cross this boundary; where they do, their existence is seldom acknowledged within the formal teaching situation. For the most part, there is a semi-permeable social membrane between the two systems. Staff have little real knowledge of the content and structure of the informal relationships among pupils, while pupils know even less about the internal characteristics of the staff room.

Whereas the membrane is particularly opaque from the students' point of view, it is part of the function of the staff to evaluate the student from the social as well as the academic point of view. It is also essential for a teacher to have a 'working knowledge' of a number of the key relationships within the class he is teaching for the purpose of controlling it.

This difference in visibility was purposefully brought about by the formal organisation. Pupils were not allowed into the staff rooms, and staff were not supposed to send boys there for books or equipment they had forgotten. When pupils were sent to the staff room (usually by a young member of staff who preferred not to leave his class) they were either sent packing or, more usually, they were dealt with but intimidated at the same time. This extract from my field notes provides a fairly typical example:

A timid knock.
  'Who's there?' (bellowed). The door opens and in comes a first-year boy.
  'Mr Jones said. . .'
  'Don't come in, just stand where you are. Now, what do you want?'
  '1C's English books, sir.' Master gets the books.
  'Who sent you?'—giving him the books.
  'Mr Jones, sir.'
  'Well, you ought to know better. Boys aren't allowed to come into the staff room. Just remember that next time!'

Alternatively, if there were loud conversation or laughter in the staff room, a member of staff might get up, open the door and shut it behind him while finding out what the boy wanted. Periodically the duty master would clear the corridor outside the staff rooms (which was out of bounds) of boys who had been told by other masters to see them at the end of break and were waiting for them to come out after having their coffee.

The masters saw boys as being morbidly interested in their free-time activities and conversations. Two boys acted as waiters to the staff at each of the house dinners. When I asked some of the teachers why they thought the boys volunteered and so missed some play time, one of the reasons suggested was that they liked to hear snippets of conversation and retail them to their mates.

On the other hand, whereas pupils rarely observed the staff as a group,[33] staff commonly observed pupils interacting in a group—in the classroom, in games, out-of-school activities, in play, etc. In all these activities there was ample opportunity to observe them interacting and to assess not only their academic but also their social characteristics. However, the transparency of the situation is to an important extent illusory. The reasons cannot be gone into fully. It will be sufficient to outline some of the factors that interfere with the staff's obtaining an objective view.

Difference in age and function are the main factors that prevent a master from entering into the boys' informal social structure. But
176

whereas the difference in age and interests merely inhibits the master from entry, the difference in *function* means that certain aspects of the pupil's informal structure must always remain hidden.

The staff and the processes of differentiation and sub-cultural polarisation

The major function of the teacher is, of course, to teach.[34] However, society also demands that he should grade and select, and it is this aspect of his role that excludes him from the aspects of the student sub-culture that would reflect unfavourably on those participating. The teacher's exclusion is far more pronounced than that of the normal adult. I was, of course, quite unable to shed my adult status during the research period, but I *was* able to shed my teacher status, and when I did I became aware of the increased flow of information about matters that had been taboo for me as a member of staff. Similarly, when I was supervising the answering of questionnaires it was rare for a group to fill them in without someone, at some time, stipulating 'You won't show these answers to any of the teachers, will you?'

A final mechanism affecting the interaction of pupils and teachers needs to be stressed at this point, for it will bring the analysis to bear on some of the major processes discussed earlier in the book, the processes of differentiation and sub-culture formation.

The factors discussed in this chapter—the large total number of pupils, the rapid succession of classes, the asymmetry of the classroom situation, the necessity for adequate classroom control and the necessity to maintain the role distance in the teacher–pupil relationship—impinge directly on the classroom situation and radically affect the sort of relationship a teacher can have with an individual pupil. The individual pupil is judged, above all, on his classroom performance (academic and behaviour). Those pupils who, in the past, have produced bad work or been badly behaved soon develop a reputation for these things which carries over into future events and other spheres.[35] Such a reputation, as we have seen, can be an important determinant of the enthusiasm and motivation which pupils bring to future tasks, and hence of the resulting performance. Of course, the pupils become aware of the rules of the game, and so the classroom also becomes a highly competitive system, the pupils competing among themselves and taking up positions within the classroom according to their reputations.

The following examples are highly selective. They are incidents which highlight the point I wish to demonstrate: that teacher behaviour, conditioned by the reputation of the pupil, is one of the central factors producing differentiation.[36] The first concerns a boy, Thornton, whose behaviour was neither difficult nor unruly but was handicapped by a number of class characteristics. He had a broad accent, his manner when addressing teachers was negative and a little surly. He mumbled. His poor reputation, however, was based mainly on his poor work and unreliability: he rarely did his homework.

Mr Bradley was demonstrating the substitution of minus numbers into equations to a bottom stream. A number of boys had failed to grasp the idea, and as he questioned round the class, getting more and more wrong answers, he became more and more irritable. Eventually, he arrived at Thornton, who was quite unable to give the correct answer. The master persevered, but the boy slipped further and further into the mire. The class groaned at his mistakes, some flung up their hands in order to answer correctly. Thornton went pale as the master, despairing of ever getting the point across, let fly. 'We've been at this now for six weeks, Thornton! My God, you're driving me up the wall. I could have taught a fox terrier more than this in six weeks. You know, Thornton, you're the stupidest boy I've ever met. Lord knows how you ever got into this school!'

Bradley calmed himself, and then followed a further attempt at explanation, step by step, with thinly veiled irritation. At each stage he asked the boy the answer and, at last, Thornton made another mistake. The master burst out, 'Now look here, Thornton, I've had enough of this. If you give me another wrong answer, I'll thrash you. I'll murder you. If you can't . . .' Thornton gave the correct answer and with obvious relief the class subsided.

The tension this incident generated was such that the boy had obviously stopped thinking about the task long before the final stages. He was so worked up that he was incapable of concentrating. In three consecutive lessons this master erupted in a similarly violent way at four boys. Their positions in class at the last examinations were twenty-fourth, twenty-sixth, twenty-seventh and thirtieth. On each occasion he could have chosen several others, but he lighted on these because they were particularly appropriate for this sort of treatment (i.e. they had the appropriate reputation).

Another time he found that Macdonald, the top boy in the form, had made a mistake in setting out a problem, and remarked quietly, privately, reasonably, 'No, lad, you'll have to do it again.' When Priestley, an anti-group pupil, made the same error he declared for the whole class to hear, 'You know, it's amazing that you've been here three years. I gave you an example of how to set it out, but you've done it differently. What's wrong with you, boy? Are you too lazy to turn back one page?'

If a pupil with a good reputation misbehaves in an insulting or unruly manner, the impact on the teacher is very great indeed. For it calls into question a whole fabric of assumptions about the class which has served as a basis for action over perhaps a long period of time. Mr Wilkins, a master with excellent discipline and control, came to me on one occasion and confessed that he had been rather upset by 5B. As he had entered the classroom, a boy had made a large 'raspberry' noise. He had immediately brought the class to order, given them a severe telling-off and threatened them all with detention if the culprit did not own up. At the end of the lesson Hodge came forward and admitted to making the noise. Wilkins was shocked and upset. He kept saying, 'I can't understand it. Hodge isn't that sort of boy. I could understand Morris, or even Larch, but not Hodge. Of course, I *had* to give him a detention.'

Later that day, Hodge came up to Mr Wilkins and apologised for the noise, but said it was quite accidental and not directed at him. He had been talking to the other boys and not noticed the teacher come into the room. The raspberry was intended for another boy and had accidentally coincided with Mr Wilkins's entry. Wilkins was relieved and obviously very pleased at this news. He let Hodge off the detention and remarked to me later, 'I knew Hodge wouldn't do something like that purposely.'

I am not concerned here with criticising these masters' actions. It would obviously have been unjust to put Hodge into detention over a mistake. Similarly, given that Mr Bradley was terribly anxious about slackness and lack of application in 2C (he remarked to me at the end of the first year, 'We have to go on to congruency and parallelograms. We've not done a tenth of the syllabus.'), he was perhaps justified in his exasperation; given that he felt an 'explosion' was needed, it must obviously be aimed at the worst offenders. I am concerned merely with its cumulative effects. All the boys mentioned in connection with Bradley's explosions left before taking O level. Morris, one of the boys mentioned by Mr Wilkins, discussed with me his reasons for wanting to leave.

Morris: What's the point of staying on? I can't do anything right in this place. Even when I do good work, I never get the credit.'

King [a friend]: That's because you've usually copied it! I agree with him really—they've all got their knife into him, especially Mr B.

Morris: We did an experiment once to prove it. I kept quiet and didn't say a thing for the first half of the lesson. Then I started to talk like everyone else. I'd only just opened my mouth and I got a detention. The whole class roared.

His final report also reflected the state of affairs:

A very unsatisfactory school career. Very early on he developed a 'chip on his shoulder' and became more and more anti-school, reflected in smoking and churlish behaviour. He has ability, but has seldom used it consistently. In athletics he has shown himself to be a very good cross-country runner. Not punctual, too many occasional absences.

Another boy who wished to leave early (before O level, but after 15 years of age) went to see the headmaster to get permission. When the Head asked him why he wanted to leave, his answer was that he hated teachers. The headmaster asked which teachers he did not get on with, but the boy replied, 'I hate *all* teachers.' The headmaster retold the conversation as a joke in the staff room. To the teachers present (including myself) the remark was amusing, because it was so categorical and unreasonable. Each of us knew that the staff included a wide range of personalities and interests. It seemed nonsensical to lump them all together. What we forgot was that the boy's experience of us *as teachers* did not contain anything like this variability. Just as *he* was viewed by most of the teachers as rather lazy, poorly behaved and lacking in strength of character, so he felt that *all* teachers disliked him, were unfair to him, and made his life miserable.

In previous chapters I have made it clear that differentiation is affected by social class simply because class-linked handicaps are taken into the classroom situation by the working-class child much more frequently than by middle-class children (the child has not done homework, is upset by differences in accents, by teachers' attitudes, and therefore lacks enthusiasm and ambition over long periods). I did not record a single instance of a child being discriminated against because he was from a working-class background. In fact, I have recorded incidents where working-class children were given special treatment because of their difficulties at home, e.g.

180

King. However, middle-class children can and do receive similar special treatment in cases of difficulty and are, perhaps, more likely to do so.

Working-class children percolate downwards in the differentiating process because they are harder to teach and more difficult to control within the classroom situation. It is a relentless, slow, grinding process. The usual resources the school can furnish to bolster the failing student are not a sufficient antidote. For example, if a master sees a boy three or four times in one week and talks to him for twenty minutes or half an hour each time, he feels he has made a large commitment of time to that child. Indeed, in terms of the number of children for whom he has a responsibility and the amount of free time he has during a normal day, he *has*—about 30 per cent of his week's supply. In fact, very few masters made this sort of commitment (encouraging, or discussing the pupil's difficulties), so that very little stood in the way of the inevitable class bias in the differentiating process.

Too often, teachers expect fairly drastic and immediate improvement from such a commitment. If it is not forthcoming, they soon become discouraged (see page 141, Lawless's reaction to Murdock and Russell). The boy is then characterised as lazy (work), or an oaf (behaviour), and further efforts to reform him can be discounted. 'Oh, I shouldn't waste any time over so-and-so, he's a lout . . .' is the sort of advice sometimes given to a new master who has problems with a pupil. This is also one reason why special agencies for maladjusted children rarely get as many referrals from teachers as they think they should. The teacher has come to see the boy with a behaviour problem as a 'bad lot' who *must* be kept under control in the classroom situation.

This mechanism is important as a protection to the teacher. He is confronted with so many problems that, should he see each as having a legitimate claim on his time, he would be inundated with this sort of counselling work. Stereotyping, therefore, cuts away the legitimacy of the problem pupil's claim to special treatment and extra time. The interference of middle-class parents (Baker), the interested teacher (King) or the research worker (Russell) was sufficient to re-establish the legitimacy of the claim to special treatment for the cases discussed.

The extent of the bias previously discussed is shown in table 60. It was constructed when the second year was being streamed. In most cases streams were allocated straightforwardly on the basis of academic merit. However, a number of border-line cases were allocated on the basis of 'those "intangibles"[37] well known to the experienced teacher but not picked up by mere examinations, and which forecast true educational promise'.

TABLE 60

THE SOCIAL CLASS BACKGROUND OF BORDER-LINE CASES WHO
WERE NOT STREAMED PURELY ON EXAMINATION RESULTS

	*Upgraded**	*Downgraded*	*Total*
1 Managerial, professional, self-employed, supervisory and white-collar workers	13	7	20
2 Skilled, semi-skilled and unskilled workers	1	11	12
Totals	14	18	32

* Boys were termed 'upgraded' if they were put into the category above the border line, when they did not merit this on the examination results. Boys were termed 'downgraded' when they were put in the category below the border line and they did not merit it on purely academic grounds.

Note: it is not necessary that the number of boys upgraded should balance the number downgraded. One boy upgraded from, say, tenth position could cause two or three boys in, say seventh, eighth and ninth positions to be classified as downgraded if they were put into the stream below the tenth boy.

These intangibles were, in fact, closely class-linked. At the time of writing, the material required to test the efficiency of these intangibles as selectors of academic promise (the GCE O level results) is not available. However, there seems little doubt from my examination of the progress of the boys concerned that the 'upgraded' ones will amply justify the teachers' faith in them.

NOTES

[1] The situation was exacerbated by two other factors: (1) a number of long illnesses among the science staff, (2) a long tradition of the dominance of the 'modern' side, which meant that new science teachers were inducted into a sub-system with lower morale, lower status, and poorer staff–student relationships.

[2] This means that nearly half the original staff had left in four and a half years. This does not relate directly to the rate of staff turnover, since many of the jobs vacated by the original nineteen have been filled and vacated a number of times since April 1963.

[3] One move was not traced.

[4] H. B. Hollingshead, *Elmtown's youth*, Wiley, 1949, page 131.

[5] *Ibid.*, page 248.

[6] For a general discussion of this difference, see G. Baron and A. Tropp,

182

'Teachers in England and America', in Halsey, Floud and Anderson, *Education, economy and society.*

[7] When the authority structure clashed with the principle of seniority, there was frequently a great deal of tension. It was fairly easy administratively to avoid placing a head of department under his own deputy. I assumed this situation was deliberately avoided.

[8] I failed to discover why two heads of houses should receive £30 a year more than the others. I suspect it was an administrative convenience related, at one time, to difficulty in dividing up responsibility allowances.

[9] 'Chores' was the term frequently used to describe these responsibilities, many of which were in fact important privileges.

[10] Table 59 illustrates another factor affecting the process of polarisation. It should be noted that the C forms are almost entirely in the hands of 'others' and the E forms are almost entirely taught by heads and deputy heads of departments in the eight academic subjects. The pupils in the C forms were well aware of this discrimination and it was frequently cited in justification of their attitudes to school and academic work.

[11] This introduced a keen sense of competitiveness into winning house points. Some boys bludgeoned masters into giving them one by their persistence, others worked the memory fiddle—'You remember last week, sir, for that homework . . .' This distortion gave rise to unexpectedly large scores in some cases, but on the whole boys got house points for good homework and test results.

[12] For reasons why teachers have to solve their own problems, see C. Wayne Gordon, *The social system of a high school*, Free Press, 1957; also H. S. Becker, 'The teacher in the authority system of the public school', *Journal of Ed. Soc.*, November 1953, pages 128–41.

[13] Most housemasters interpreted the rule loosely.

[14] One extra free period a week—the same as heads of departments.

[15] The housemasters who were most enthusiastic were those for whom the position was most likely to be a stepping stone in their career, e.g. towards a headship or head of house in a comprehensive school. Those who were least enthusiastic had no ambitions in this direction.

[16] In order to gain sufficient support for the system in the first place, the headmaster had had to bide his time and wait for the opposition to 'die or retire'.

[17] The implication here is that they wished to be loved by the pupils, not by the staff.

[18] Willard Waller, *The sociology of teaching*, Wiley, 1965, page 10.

[19] See B. Wilson, 'The role of the teacher', *B.J.S.*, 1962, for an otherwise more exhaustive analysis of the role and functions of the teacher. Wilson does mention the clash between the affective and disciplinary aspect of the teacher's role, but he does not give full recognition to the stresses the disciplinary role imposes.

[20] *Ibid.*, 'He [the teacher] must occupy a place in the child's scheme of things which makes the transmission of values, standards and attitudes of mind one which can occur *easily* and *naturally*. They must occur in a *favourable climate* where the teacher can *cultivate* children' [my italics].

[21] In the Mertonian sense. They do not necessarily form a clique. In fact, they are frequently isolates.

[22] See chapter 8, 'Community control'.

[23] Reports were filled in at the end of each term. It was quite frequent at Christmas and even the spring term for masters to break the silence of the work room with the question 'What does so-and-so look like? Anyone here teach so-and-so?'

[24] C. Wayne Gordon, *The social system of the high school*, makes the same point

for the American high school (page 47): 'They taught for 30 hours a week, meeting between 130 to 150 students daily. The necessity to reduce the stress was considerable.'

[25] The pupils were examined in English Language in the GCE, which represented a relatively small burden in terms of the timetable allocation of five periods a week.

[26] While teaching at the school, I frequently involved pupils in this type of conversation, in my capacity as a research worker. The situation was sometimes interpreted by both staff and pupils as a reprimand situation. Staff would ask, 'What's so-and-so been up to?' and pupils passing by frequently made signs which made it clear they thought the boy was in trouble. This was only one of the role conflicts inherent in combining the role of teacher with that of research worker.

[27] On several occasions I was in the position of having to interfere with this process. Boys who were failing to hold their own in the school sometimes had periods of crises (e.g. Buttle) and during this time incurred numerous detentions, sometimes canings. The system of punishment tended to be cumulative, e.g. more than two detentions a week was followed by a caning. On two occasions, in particular, a whole series of such events culminating in the probable expulsion of the boy, hung on the question of whether a young master gave a boy a detention. In both cases, it was no easy matter for the master to rescind the punishment. Not because the crime was a heinous one—in one case, talking out of turn; in the other, failure to hand in homework—but because the master had drawn his line at that point. 'I told the class the next person to talk would get a detention.' Even when the masters knew the effect of the detention, they found it difficult to withdraw it. 'If they know Murdock can get away with it, they will all try.' The masters saw my interference as the thin end of the wedge that could damage their standing with the class. (It is to their credit that they withdrew the detentions despite the probable consequences.)

[28] See A. K. Cohen, *Delinquent boys*, Free Press of Glencoe, 1955, page 50 ff., for a description of the processes by which customs and experience reduce the pressures implicit in taking even small, everyday decisions.

[29] If the anti-group is violently suppressed, a whole series of problems emerge. The records of Hightown Grammar School were full of the after-effects caused by a master who left before I arrived: he had attempted to improve the examination results in his subject by caning every boy who got less than seven out of ten in a weekly test. Some of his pupils paid a high price in disturbed behaviour for a marginal improvement in their examination results.

[30] W. Waller, *The sociology of teaching*, page 164. The fear Waller refers to is the fear the teacher has of disorder and chaos (my emphasis).

[31] I am not suggesting that the teacher is necessarily forced into a formal and rigid approach. Even an informal or 'child–centred' approach involves the use of these elements.

[32] This revue can be described as a 'ritual of rebellion': see M. Gluckman, 'Rituals of rebellion in south-east Africa' in *Order and rebellion in tribal Africa*, Cohen & West, 1963.

[33] The major exception was morning prayers, but the staff did not interact in this situation.

[34] B. R. Wilson, 'The teacher's role: a sociological analysis', *B.J.S.*, vol. 13, 1962. Wilson makes a useful distinction between the socialising and instructional aspects of the role.

[35] In games, for example, badly behaved boys who were good at sports were a constant source of difficulty and embarrassment to the school.

[36] I do not wish to suggest that all methods of teaching have the same result. A

good teacher can modify the differentiation his behaviour produces. Nevertheless, as long as teachers are under these sorts of pressure, a high proportion of them will continue to give rise to the type of incident described.

[37] The 'intangibles' were made available to the headmaster through recommendations by teachers who had taught the pupils in question, i.e. these recommendations emanated from their experience of the children in the classroom situation. The quotation is from the headmaster.

9 Conclusion

In this concluding chapter I select and refine some of the theoretical points arising out of the analysis presented in preceding chapters. I show their relevance to two problems of broader educational and sociological interest: (1) the disappointing performance of working-class boys in grammar schools since the 1944 Education Act, and (2) the deferred gratification pattern. Further possible developments in this type of research are indicated.

The performance of working-class boys

The school is an example of a socialising organisation and as such is particularly sensitive to changes in the structure of its parent society. The recent changes in English society from predominantly locally based, locally owned industry with relatively low levels of technical expertise and small managerial elites to predominantly nationally and internationally based companies, with high degrees of expertise and division of labour, and large, powerful, highly qualified managerial elites, is well documented.[1] Equally well known is the general effect of this fundamental change on the socialising organisations.[2] They have expanded enormously, to deal with the increased demand for highly trained personnel.[3]

Socialising organisations have become major stratifying devices within society. The qualifications they distribute have been likened to tickets for the journey through life, with the implication that a first-class ticket ensures a first class journey. The chances of career mobility for a person with a low-ranking ticket have been shown to be diminishing.[4] Some sections of the literature of education emphasise the increasing competition within these socialising organisations[5] and the strain upon the competitors during certain diagnostic periods which will shape their future.

186

In chapter 2 these general trends were examined in the context of Hightown. The changing social situation described above was divided into three stages and the participation and success of the various class groupings within the Grammar School were analysed for each of those stages. The results showed that the variation in social class participation in Hightown has not been smooth or entirely predictable. It was found that in the 1930's the working-class contingent performed as well as the lower middle class contingent, and that this was also true in south-west Hertfordshire and in Middlesbrough. At the same time there was little evidence to show that the working-class intake had been purged of marginal candidates by the economic depression. In fact the working-class intake in Hightown had been stable since the opening of the school, and in Middlesbrough the working-class contingent reached new heights that were not sustained in 1953. In chapter 2 a number of factors were discussed that may have caused the relatively high performance of working-class boys in the 1930's. These can now be assessed in the light of the later accounts of the internal processes of the school (chapter 4) and the relation between the home and the school (chapter 7).

In chapter 4 it was shown that 'differentiation' and 'polarisation' occurred as pupils moved through the school, and the resulting pro- and anti-school sub-cultures were also linked to class differentiation. The situation can be depicted as in Fig. 18.

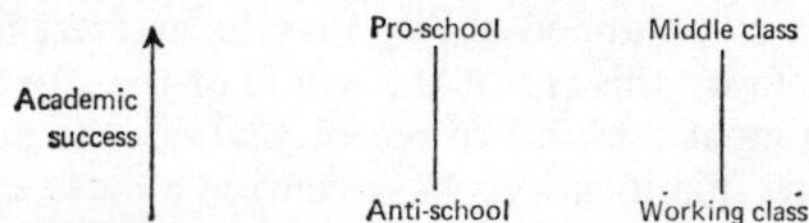

Fig. 18. Class differentiation and the pro- and anti-school sub-cultures.

In the 1930's, however, an additional factor complicated the picture. Evidence from 'old boys' who were at the school during this period underlined the importance of the fee-payer–scholar dichotomy. The informants pointed out that while at school they were very conscious of their working-class scholar status, and felt the need to

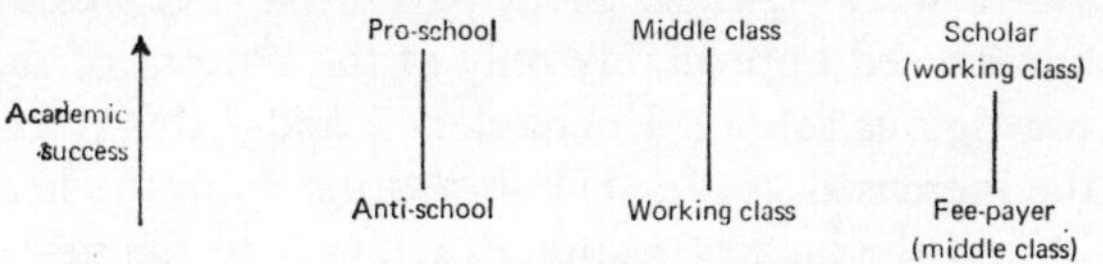

Fig. 19. The fee-payer–scholar dichotomy.

187

work hard and to succeed academically. In their eyes, many of the middle-class fee-payers were lazy and badly behaved because they were supported by well-off parents who could secure their children's future. The situation can be depicted as in Fig. 19. The existence in the school of an important working-class scholar reference group associated with academic success, and an important middle-class fee-payer contingent associated with anti-school attitudes,[6] would certainly affect the processes of differentiation and polarisation described in chapter 4.

A second factor affecting the internal organisation of grammar schools in the district in the 1930's[7] was brought to my notice by old boys of nearby grammar schools. They reported the existence of arrangements whereby successful working-class boys could jump a year in order to take external examinations a year earlier. This method of combating early leaving was reported to be the origin of an express stream[8] in one nearby grammar school. The two factors of scholar status and express stream preference could have enhanced the position of working-class boys in Hightown Grammar School in the 1930's.

After the second world war the fee-payer–scholar distinction was abolished in local education authority schools, and all grammar school places were thrown open to competition. The expected flood of able working-class boys who were previously prevented from taking up grammar school places never materialised.

While the reserves of untapped ability may be greatest in the poorer sections of the community this is not the whole of the story. It is sometimes imagined that the great increase in recent years in the numbers achieving good school-leaving qualifications has occurred almost entirely among the children of manual workers. *This is not so*. The increase has been almost as great among the children of professional parents, where the pool of ability might have been thought more nearly exhausted. In those groups the performance of a given measured ability has in fact continually improved . . .[9]

In Hightown the number of grammar school places for boys increased from 500 in 1945 to 1,180 in 1964.[10] At the same time the town's population has declined rapidly. Even in these circumstances the increase in working-class participation has been disappointing, and it has increased appreciably only at the bottom of the scale, in the least prestigious school. In chapters 2 and 7 this is explained in terms of the increased academic competition from the lower middle class pupils and the lack of resources relevant to the new, increased competition on the part of working-class family units.

188

There are a number of speculative elements in this analysis, which can, however, be tested in further research. The following avenues have yet to be exploited and would yield data relevant to these problems.

1 *Research into the private school system.* The fee-payer–scholar dichotomy still exists in these schools, and in some girls' schools of this type the 'finishing school' function is still dominant.
2 *Research into grammar schools in middle-class areas* and into the prestigeful direct grant schools.[11] The academic pressures in these schools can be expected to be very great and to give rise to anti-groups which are not dominated by working-class norms.
3 *Historical and statistical research.* There is a large amount of data in local education offices and the records of grammar schools that has yet to be exploited. This is also true of the data amassed by the various Government surveys.

The deferred gratification pattern

The model of the school presented in chapter 4 contrasts with the idea of the 'deferred gratification pattern'. In chapter 4 the school is described as an arena in which teams compete for rare resources, the rare resources being a flow of *short*-term gratifications. The deferred gratification pattern was recognised by Schneider and Lysgaard[12] in 1953 as being implicit in the explanation offered by Dolland,[13] Kinsey,[14] Whyte,[15] Hollingshead[16] and many others for differences in class behaviour. It refers to a cultural pattern which characterises a large number of fields of middle-class behaviour. The middle class is seen as renouncing immediate gratifications in sexual activities, economic and employment spheres, etc., in order to obtain much higher rewards later on. 'But it is not necessarily implied that deferment of gratification is always worth while. . . .'[17]

Schneider and Lysgaard take the idea further:

The deferred gratificaton pattern appears to be closely associated with impulse renunciation. Thus, some of the pertinent current literature emphasises, by way of example, middle-class renunciation of impulses towards violence . . .

and

A more important point is the *normative* character of the deferred gratification pattern. Middle-class persons feel that they *should* save, postpone, and renounce a variety of gratifications.[17]

189

It is clear that Schneider and Lysgaard feel that deferred gratification is not just a behaviour pattern brought about by structural features associated with a stratified society. It is, for them, a normative value orientation of the middle class, adhered to for its own sake, which therefore plays a major role in determining attitudes to education and academic achievement. At the other end of the class scale, absence of deferred gratification brings out

relative readiness to engage in physical violence, free sexual expression (as through intercourse), minimum pursuit of education, low aspiration level, failure of parents to identify the class of their children's playmates, free spending, little emphasis on being well mannered and obedient.[18]

In their study Schneider and Lysgaard find that a number of their indicators representing (for example) saving, good manners and college plans, correlated with social class. However, they give no evidence that deferred gratification is a *causal* factor in these correlations nor that any *pattern* exists.

Subsequent research by Strauss[19] and Caro[20] has also failed to give support to the deferred gratification pattern concept. Strauss shows that there is very little correlation between the variables that make up the so-called *pattern*. The idea of a pattern is therefore tenuous. Building on the work of Beilin[21] and Rodman,[22] Caro investigated the idea of deferment. He argued that *deferred* gratification involves the renunciation of some perceived and preferred *immediate* activity for some preferred *distant* goal or activity. He examined the extent to which working-class and middle-class students perceived college-going as involving this sort of conflict between long-term and short-term goals. He found that

at least from the perspectives of the youths involved, possible differences in willingness to defer are largely irrelevant as an explanation of class differences in rates of initial college attendance.[23]

The evidence presented in this book, in particular the case studies,[24] has relevance to the above discussion, although it must be remembered that the material is from a selected section of the population. The model constructed in chapter 7 provides an explanation of the case study material. In the process of developing the model, some fifty or sixty detailed case histories were examined. These cases provided very little evidence to support the idea that the deferred gratification pattern played an important part in the differential success of pupils. The pupils brought their talents and

190

resources to the situation (the school) and competed for what I have termed the 'flow of short-term gratifications'. External resources, including value orientations, were of course important factors in the competition, but I have also demonstrated (Cready) that the successful management of the internal factors (classroom situation, choice of friends, etc.) could be of critical importance in the competition.

For some pupils, competition inevitably brought about the cessation of the flow of short-term gratifications from the school. This misfortune[25] fell on both working-class and middle-class pupils, but its effect and the problems it posed differed in relation to the resources of the competing units. The Bakers' solution to the problem —to utilise their considerable resources to help their son stay on at school—cannot be characterised as deferred gratification, because the immediate alternative—to withdraw him from the school—was not an alternative gratification. While Baker's parents felt they could cope with the situation, they preferred to keep the boy at school. The parents supported him in this difficult situation by encouraging him, taking him out more often, getting him to invite school friends home and maintaining close contact with the school. The parents and the boy derived short-term gratification from the improvement in the situation that subsequently developed.

Conversely, the Dockers' decision to remove their boy cannot be characterised as impulse gratification (lack of deferred gratification). They had exhausted their resources. Mrs Docker would have liked Peter to stay,[26] but she lacked the energy and know-how (psycho-cultural resources) to achieve her desire, and saw unbearable pressures mounting as a consequence of his difficulties at grammar school. She terminated his career there because she felt she had no alternative: 'either him or I will have a nervous breakdown.'

Rodman[22] has developed what he calls the 'value stretch' hypothesis to describe this situation. He suggests that the working class has internalised similar achievement norms to the middle class, but may in fact be *satisfied* with less actual achievement, that is, it has greater value stretch.[27] My own explanation of the case study material and Caro's research on college attendance both support Rodman's hypothesis. A number of important implications arise from this discussion:

1 The greater 'value stretch' of working-class family units is a rational adjustment to their position in a stratified society. In

terms of the competition model (chapter 7), working-class aspiration and achievement is viewed as a *rational assessment* of what is possible, given the more limited socio-cultural resources of the working-class family units. A major advantage of the resources–competition model over the deferred gratification pattern is therefore its parsimony. Working-class and middle-class behaviour are both explained in terms of rational behaviour. (Deferred gratification *v.* impulse gratification implies rationality *v.* irrationality.)

2 Caro shows that the argument over the deferred gratification pattern has relevance for the Davis[28]–Tumin[29] debate on the merits of the Davis–Moore functional theory of stratification. In fact the implications of this discussion also extend into the major problems facing education today. Davis and Moore[30] assert that positions in society which 'have the greatest importance for society and require the greatest training and talent'[31] have the highest ranks. For many of the most important posts in society, 'talent is fairly abundant in the population but the training process is so long, costly and elaborate that few can qualify'.[32] Few would undertake burdensome and expensive training if the position 'did not carry a reward commensurate with the sacrifice'.[32]

The last quotation implies that as the division of labour proceeds and society requires more advanced and arduously acquired skills, it will also have to provide larger rewards. This will lead to greater societal differentiation.

The lesson to be drawn from the evidence presented in this book contradicts the implication of the Davis–Moore analysis. The study has uncovered evidence of tremendous energy and drive towards academic achievement.[33] Much of this energy and talent is frittered away because the effects of relative failure in the competitive process are allowed to demoralise a large section of the competitors. An anti-group sub-culture develops which constantly erodes the competitive ability of a high proportion of the students. In other words, the erosion comes from the competitive process brought about by the organisation of the school, *not* from a lack of differential rewards outside the school. It follows from my arguments that an increase in differential rewards within society could have a deleterious effect. There would be a larger number of families with relatively low

192

'resources' and these families, as we have seen, are more vulnerable to erosion from within the system.

It is outside the scope of this book to point to the detailed practical implications of the arguments presented here. I make only two suggestions for consideration:

1 A modification of the streaming system, commensurate with the problems of teaching groups of varied ability—through setting, for example.

2 A modification in the role of a proportion of the teaching staff. For example, the introduction of a specially trained group of teacher–social workers who would teach only first- or second-year classes on a half-time basis and thus be freed from some of the pressures of the teaching situation outlined in chapter 8. Their job would be to pick out, early on, cases that would require additional help and supervision, to encourage parents and, where necessary, to supplement the parent role by providing an additional source of help and encouragement.

The general direction is clear. The major objective for those interested in increasing the supply of highly trained personnel from our schools must be the anti-group sub-cultures within secondary schools.

NOTES

[1] S. M. Lipset and R. Bendix, *Social mobility in industrial society*, University of California Press, 1959.

[2] See, for example, R. Perrucci, 'Education, stratification and mobility', in *On education—sociological perspectives*, ed. D. A. Hansen and J. E. Gerstl, Wiley, 1967.

[3] For example, local education authority grants for students in further education (all forms) rose by 90 per cent in the four years ending 1965–66, and more than doubled by December 1966.

[4] R. V. Clements, *Managers: a study of their careers in industry*, London, 1958.

[5] B. R. Clark, 'The cooling-out function in higher education', in *Economy, education and society*, ed. Floud, Halsey and Anderson. Clark describes a method of deflecting resentment among those who do not succeed.

[6] Middle-class fee-payers exploiting the 'finishing school' function of the grammar school could be expected to develop anti-academic attitudes.

[7] I have no confirmation that a similar arrangement existed at Hightown Grammar School, but table 70 shows that working-class boys gained their examination successes at an earlier age than middle-class boys.

[8] This contrasts with the main function of the express stream in the post-war period, which was to enable the development of a third-year sixth to try for Oxford or Cambridge open scholarships. By this time the express stream was dominated by middle-class boys.

[9] *Higher education* (the Robbins report), H.M.S.O., Cmnd 2154, page 53.

[10] Total number of places at Hightown Grammar School and the Technical High School.

[11] More is known about secondary modern schools than either private girls' schools or direct grant schools.

[12] L. Schneider and S. Lysgaard, 'The deferred gratification patterns: a preliminary study', *Am. Soc. Review*, 18, 1953, pages 142–9.

[13] J. Dollard, *Caste and class in a southern town*, Harper, New York, 1949.

[14] A. C. Kinsey, W. B. Pomeroy and C. E. Martin, *Sexual behaviour in the human male*, Philadelphia and London, Saunders, 1948.

[15] W. F. Whyte, *Street corner society*, University of Chicago Press, 1943.

[16] A. B. Hollingshead, *Elmtown's youth*, Wiley, New York, 1949.

[17] Schneider and Lysgaard, *op. cit.*, page 142.

[18] Schneider and Lysgaard, *op. cit.*, page 143.

[19] M. A. Strauss, 'Deferred gratification, social class and the achievement syndrome', *Am. Soc. Review*, 27, 1962, pages 326–35.

[20] F. G. Caro, 'Deferred gratification, time conflict and college attendance', *Soc. of Ed.*, 38, 1965, pages 332–40.

[21] H. Beilin, 'The pattern of postponability and its relation to social class mobility', *Jnl. of Soc. Psych.*, 44, 1956, pages 33–48.

[22] H. Rodman, 'The lower class value stretch', *Social Forces*, 42, 1963, pages 205–15.

[23] Caro, *op. cit.*, page 339.

[24] This evidence has been followed up in the survey of parents mentioned earlier. When the analysis of the survey is completed, a quantification of some aspects of the problem will be possible over the full social class range.

[25] There were of course degrees of failure and perception of failure.

[26] She spent much time and energy encouraging him to get there. He was the only boy from his junior school to pass the eleven-plus examination.

[27] One of the indicators used by Plowden, *Children and their primary schools*, vol. II, H.M.S.O., page 123, table 32, confirms the greater tolerance of the working-class parent for practically all types of school:

Type of school particularly liked	Parents' occupation (%) Professional	Unskilled
1 Grammar	–	1
2 Secondary Modern	27	3
3 Comprehensive	6	–
4 Independent	2	–
5 Mixed	8	3
6 Religious	2	2
Total	46	9

[28] K. Davis, 'Reply to Tumin', *Am. Soc. Review*, 18, 1953, pages 394–7.

[29] M. Tumin, 'Some principles of stratification: a critical analysis', *Am. Soc. Review*, 18, 1953, pages 387–94.

[30] K. Davis, and W. Moore, 'Some principles of stratification', *Am. Soc. Review*, 10, 1945, pages 242–9.

[31] *Ibid.*, page 243, as quoted by Caro, *op. cit.*, page 335.

[32] *Ibid.*, page 244.

[33] It would seem that the present reward differentials in society are ample to secure enthusiasm for the training process.

Appendix 1

TABLE 61

LENGTH OF SCHOOL LIFE OF SONS OF 'QUALIFIED'
AND 'PROPRIETARY' MIDDLE CLASS, 1917–20*

	Early leavers	Completed	Stayed on	Totals
Qualified middle class:				
professional and higher technical, clerical and miscellaneous	(20) 18·4%	(47) 43·1%	(42) 38·5%	(109)
Proprietary middle class:				
business and managerial, foremen and shopkeepers	(22) 30·1%	(34) 46·6%	(17) 23·3%	(73)
Totals:	(42)	(81)	(59)	(182)

* The distinction between the 'qualified' and 'proprietary' groups of the middle class is very similar to that made by Frankenberg using Merton's terminology, 'locals' and 'cosmopolitans'. See R. Frankenberg, *Communities in Britain*, Penguin Books, 1966, pages 162–4: 'Locals are committed to the town through their business interests . . . their key question is one about ascription. Who is he? What is his family? Locals have a total status.' Cosmopolitans 'have their frame of reference in a wider society. Their key question is one about achievement. What does he do? What has he done?'
It also corresponds closely with Watson's 'spiralists' and 'burgesses'. See W. Watson, 'Social mobility and social class in industrial communities' in *Closed systems and open minds: the limits of naivity in social anthropology*, ed. M. Gluckman.

TABLE 62

DISTRIBUTION OF FEE-PAYERS AND SCHOLARS AMONG THE
'QUALIFIED' AND 'PROPRIETARY' MIDDLE CLASS (LEAVERS, 1917–20)

	Fee-payers	Scholars	Totals
Qualified middle class:			
Professional, technical, clerical and miscellaneous	47 (41·6%)	66 (58·4%)	113 (100%)
Proprietary middle class:			
business, managerial, foremen and shopkeepers	40 (50%)	40 (50%)	80 (100%)
Totals:	87	106	193

195

Fee-payers are found disproportionately among the 'proprietary' middle class (see table 62), so it is necessary to see whether this alone accounts for the difference between the two groups.

Table 63 shows that when fee-payers and scholars are taken separately, the 'proprietary' middle class is still more likely to leave early and less likely to stay on, in both categories:

TABLE 63

LENGTH OF SCHOOL LIFE OF THE QUALIFIED AND PROPRIETARY MIDDLE CLASS FOR FEE-PAYERS AND SCHOLARS, TAKEN SEPARATELY (LEAVERS, 1917–20)

	Early leavers	Completed	Stayed on	Total
Fee-payers:				
Qualified middle class	11 (23·9%)	18 (39·1%)	17 (36·9%)	46
Proprietary middle class	16 (43·2%)	17 (45·9%)	4 (10·8%)	37
Total				83
Scholars:				
Qualified middle class	9 (14%)	29 (46%)	25 (40%)	63
Proprietary middle class	6 (17%)	17 (47%)	13 (36%)	36
Total				99

The difference is, however, much less marked among the scholars. This clear disparity between the two groups taken as a whole, from the point of view of length of school career, is *not* mirrored in jobs that they were able to achieve on leaving school (see table 64):

TABLE 64

PERCENTAGES OF 'PROPRIETARY' AND 'QUALIFIED' GROUPS GOING INTO HIGHER TECHNICAL AND CLERICAL JOBS, FURTHER EDUCATION AND FATHER'S BUSINESS (LEAVERS, 1917–20)

	Higher technical	*Higher clerical*	*Higher clerical and technical as a percentage of total**
Qualified middle class	16	7	23·4
Proprietary middle class	7	6	22·4

	Further education	*Father's business*	*Total*
Qualified middle class	13 (12·9%)	3 (2·7%)	101
Proprietary middle class	9 (13·0%)	11 (13·7%)	69
Totals	22	14	

* Sons going into fathers' business are not included in the percentage total, since they might well include jobs leading to a high status position.

The evidence suggests that the local influence and connections of the 'proprietary' group were able to make up for their poorer performance at school when it came to obtaining jobs. It therefore supports the 'finishing school' hypothesis because it demonstrates that the group best placed to exploit the 'finishing school' mechanism in fact does so.

Appendix 2

TABLE 65

LENGTH OF SCHOOL LIFE OF THE BOYS IN
EACH CLASS CATEGORY, 1917–20

Occupation	Early leavers (less than three years)	Completed three years	Stayed on (more than three years)	Totals
Professional and higher technical, business owners and managers	4 }5 1	9 }14 5	10 }13 3	23 }32 9
Clerical workers foremen and shopkeepers miscellaneous non-manual	3 21 }37 13	14 29 }67 24	11 14 }46 21	28 64 }150 58
Skilled manual, unskilled manual	19 }24 5	32 }44 12	16 }21 5	67 }89 22
Not stated	4	3	4	11
Totals	70	128	84	282

Note: transfers, i.e. boys leaving to go to other grammar schools (13), have been removed.

198

Appendix 3

The following three points are taken in turn to show that they are not in themselves sufficient explanation of the reversal of the normal class fortunes, discussed in chapter 2:

1 The low performance of the middle class could be due to the fact that a high proportion of the middle-class boys are fee-payers.[1] As we have seen—fee-payers do not perform as well as scholars.
2 The high performance of the working class could be due to the fact that a proportion of marginally qualified working-class children refused their places in the grammar school due to the economic situation, which affected the working-class families disproportionately. The resulting working-class contingent was thus more highly selected.
3 The class structure of the community could have changed.

1 Low performance of the middle class

The evidence from Hightown regarding the difference in performance between scholars and fee-payers does not support the hypothesis that the reversal of fortunes is due solely to fee-payers depressing the middle-class performance.[2] Table 66 shows that, if scholars are taken separately, the

TABLE 66

PERCENTAGE OF SCHOLARS IN EACH CLASS CATEGORY WHO 'LEFT EARLY', 'COMPLETED THE COURSE' OR 'STAYED ON' AT HIGHTOWN GRAMMAR SCHOOL, 1934–39

Class	Early leavers %	Completed %	Stayed on %	No. of scholars
Upper middle	17·1	41·5	41·5	41
Lower middle	20·4	55·3	24·3	103
Working	20·4	57·0	22·6	93
				237

lower middle class and working class are almost indistinguishable on the basis of length of school life. This is confirmed by the analysis of examination results for scholars in table 67.[3]

TABLE 67

PERCENTAGE OF SCHOLARS IN EACH CLASS CATEGORY OBTAINING
SCHOOL CERTIFICATE, MATRICULATION, HIGHER SCHOOL CERTIFICATE
OR NO EXAMINATION AT HIGHTOWN GRAMMAR SCHOOL, 1934–39

Class	No exam %	School certificate %	Matriculation %	HSC %	scholars
Upper middle	23	78	38	20	40
Lower middle	36	64	18	13	105
Working	38	62	22	13	93
					238

The evidence from south-west Hertfordshire and Middlesbrough cannot
be assessed as readily, because the statistics for scholars are not published.
However, there is a certain amount of evidence which shows that the over-
representation of fee-payers in the middle-class groups could not have
depressed the middle-class performance very much. First, the fee-payers
were by now staying longer at school and their performance had improved:

There was a marked tendency in the middle thirties for fee-payers to lengthen
their school life, and this was particularly striking in South-west Hertfordshire;
in the period 1934–38 the proportion of fee-paying boys staying at school to the
age of 17 or over was half as great again (44 per cent) as that of free-place holders
(28 per cent).[4]

Coupled with this trend to stay at school longer was a trend to greater
success at examinations, as is shown by table 68. At south-west Hertfordshire, fee-payers still did less well at school certificate and Higher School

TABLE 68

PERCENTAGE OF SCHOLARS AND FEE-PAYERS GAINING SCHOOL CER-
TIFICATE, HIGHER SCHOOL CERTIFICATE AND FURTHER EDUCATION
IN SOUTH-WEST HERTFORDSHIRE AND MIDDLESBROUGH*

	No. of leavers (excluding transfers)		Percentage obtaining school certificate or HSC				University and other further education	
	S	F	S	F	S	F	S	F
South-west Herts	89	177	87	70	15	11	2	19
Middlesbrough	183	111	72	59	5	5	5	14

S: free and special place holders.
F: fee-paying pupils.

* From Floud, Halsey and Martin, *Social class and educational opportunity*, page
121 (simplified).

Certificate than the free or special place holders, but in Middlesbrough they
did as well as free-place holders at Higher School Certificate. This means

that the fee-payer argument cannot be used to explain the superiority of working-class boys in Middlesbrough at the Higher School Certificate level. Also, it would appear that by this time the superiority of the 'scholars'' ability to pass examinations was only slight,[5] so that although this could account for the superiority of the working-class group over the lower middle class group[6] it would do so only by a very narrow margin, especially if a moderate number of fee-payers were among the working-class categories.[7]

Floud, Halsey and Martin failed to lay stress on this finding because they used a second indicator, 'age of leaving school', which did not produce the same result:

With few exceptions, the proportion of free-place holders leaving under 16 decreases with each step up the occupational scale, while the proportion of those remaining at school until 17 or over increases.[4]

It is fairly easy to show that 'age of leaving school' is not at this time a good indication of success in a school career. A far better indicator is whether or not the course has been 'completed', 'not completed', or whether the student has 'stayed on'. For example at Hightown, of the 92 boys who left under the age of 16 in 1934–39, 66 had not completed the course, but 26 had completed; of these, 22 gained a school certificate. The age of leaving school figures reported by Floud, Halsey and Martin therefore only make the examination success of the working-class boys more surprising because they show that it was gained on average at an earlier age (see table 69).

TABLE 69

PERCENTAGE OF EACH CLASS CATEGORY LEAVING SCHOOL
(1) UNDER 16 AND (2) AT 17 OR OVER

	Leaving under 16	Leaving at 17 or over
South-west Herts, 1934–38		
Upper middle class	6	62
Lower middle class	29	36
Working class	18	25
Middlesbrough, 1935–37		
Upper middle class	16	39
Lower middle class	17	27
Working class	33	18
Hightown, 1934–39		
Upper middle class	20·4	22·5
Lower middle class	26·0	13·0
Working class	31·2	8·3

In fact the Hightown figures, which show a marked differentiation between the class categories—particularly in the 17 and over age range—are hardly supported at all by the examination results (see table 70).

TABLE 70

PERCENTAGE OF PUPILS LEAVING AT 17 OR OVER COMPARED WITH
PERCENTAGE GAINING HIGHER SCHOOL CERTIFICATE, FOR EACH CLASS
CATEGORY

Hightown, 1934–39	Leaving at 17 or over	Gaining HSC
Upper middle class	22·5	16·7
Lower middle class	13·0	11·2
Working class	8·3	12·4

2 High performance of the working class

The probability must now be examined that the depressed economic
situation at large affected the working-class enlistment to the school,
which in turn affected the success of the working-class contingent. It would
seem that this factor would, in all probability, affect working-class recruitment more than recruitment from the other class categories. Among those
working-class boys dissuaded from competing for, or taking up, scholarships would be a greater proportion of boys who were least persuaded of
the importance of academic achievement and therefore least likely to do
well.[8] However, it is important to assess the size of this factor by looking
at its effects on recruitment, rather than by dwelling on its logic. The effects
of the economic recession were felt more strongly in Middlesbrough, and
so it is there that we would expect to find the maximum effect on working-
class recruitment. The reverse is the case. In Middlesbrough between
1922–30 and 1935–38 the working-class representation at grammar school
increased from 37·5 to 45·6 per cent, the number of unskilled workers' sons
rising from 10·5 to 16·1 per cent. This is a higher level than in 1953, when
working-class representation fell to 44·6 per cent and the number of
unskilled workers' sons at the school fell to 13·8 per cent. Conversely, in
south-west Hertfordshire the proportion of unskilled workers' sons at
grammar school fell from 19·3 per cent in 1922 to 16·1 per cent in 1934–38.

At Hightown, we have no figures for the 1920's, but if the period 1934–36
is compared with 1936–39 (that is, if the number of pupils recruited before
the cut-backs in scholarships are compared with those recruited afterwards) there is no substantial proportional decrease in working-class
representation.

3 Class structure of the community

It is obvious from the previous sections of this appendix that the class
structure of Hightown was undergoing considerable change. It is not
possible to trace the exact nature of this change from the data available.
It is unlikely that the changes were the same as those going on in south-
west Hertfordshire, where there was a large influx of middle-class population in what was quickly developing into a commutor suburb of London.
The class structure of Middlesbrough was also sufficiently different from
Hightown's to rule out the likelihood that some set of unique changes in the

class structures of these communities could account for the phenonemon we are discussing. Any explanation must therefore be consistent with any general changes in the class structure taking place at that time.[9]

NOTES

[1] Floud, Halsey and Martin imply this in their last paragraph on page 118 of *Social class and educational opportunity*.

[2] If it were true, this would still have important implications for the processes of differentiation and polarisation and the character of the anti-group sub-culture (see page 187).

[3] The slight variation in the totals of scholars is due to the fact that a small number of record cards contained only partial information.

[4] Floud, Halsey and Martin, *Social class and educational opportunity*, page 118.

[5] It can be expressed conveniently as a ratio:

$$\frac{\text{Percentage of scholars passing school certificate}}{\text{Percentage of fee-payers passing school certificate}}$$

= 87/70 or 1·24 in south-west Hertfordshire and 72/59 or 1·22 in Middlesbrough.

[6] The ratio:

$$\frac{\text{Percentage of working-class boys obtaining school certificate}}{\text{Percentage of lower middle-class boys obtaining school certificate}}$$

shows the strength of the reversal: south-west Hertfordshire, 82/69 or 1·2; Middlesbrough, 69/61 or 1·13.

[7] It must be remembered that during the earlier period, 1917–20: (1) fee-payers were more numerous, especially in south-west Hertfordshire and Middlesbrough, but also in Hightown; (2) their performance was well below that of the scholars; (3) these factors were not sufficient to cause a reversal of the expected correlation.

[8] Floud, Halsey and Martin point out (page 35 ff.) that the proportion of free places going to the sons of manual workers declined in both Middlesbrough and south-west Hertfordshire. However, this was partly due to increases in the number of free places available. A similar decrease took place between 1943 and the post-war years, when a substantial number of extra free places were made available. In fact the highest proportion of free places *ever* held by working-class children was in the period 1922–30 in both schools.

[9] For example, the expansion of the professional and clerical middle classes. For the growing importance of examinations for qualifying for a position with these growing sections of the middle class, see D. Lockwood, *The blackcoated worker*, Allen & Unwin, 1958, and G. Millerson *The qualifying associations*, 1964.

Appendix 4

TABLE 71

SOCIAL CLASS COMPOSITION OF HIGHTOWN TECHNICAL
GRAMMAR SCHOOL, 1956 AND 1959 INTAKES

	1956	1959	Total	Percentage
Manual	40	48	88	67·2
Non-manual*	21	22	43	32·8
Unclassifiable	6	14	20	–
Totals	67	84	151	100·0

* Less than 5 per cent of the non-manual category could be classified as upper middle class, and all those fall into the business and managerial category.

TABLE 72

ACADEMIC SUCCESS OF THE MAJOR CLASS CATEGORIES

1 *South-west Hertfordshire, including fee-payers in 1935–38*

	1935–38		1948–51	
	School certificate	*HSC*	*School certificate*	*HSC*
Upper middle class	82	13	88	51
Lower middle class	69	14	86	37
Working class	82	11	80	26

2 *Middlesbrough, including fee-payers in 1935–37*

	1935–37		1948–50	
	School certificate	*HSC*	*School certificate*	*HSC*
Upper middle class	76	4	88	32
Lower middle class	61	5	78	20
Working class	69	6	71	13

Appendix 5

The clubs run by the school included the Scouts, a chess club, a geographical society, a film club, the Duke of Edinburgh Award Scheme, a table-tennis club, a judo club, dramatic and art groups, a school choir, a school orchestra, a debating society and various house sports teams. The activities were clearly within the jurisdiction of the school, and although they provided a useful opportunity to meet members of staff in a relaxed and less formal atmosphere they were in no sense a release into an adolescent-controlled world. This point has relevance to an indicator used by Coleman.

Coleman asks whether or not pupils would join a particular club at school if their parents did not approve of the group, and uses the answer to this question as a 'good indicator' of the degree to which a pupil is 'released' from the family's demands into the adolescent sub-culture. The question would yield meaningless information in the context of Hightown Grammar School. To conceive of a club run by the school which parents would object to would be difficult. In a hypothetical form the question would tell the investigator more about the child's loyalty to the school or to abstract ideas of the liberty of the individual than about his allegiance to the adolescent sub-culture.

Sugarman[1] points to an important difference between American and British adolescent culture. For American youth the institutional focus of the adolescent sub-culture is the high school. This difference may explain why Coleman is able to attempt to obtain indices of participation in the adolescent sub-culture from questions relating to the school situation. However, while Sugarman's point may be true it is still important that the role of pupil is kept conceptually distinct from the more general role of adolescent. Many of Coleman's indices confuse social status in the school (pupil role) with social status in the *adolescent sub-culture* (adolescent role).[2]

[1] B. Sugarman, 'Youth culture, academic achievement and conformity', *Brit. Journ. Soc.*, vol. XVIII, No. 2, June 1967.

[2] J. S. Coleman and E. L. McDill, 'Family and peer influences in college plans of high school students', *Sociology of Education*, vol. 38, 1965, pages 112–26. In

this article, the index used to measure peer influences is membership of the 'leading crowd' (2+ choices). However, membership of the leading crowd is to some extent determined by academic performance and college orientation. Hence the variables are partially confounded. On page 125 the authors recognise that membership of the 'leading crowd' is a measure of social status in school but go on to equate this with peer group influences. Their conclusion that the relative effects of family background and peer influences on changes in the college plans of high school students must be reassessed in favour of peer influences, is not therefore substantiated.

Bibliography

Besides the works mentioned in the text, the following have been consulted and found useful during the research:

A. J. ALLAWAY, 'Social and educational change since 1900'. *Sociological Review*, vol. 43, section VIII, 1951.

D. H. ALLCORN, *The social development of young men in an English industrial suburb*, unpublished Ph.D. thesis, Manchester University 1955.

G. BARON and A. TROPP, 'Teachers in England and America', in *Education Economy in Society*, ed. J. E. Floud, A. H. Halsey and C. A. Anderson. Free Press of Illinois, 1961.

Z. BAUMAN, 'Values and standards of success of the Warsaw youth'. *Polish Sociological Bulletin*, January–June 1962, pages 77–90.

H. S. BECKER, 'Social class variations in the teacher–pupil relationship'. *Jnl. of Ed. Soc.*, vol. 25, No. 8, 1952.

H. S. BECKER, 'The teacher in the authority system of the public school'. *Jnl. of Ed. Soc.*, vol. 27, No. 3, 1953.

E. BENE, 'Some differences between middle-class and working-class grammar school boys in their attitudes towards education'. *Brit. Jnl. of Soc.*, vol. X, No. 2, 1959.

B. BERNSTEIN, 'Language and social class'. *Brit. Jnl. of Soc.*, vol. XI, No. 3, 1960.

W. A. L. BLYTH, *English primary education: a sociological description*, 2 volumes, London, Routledge & Kegan Paul, 1965.

W. A. L. BLYTH, 'Sociometry, prefects and peaceful coexistence in a junior school'. *Soc. Review*, vol. 6, No. 1, 1958.

W. A. L. BLYTH, 'The sociometric study of children's groups in English schools'. *Brit. Jnl. of Ed. Studies*, vol. VIII, No. 2, 1960.

M. S. BROWN, 'A sociological study of a grammar school in a working-class community', unpublished Ph.D. thesis, London University, 1951.

B. R. CLARK, *Educating the expert society*. Chandler Publishing Co., 1962.

M. COLLINS, 'The causes of premature leaving from grammar schools'. *Brit. Jnl. of Ed. Psych.*, vol. 24, No. 3, 1954.

S. COTGROVE, 'Education and occupation'. *Brit. Jnl. of Soc.*, vol. XIII, No. 1, 1962.

H. O. DAHLKE, *Values of culture and classroom*. Harper & Bros., New York, 1958.

A. DAVIS, *Social class influences upon learning*. Harvard University Press, 1948.

J. A. M. DAVIS, 'Secondary schools as communities'. *Educational Review*, vol. 9, No. 3, 1957.

L. DAVISON, 'The secondary modern school and its staff'. *Forum*, vol. 4, No. 2, 1962.

F. ELKIN and W. A. WESTLEY, 'The myth of adolescent culture'. *American Sociological Review*, vol. XX, 1955, pages 680–4.

J. H. FICHTER, *The parochial school: a sociological study*. University of Notre Dame Press, 1958.

J. FLOUD, 'The educational experience of the adult population of England and Wales as at July 1949', in *Social mobility in Britain*, ed. D. V. Glass. Routledge & Kegan Paul, London, 1954.

E. FRAZER, *Home environment and the school*. University of London Press, 1959.

M. GOLD, 'Power in the classroom'. *Sociometry*, vol. XXI, No. 1, 1958.

D. GOTTLIEB and J. REEVES, *Adolescent behaviour in urban areas*. Free Press, 1963.

H. J. HALLWORTH, 'Sociometric relationships among grammar school boys and girls between the ages of 11 and 16 years'. *Sociometry*, vol. XVI, Feb. 1953.

A. H. HALSEY, 'Genetics, social structure and intelligence'. *Brit. Jnl. of Soc.*, vol. 9, No. 1, 1958.

A. H. HALSEY and L. GARDNER, 'Selection for secondary education and achievement in four grammar schools'. *Brit. Jnl. of Soc.*, vol. 4, No. 1, 1953.

H. T. HIMMELWEIT, 'Social status and secondary education since the 1944 Act: some data for London', in *Social mobility in Britain*, ed. D. V. Glass. Routledge & Kegan Paul, London, 1954.

H. T. HIMMELWEIT, A. H. HALSEY, and A. N. OPPENHEIM, 'The views of some adolescents on the social class structure'. *Brit. Jnl. of Soc.*, vol. III, No. 2, 1952.

E. HOYLE, 'Organisational analysis in education'. *Educational Research*, vol. VII, November 1955.

B. JACKSON and D. MARSDEN, *Education and the working class*. Routledge & Kegan Paul, London, 1962.

G. JAHODA, 'Social class attitudes and levels of occupation aspiration in secondary modern school leavers'. *Brit. Jnl. of Psych.* vol. XLIV, No. 2, 1953.

A. KOBBEN, 'Why exceptions?' International Social Science Council: round table conference on comparative research, Paris, 22–4, April 1965.

MINISTRY OF EDUCATION, *Early leaving*, a report of the Central Advisory Council for Education (England). H.M.S.O., London, 1954.

MINISTRY OF EDUCATION, *Report of the Central Advisory Council for Education in England and Wales, 15–18* (the 'Crowther report'). H.M.S.O., London, 1959–60, two volumes.

F. MUSGROVE, 'A survey of attitudes to and expectations of the school among parents of children in the last two years of junior schools'. *Soc. Review*, vol. 9, No. 2, July 1961.

B. L. NEUGARTON, 'Social class and friendships among schoolchildren'. *American Journal of Sociology*, vol. LI, No. 4, 1946.

S. NOWAK, 'Social attitudes of Warsaw students'. *Polish Sociological Bulletin*, January–June 1962, pages 91–103.

A. N. OPPENHEIM, 'Social status and clique formation amongst grammar school boys'. *Brit. Jnl. of Soc.*, vol. VI, No. 3, 1955.

A. K. C. OTTAWAY, 'Social relations in the school'. *Researches and Studies*, No. 4, 1951.

T. PARSONS, 'The school class as a social system—some of its functions in American society', in *Education, economy and society*, ed. Halsey *et al.*

H. REE, *The essential grammar school*. Harrap, London, 1956.

W. H. SEWELL, A. O. HALLER, and M. A. STRAUSS, 'Social status and educational and occupational aspiration'. *American Sociological Review*, vol. 22, 1957, pages 67–73.

M. SMITH, 'Some factors in friendship selection'. *Sociometry*, vol. VII, No. 3, 1944.

A. TROPP, *The schoolteachers* (Kingswood Social History Series). London, Heinemann, 1957.

R. H. TURNER, 'Sponsored and contest mobility and the school system'. *American Sociological Review*, vol. XXV, No. 5.

W. L. WARNER, R. J. HAVIGHURST and M. B. LOEB, *Who shall be Educated? The challenge of unequal opportunities*. London, Routledge & Kegan Paul, 1946.